Don Browning and Psychology

Don Browning and Psychology

Interpreting the Horizons of Our Lives

Terry D. Cooper

MERCER UNIVERSITY PRESS

MACON, GEORGIA

MUP/

© 2011 Mercer University Press
1400 Coleman Avenue
Macon, Georgia 31207

First Edition

Books published by Mercer University Press are printed on
acid-free paper that meets the requirements of American
National Standard for Information Sciences—Permanence of
Paper for Printed Library Materials.

Mercer University Press is a member of Green Press
Initiative (greenpressinitiative.org), a nonprofit organization
working to help publishers and printers increase their use of
recycled paper and decrease their use of fiber derived from
endangered forests. This book is printed on recycled paper.
Library of Congress Cataloging-in-Publication Data

Cooper, Terry D.
 Don Browning and psychology : interpreting the horizons of our lives /
Terry D. Cooper. -- 1st ed.
     p. cm.
 Includes bibliographical references and index.
 ISBN 978-0-88146-254-8 (pbk. : alk. paper)
 1. Browning, Don S. 2. Psychology and religion. 3. Psychology, Religious.
4. Christianity--Psychology. I. Title.
 BL53.C654 2011
 201'.615--dc23
                              2011024531

Contents

Introduction / 1

1: "Mere" Psychology / 6

2: Basic Instinct(s): Human Nature and Culture / 59

3: Identity, Self-Injury, and Generativity / 116

4: Jung, Self-Realization, and Evil / 165

5: Browning's Contributions:
Interview and Concluding Statement / 192

Index / 223

For

Carol Browning

Introduction

Psychologist of religion, ethicist, theological psychologist, cultural critic, philosophical anthropologist, marriage and family expert, practical theologian, and progressively a religion and law scholar—these are some of the many labels one could use to describe the history of Don Browning's work. Indeed, when I attended Browning's retirement celebration at the University of Chicago, a panel of scholars represented the various stages of his work. The scholars' orientation and academic tasks were very different, so much so that it was hard to believe that one thinker had influenced all of these directions. They shared one important element, however; they had all been students of Browning.

I would like to suggest, however, that in spite of the changes in Browning's focus, one can clearly identify abiding themes and central concerns. In fact, I think the title that fits him most adequately is that of "horizon analyst." By this, I simply mean that Browning is always at his best when he is helping us see the world of implicit assumptions and normative images that govern various perspectives. He has an eye for metaphors, which as his mentor, Ricoeur, famously said, give rise to thought. He carefully sifts through layers of theory and provides an in-depth analysis of the origin of theories and, particularly, what they imply about the human condition. He is equally at home among theologians, ethicists, social scientists, legal scholars, economists, cultural critics, social theorists, and philosophers. He also has made important contributions to science and religion, contributions recently recognized as Browning was invited to give the prestigious Templeton Science and Religion Lectures. There have been several occasions in conversation with Browning in which I have wondered how in the world he could be so widely read and conversant in so many disciplines. Browning is able to quickly and accurately get to the heart of ideas. While many of us would need to labor over a concept for a lengthy time, Browning sees its underlying assumptions and implications very quickly.

Perhaps it would be helpful if I contextualize this book in terms of a couple of previous publications, as well as my work with Browning. This book is the third in a series I've done with Mercer University Press. The focus has been on bringing theology and psychology into fruitful dialogue. The first book was predictable enough, *Paul Tillich and Psychology*. Clearly, Tillich, more than any major twentieth-century theologian, seriously engaged the psychological, and particularly the psychotherapeutic, disciplines. I attempted to bring his theological anthropology into contact with key psychotherapeutic themes and analyzed Tillich's involvement with the New York Psychology Group, which met regularly during World War II. I then turned to Tillich's colleague, Reinhold Niebuhr, whom I believe offers important insights for psychological perspectives on the human condition, and produced *Reinhold Niebuhr and Psychology*. If Tillich seemed a likely candidate for such a discussion, Niebuhr perhaps did not. While many appropriately connect Niebuhr to political theory and social ethics, I brought Niebuhr into a discussion with psychological theory. I continue to believe that his work contains enormous insight into our anxieties and struggles. This conviction is also deeply shared by Don Browning. This book, *Don Browning and Psychology*, concludes the trio of books. It is hardly a stretch to write on Browning's interest in psychology because he has been one of the most significant contributors to the psychology-and-religion dialogue for nearly half a century. I am making a huge vote of confidence in Browning's importance as I place him within the company of two theological giants, Tillich and Niebuhr. Browning himself draws upon the work of these two mentors but links their thought to specific psychological concerns and theories in a manner that goes beyond the discussions that Tillich and Niebuhr had with psychology. In short, at the theoretical level, I consider Browning to be the most important interpreter of the psychology and religion discussion of the past fifty years.

I was not officially one of Browning's students. While I read carefully his work, I met him for the first time at the 1998 American Academy of Religion meeting in Orlando, Florida. He and his wife, Carol, were coming out of a restaurant as I approached them. I told Don that I was working on a second doctorate, this time in theology and psychotherapy, and that I was focusing primarily on Niebuhr. I expressed how impressed I had been with his 1987 book, *Religious Thought and the Modern Psychologies*, and how it had guided much of my thinking. By the end of this conversation, Browning, who was very busy at that time, agreed to read my dissertation. He read it and offered a much-valued affirmation. A couple of years later, I was approaching a sabbatical and contacted Browning about coming to Chicago to study with him. We met in Hyde Park, had an excellent conversation over lunch, and decided it would be a good match. Three weeks later, I found out from Browning that he was going to be a visiting professor in the law school at Emory during this time. I quickly changed my plans and headed to Atlanta rather than Chicago. So I spent Spring 2002 working with Don, who was located in Emory's law school.

During an early meeting with Don at Emory, he invited me to help him revise *Religious Thought and the Modern Psychologies*. More specifically, I added sections on the cognitive therapies of Albert Ellis and Aaron Beck, family systems theorist Murray Bowen, and the important dialogue between evangelicals and mainliners on the theology and psychology connection. I also helped him reframe the earlier discussion into a more explicit critical hermeneutical approach. This partnership worked well and I was able to watch Don work. We have also co-authored articles, and Don has been enormously supportive of my book projects. I have spent time in his home and been the fortunate recipient of Don and Carol's generosity.

Throughout Browning's work, he has been particularly struck by the importance of Ricoeur's term "distanciation." Distanciation is the process of critically distancing oneself from a theory for the purpose of description, analysis, and evaluation. Distanciation is not the same as objectivity. Browning has long ago given up on the foundationalist assumption that one can empty oneself of all preconceptions and read a text with no orienting assumptions. He is steeped in hermeneutical theory and believes that we always bring our personal histories to the text. That history has been formed by classics, images, and symbols from a tradition. Nevertheless, Browning advocates a *critical* hermeneutical approach to emphasize that it is both possible and necessary to attempt some distance from one's orienting assumptions and examine them as carefully as one can. I will attempt to employ this method to understand Browning's own work. I would not be doing him justice if I simply set forth his own views and said "Amen." I will spend a great deal of time describing Browning's work and attempting to connect central themes over the course of his intellectual development. Yet I will also attempt more than explication; I will bring Browning into discussion with other perspectives that may not conform with his own assumptions. My hope is that this presentation of his ideas is clear and helpful to faithful Browning readers, as well as those who decide to start reading him.

The more familiar I become with Browning's work and life, the more I realize how much the University of Chicago has shaped him. Don received his Ph.D. from Chicago and began teaching there not long afterward in the mid-1960s. His son, Christopher, holds a Ph.D. in sociology from Chicago; his daughter Elizabeth holds an M.S.W. from this institution; and his son-in-law is also a Ph.D. graduate of Chicago. His wife, Carol, is the lone Northwestern graduate in the family although she has lived in Hyde Park for a long time and has been intimately associated with the university. In addition to being an accomplished musician, Carol has been an important consultant and collaborator with Don, particularly with the Religion, Culture, and Family Project.

The Divinity School at Chicago sits in a high-profile part of the campus. Because of its location and reputation, Swift Hall is not easily ignored and the faculty within its walls do their work with a keen interest in how their efforts will be received by a critical, public discussion. Chicago has always been known more for its academic rigor than its confessional and churchly ties. This public, highly academic, and critical stance has been absorbed and perpetuated in Browning's work. As we shall see, while Don believes that all thought begins with faith assumptions, he also believes that these assumptions should risk public discussion and not remain strictly within the confines of the confessional community. This theme will be a prominent discussion within this book.

This book is an attempt to be fair-minded, clear, and informative as I investigate the very significant contribution Browning has made. I begin with no pretension that I do not already hold a fondness and deep appreciation for Don's intellectual skill and generous disposition toward those of us trying to find our way in the psychology and religion discussion.

On 3 June 2010, Don Browning succumbed to cancer after a brave battle. His death has been deeply felt by the numerous people whose lives he touched. Don Browning was not only aware of this book on his thought, he carefully read it and strongly affirmed its contents. In fact, I once went over the manuscript with Don while he was literally undergoing chemotherapy at the University of Chicago Medical Center. I was at first reluctant for fear that this might be physically uncomfortable for him. But Don was not in much pain at the time and insisted on using this time "constructively." His friend and colleague, John White, from Emory Law School, had the same experience with Don as they, too, looked over a manuscript. I will never forget the tenacious focus of Don, even as he maintained a pleasant and humorous relationship with his nurses, while not knowing the outcome of the chemotherapy. Warmth with deep insight, critical thinking with a robust commitment, energetic motivation to follow-through on projects and an enthusiastic enjoyment of watching his students and mentees flourish—this was Don Browning.

1

"Mere" Psychology

> "...psychology becomes more than psychology. It becomes an arena for the exercise of our unsuppressible and unquenchable thirst for religious myth and moral order. Without the utmost stringency in curbing our religious and moral proclivities, we will project them into our supposedly secular mental endeavors." —Don Browning

If one is looking for a "practical theologian" who uncritically takes the latest discoveries in the human sciences and makes them relevant for current issues facing the church, a person who creatively but unquestioningly absorbs psychological and social concepts and then unhesitatingly applies them to so-called religious problems, Don Browning is not the person to consult. Browning's work is, as much as anything else, profoundly archaeological in character. He is an archaeologist of concepts, one who digs deeply into the subsoil of the social sciences and exposes the underlying assumptions about the nature of health, ethics, human possibilities, and ultimate reality. Put another way, Browning is not very good at taking things at face value. Much like a psychoanalyst who wants to get to the primary sources of behavior, Browning will not leave theories alone without an exhaustive investigation into their underlying assumptions. He is convinced that because most things are more complicated than they may at first appear, they therefore require a "thicker' interpretation. Browning is incurably philosophical in his approach to the social sciences. Like Reinhold Niebuhr and Paul Tillich, Browning always wants to know what sort of image of humanity a thinker is employing. Further, what assumptions is the thinker making about human needs? Also, how do the underlying ethical assumptions guide the thinker's vision of human flourishing? And how does the thinker view the ultimate context of our lives? In other words, how do the concrete details of our lives relate to this much larger vision about the nature of the world?

To state it differently, Browning is not one who lets people "off the hook" ontologically. This ontological detective work can be seen from the beginning of his writing career in 1966 with the book *Atonement and Psychotherapy*.[1] In this, Browning's first book, we see a strategy that has persisted. While many were content to transfer the psychotherapeutic insights of Carl Rogers to pastoral counseling, Browning instead asked about the conceptual world out of which Rogers operated, and particularly, whether Rogers made ontological assumptions similar to Christian convictions about the nature of Divine acceptance. Browning concluded that there were indeed tacit ontological assumptions about human acceptability in Rogers, assumptions that were clearly trans-empirical. Rogers implicitly assumed that human beings are acceptable not simply before a therapist, or even a community of acceptance, but instead, acceptable before the very source of life. This transformational message that life or ultimate reality accepts the client smuggled in a quasi-theological assumption about Divine acceptance. While many were interested in exploring what Rogers had to say to theologians, Browning was interested in exposing how Rogers was *already functioning*, implicitly, as a theologian. How does Rogers know that life itself is accepting? Who grants him the authority to declare someone acceptable? This Rogerian acceptance became a way of understanding and experiencing the deeper reality of God's grace.

Throughout his career, Browning continued to hone and develop these skills of philosophical investigation into the world beneath a "simply" empirical approach. His earlier work expanded and grew into a multilayered analysis that often explores the hidden

---

[1] Don S. Browning, *Atonement and Psychotherapy* (Philadelphia: Westminster Press, 1966).

assumptions of a theory, assumptions of which the theorist him/herself may not be completely aware. Browning has shown on many occasions that even thinkers who do not consider themselves theologians often carry theological, or at least quasi-theological, assumptions.

For persons who simply want to get on with the business of helping people, Browning's work might prove annoying. But if one wants to pause long enough to ask about the ethical assumptions one is implicitly endorsing, the image of human flourishing one is accepting, and whether the perspective is compatible with a Jewish and Christian conception of the Divine, Browning's work can be extremely enlightening.

Browning's work can also be frustrating if we want simply to "learn the facts" about human life or achieve a state of pure, empirical objectivity as we allow the social sciences to tell us "the way things are." For Browning, we are hardly blank slates awaiting the social sciences to define us. We are instead always interpreting, and this interpretation inevitably involves our previous experience with the world. Complete objectivity is a foundationalist illusion. Richard Bernstein provides a description of the type of "objectivity" Browning rejects:

> By "objectivism," I mean the basic conviction that there is or must be some permanent, ahistorical matrix or framework to which we can ultimately appeal in determining the nature of rationality, knowledge, truth, reality, goodness, or rightness. An objectivist claims that there is (or must be) such a matrix and that the primary task of the philosopher is to discover what it is and to support his or her claims to have discovered such a matrix with the strongest possible reasons. Objectivism is closely related to foundationalism and the search for the Archimedean point. The objectivist maintains that unless we can ground philosophy, knowledge, or language in a rigorous manner we cannot avoid radical skepticism.[2]

---

[2] Richard Bernstein, *Beyond Objectivism and Relativism: Science, Hermeneutics, and Praxis* (Philadelphia: University of Pennsylvania Press, 1985) 8.

This form of objectivity, for Browning, is not humanly possible. We cannot step outside of our own histories any more than we can step outside of our own skins. This personal history of ours also includes a *conceptual* history. Before we begin to think critically about most ideas, we have already been exposed to assumptive worlds about those ideas. We bring that preunderstanding with us. We cannot start from scratch, empty ourselves of our assumptions, and engage in totally objective, factual thinking. In fact, we wouldn't even have a framework for understanding a concept without this history. We would not be able to make sense of the concepts. We wouldn't have the orientation necessary to grasp the ideas. Thus, Enlightenment objectivity is not possible. We are each parented and nurtured by assumptive worlds even before we begin our "official" theorizing. Stated differently, *we are all children of traditions*. The questions we ask and the options we are willing to entertain are already deeply influenced by those traditions. Cognitively speaking, no one is truly homeless. All interpretation begins with what the German philosopher Hans-Georg Gadamer frequently called an "effective history," a fund of meanings that has already become part of our way of approaching the world. While preunderstanding is personal, it has been socially and culturally informed. We never approach a text as totally autonomous readers or conceptual virgins. When we act, judge, understand, or even simply experience life, we are *already interpreting*. This is why all practice is inevitably informed by theory. And this theory emerges from images and symbols embedded within a particular community of discourse.

> Without the prior state of belonging to these historically mediated images—without this prior inheritance—we would have nothing to reflect on, nothing to understand. For when we study human behavior, we never study it in the raw; we study it through

linguistically and historically mediated images that influence both our subjects and the perceptions of scientific endeavors.[3]

Complete emancipation from these traditions is not possible or even desirable. We are interpreting human beings and not analyzing robots.

Psychology, like all disciplines, is also "tradition saturated" in the sense that we have already been shaped by images of the human condition before we start formally theorizing about it. We have all been lay psychologists long before we officially begin studying the discipline of psychology. Again, investigation into the human psyche or life in general is not even possible without these images. As Browning puts it, "Even its most objectivist forms—neuropsychology or experimental behaviorism—only find meaning and relevance with reference to the historically mediated images of the human from which they gain relative distance in their scientific work."[4] Both our scientific and philosophical thought emerge out of inherited symbols and metaphors that have shaped our consciousness. These assumptions orient our investigative procedures and make reflection possible. *Just as Reinhold Niebuhr masterfully exposed the image of human nature operating in political thought, so Browning exposes the assumptions about the human condition, the normative images of health, the sense of moral obligation, and the possibilities of transcendence in psychological thought.* Psychology works on the basis of an inherited pool of religio-cultural images of what it means to be human. Browning's work can be seen as a long, persistent attempt to pull back the curtain and expose these assumptions before comparing them with alternative frameworks. Put another way, Browning wants to push the discussion back to the level of philosophical anthropology. The metaphors and images lurking beneath psychological approaches must be made explicit and critically examined. Browning opposes the

---

[3] Don S. Browning, "Can Psychology Escape Religion? Should It?," *International Journal for the Psychology of Religion* 7/1 (1997).

[4] Ibid., 2.

claim that these empirical approaches are void of such assumptions. He never tires of questioning empirical psychologists whose mantra seems to be, "We are scientists who simply operate on empirical grounds without a need for an underlying philosophical framework. We are modest empiricists who merely report the facts of life. While religion may need 'faith,' we have completely eradicated such a need and work strictly on the basis of science." Consistently and insightfully, Browning rejects this empiricist claim while simultaneously respecting empirical contributions to a larger understanding of the world.

If one believes this type of scientific foundationalism died with positivism, one hasn't been paying close attention to contemporary culture. The current spate of books on atheism, for instance, argues for a resurrection of this enlightenment hope for complete objectivity.[5] The title of Sam Harris's book, *The End of Faith*, is perhaps the most telling: By "ending" faith, we can get back to "pure" evidence. Yet Harris's "pure" evidence ignores the very faith that makes such evidence possible. Harris's philosophical views are not modestly and empirically taken from his investigative efforts. Instead, his philosophical assumptions serve as gatekeepers for what is plausible and what is not. In fact, there is an interesting parallel between the atheistic trio of Dawkins, Hitchens, and Harris and the resistant patient in psychotherapy: Just as the patient claims he or she does not bring any "emotional baggage" to new relationships, so Dawkins, Hitchens, and Harris claim they bring no philosophical "baggage" to their strictly empirical findings. In both cases, denial is prominent. All forms of scientism deny the need for interpretation. In fact, the scientism underlying much of contemporary atheism denies its own historicity and claims to speak, even about ultimate matters, from an ahistorical point of scientific certainty. Dawkins switches from a scientific hat to a philosophical hat so easily that many don't

---

[5] See, for instance, Richard Dawkins, *The God Delusion* (Boston: Houghton Mifflin, 2006); Christopher Hitchens, *God Is Not Great: How Religion Poisons Everything* (New York: Twelve, 2007); Sam Harris, *The End of Faith* (New York: W. W. Norton, 2005).

recognize the enormous shift that has been made. While making metaphysical claims, he presumes to be speaking still as a scientist.[6]

Perhaps this can be stated even more directly: Dawkins and those of similar perspective claim to speak out of a *horizon-less* world. They think science has no background, no historical context, and no contextual limitations. Yet Dawkins in his all-out attack on "faith" reveals a kind of scientific fundamentalism that refuses any form of dialogue. Alister and Joanna McGrath put this in a humorous, but pointed, manner:

> Dawkins simply offers the atheist equivalent of slick hellfire preaching, substituting turbocharged rhetoric and highly selective manipulation of facts for careful, evidence-based thinking. Curiously, there is surprisingly little scientific analysis in *The God Delusion*. There's a lot of pseudoscientific speculation, linked with wider cultural criticisms of religion, mostly borrowed from older atheist writings. Dawkins preaches to his god-hating choirs, who are clearly expected to relish his rhetorical salvoes and raise their hands high in adulation. Those who think biological evolution can be reconciled with religion are dishonest! *Amen!* They belong to the "Neville Chamberlain school" of evolutionists! They are appeasers! *Amen! Real* scientists reject belief in God! *Hallelujah!* The God that Jews believed in back in Old Testament times is a psychotic child abuser! *Amen! You tell them, brother!*[7]

When *any* thinker claims that his or her thought has no horizon, no background world of philosophical assumptions, it can become dangerously narrow. It is a short step from saying that one has no horizon to saying that one speaks from a God-like perspective. Finitude is denied and one's own perspective is embraced as absolute truth. Niebuhr's words are worth noting:

---

[6] For a good critique of Dawkins, see Alister and Joanna McGrath, *Dawkins' Delusion: Atheist Fundamentalism and the Denial of the Divine* (Downers Grove IL: InterVarsity Press, 2007).

[7] Ibid., 11–12.

Therefore man is tempted to deny the limited character of his knowledge, and the finiteness of his perspectives. He pretends to have achieved a degree of knowledge, which is beyond the limit of finite life. This is the "ideological taint" in which all human knowledge is involved and which is always something more than mere human ignorance. It is always partly an effort to hide that ignorance by pretension…. Each thinker makes the same mistake, in turn, of imagining himself the final thinker.[8]

This conviction that one has eliminated life's ambiguity typically involves an aggressive protest to anyone who thinks otherwise.

A Nonfoundationalist Use of Science

As I have mentioned, Browning welcomes and supports scientific approaches to life. He deeply values the empirical findings of science and further believes that these findings can serve as a corrective to misguided theological beliefs. Yet, again, he asks scientists to be honest about the turf on which they are standing. If they speak about specific, empirical claims, then by all means, announce them as scientific. But when scientists of any discipline wander into the realm of questions of ultimate meaning, purpose, and ethics, they need to be clear that they are now speaking as philosophers and not as scientists. Browning welcomes them *as philosophers* to the conversation and believes they may very well have important contributions to make. But they should not enter the conversation claiming an epistemological privilege because they speak as "pure" scientists. They have in fact left that tidy world of empirical findings and are now facing much larger questions about the context of our lives. While this conversation can be aided by their empirical findings, it will inevitably go beyond the narrow confines of their empirical discoveries. Thus, when we hear scientists move from modest empirical findings to universal and ultimate claims about life, we should be alerted that they've changed roles. This shift

---

[8] Reinhold Niebuhr, *The Nature and Destiny of Man*, vol. 1 (New York: Charles Scribners, 1964) 182–95.

frequently involves some form of reductionism. The complex and ambiguous parameters of life are squeezed into a narrow empiricism. David Tracy describes this approach as the dream of positivism:

> The dream of positivism was to discover a reality without quotation marks: a realm of pure data and facts, red spots "out there" and sharp pains "in here." This realm—"science" it was named—gave us reality. Other realms—art, morality, religion, metaphysics, and common sense—gave us merely interpretations. But interpretations are not reality.[9]

By contrast, Tracy argues that science *interprets* the world; it does not merely "find the facts" as if they are already bundled in a nicely interpreted package. As he puts it, "Reality is what we name our best interpretation."[10]

David Tracy's Influence on Browning

When discussing the way in which our preunderstanding affects our theorizing about life, Browning draws upon the concept of "the classic," particularly as it is developed in Gadamer and Browning's colleague, David Tracy.[11] Following Gadamer, Tracy, in discussing the concept of the "classic," refers to any text, event, image, ritual, or symbol that grasps us so convincingly that we must recognize it as truth. Classics command attention; they provoke, challenge, and transform us. They may very well turn upside down conventional understandings and usher in a new way of viewing the world. They are disclosures that reveal such insight into the human condition that we feel compelled to name them as "classics." They become normative. Even nihilistic thinkers who refuse to recognize classics in our cultural experience typically smuggle in their own classics in an

---

[9] David Tracy, *Plurality and Ambiguity: Hermeneutics, Religion, and Hope* (San Francisco: Harper and Row, 1987) 47.

[10] Ibid., 48.

[11] Hans-George Gadamer, *Truth and Method* (New York: Crossroad, 1982); David Tracy, *The Analogical Imagination: Christian Theology and the Culture of Pluralism* (New York: Crossroad, 1981); Tracy, *Plurality and Ambiguity.*

effort to understand life. Even the most radically countercultural movements have their own revelatory figures and texts. Classics are *both* personal and public. Further, the religious classics are also public *in so far as they are also cultural classics.* They have affected so-called secular understandings as well. Put another way, one cannot grow up in Western culture without being influenced by images, metaphors, and symbols within the Jewish, Christian, and Muslim traditions. Again, they are not just *religious* classics; they have also become *cultural* classics. This, by the way, is one of the reasons the study of religion is absolutely essential to an understanding of culture. Trying to understand Western culture, for instance, without understanding the monotheistic traditions is utterly futile. Christian symbols, for instance, emerge frequently as a part of general culture, not just in a sacred sphere separate from cultural transmission. Thus, the classics are, as Tracy puts it, "grounded in some realized experience of a claim to attention, unfolding as cognitively disclosive of both meaning and truth and ethically transformative of personal, social, and historical life.... Who can deny any classic's claim to a real, even sometimes a paradigmatic, public status?"[12] The meaning and truth disclosed in a classic are available, at least in principle, to any human being searching for meaning and truth in life. Classics help ground and shape culture. They also bear an "excess" of meaning in the sense that they can be reinterpreted over and over again. There is no once-and-for-all interpretation of a classic. They continue to invite, challenge, and provoke further reflection. While classics may be highly particular in their origin, they contain the capacity to be universal in their impact. They may be temporarily forgotten in a cultural era, but they will reappear with a new capacity to claim our attention. When a classic "taps us on the shoulder" it is difficult to ignore. As Tracy puts it, they are not easily tamed.[13]

Yet these texts do not simply invade our consciousness and demand a particular interpretation. The mind is hardly a passive

---

[12] Tracy, *The Analogical Imagination*, 132.
[13] Tracy, *Plurality and Ambiguity*, 15.

receiver, a blank slate, on which the text simply writes. While we approach the text already having been influenced by the text, we nevertheless actively inquire and question it. Put another way, there is always a *conversation* between our particular situation and the text. Again, we bring specific and personal questions and issues to the text. Understanding does not occur by passively receiving a text; instead it necessitates a dialogue and active engagement. This is the mistake made by fundamentalist readings of sacred literature. The sacred text is approached as a "deposit" of revelation that the mind passively receives. Our presuppositions must be cleared away to let the text speak for itself. The conversation is all one way as we simply receive the never-to-be-questioned final word of the text. This, of course, leads to a stale and stagnant dogmatism that does not breath life into our existence. Yet invariably, even in the most extreme forms of biblicism, aspects from our own experience and life situation will invariably influence the focus we place on the text. The mere fact that we pay greater attention to one part of sacred literature than other parts already shows that we are not merely passive readers. Instead, we seek a conversation with the text, a conversation that can open new possibilities for the life we *currently* live. Our current life circumstances set the stage for our engagement with the text.

> My present situation is always one where I possess a finite, temporal horizon within which all that I encounter—persons, texts, images, events, symbols have their initial meaning for me. To stay in that horizon by refusing the risk of interpretation of the classics of the tradition—in the manner of authoritarian theologies of mere repetition and reconstruction—is to hand myself and my tradition over to the dustbin of history. It is to insist, in effect, that the properly human task and hope is not understanding but certitude; that so obvious, so familiar are the responses that the fundamental questions constituting the responses need not to be struggled with; that my present horizon is so clear and distinct that no effort of interpretation is required for it to be relocated by the classics of the tradition; that so eternal is the tradition that I, too, somehow partake in its tem-

porality—now in the increasingly brittle form of an ahistorical certitude.[14]

Browning also endorses Tracy's widely known *revised correlational approach*. In this approach, Tracy appreciates but goes beyond Paul Tillich's famous correlational method of doing theology. For Tillich, we need to pay very close attention to the existential situation in which we find ourselves and allow philosophical questions to emerge from that situation. These questions raised by philosophy are then answered by theology. Philosophy can be trusted to ask the important questions in its analysis of the problems of human existence. Theology then addresses those specific questions. This approach, of course, differed radically from the highly influential Protestant neo-orthodox theologian Karl Barth, who believed that natural reason is not even capable of asking the right questions. Further, argued Barth, why should we allow these questions to set the agenda for what theology has to say? For Tillich, any theology that doesn't take the existential questions of its own situation seriously will soon be dead. We have a common ground with persons asking such questions, and in fact, those questions rise up within ourselves as well. Without a rich cultural analysis, we may be addressing questions that have never even been asked.

Tracy believes that Tillich's correlational approach needs to be appreciated but expanded. More specifically, the theologian needs to take into consideration not just the *questions* raised by the philosophical analysis of human existence but also the *answers* it also proposes. Various analyses of our situation—sociological, psychological, Marxist, Freudian—do not simply stop with questions; they instead offer interpretative answers. For Tracy, we need a correlation and comparison of the answers offered by *both* Christian thought and these alternative perspectives. Theology is not simply the teacher who supplies answers to the culture's questions. Culture brings a variety of answers to the table also. For Tracy, "Tillich's method does

---

[14] Tracy, *The Analogical Imagination*, 103.

not actually correlate; it juxtaposes questions from the 'situation' with answers from the 'message.'"[15]

Yet when we look at the actual manner in which Tillich approached his dialogue partners, we see that he was interested in their interpretative answers as well as their questions. Tracy states this quite directly:

> The fact is that Tillich does allow the answers (and not just the questions) of psychoanalysis, socialist theory, existentialism, and his own "self-transcending" naturalism to provide answers, not only questions, in his theology.... In some, the method of correlation is better formulated not as he usually formulated it, but as he actually employed it: an interpretive correlation of the questions and answers of the message and the questions and answers of the situation.... This interpretation of Tillich's method is, I believe, not only more faithful to his own use of the method but also more in keeping with the hermeneutical character of all contemporary theology.[16]

As I have previously argued in *Paul Tillich and Psychology*, I, too, believe that Tillich *actually practiced* a method closer to the revised correlational approach.[17] Tillich engaged both questions and answers. Perhaps this is most revealing in his many dialogues with psychotherapists and particularly his involvement with the New York Psychology Group, a group of elite social scientists who met monthly from 1941–1945.[18]

It is important to note that, following Tillich, both Tracy and Browning argue that a correlation between culture and the Christian tradition will involve a comparison of "faith." This is a central claim: No one is without some form of faith, some trust in the assumptive world that grounds existence. We can only criticize a notion of faith

---

[15] David Tracy, *Blessed Rage for Order* (Chicago: University of Chicago, 1996) 46.

[16] David Tracy, "Tillich and Contemporary Theology," in James Luther Adams, Wilhelm Pauk, and Roger Shinn, eds., *The Thought of Paul Tillich* (San Francisco: Harper and Row, 1985) 266.

[17] Terry D. Cooper, *Paul Tillich and Psychology* (Macon GA: Mercer University Press, 2006).

[18] See Ibid., chs. 4, 5.

from another location of faith. In other words, we should not allow any cultural perspective to announce itself as "free of faith" or "faithless." It is pretentious, condescending, and impossible to claim that one judges the "faith" of another perspective from the standpoint of pure, objective, scientific observation.

It is here that Tracy may sound a bit different to some from how he sounded in his earlier work, *Blessed Rage for Order*, which was published in 1975.[19] In the 1995 preface to a new edition of this book, Tracy states that hermeneutics was important to him in 1975, but it was not yet "the very heart of my concept of theology."[20] In what may be the most revealing paragraph conveying his embrace of a hermeneutical approach, Tracy puts it this way:

> Indeed, a hermeneutical understanding of reason, history, and theology has defined, for me, how to understand reality and thought most adequately. Inevitably, as all my subsequent work on hermeneutics argues, modern "rationality" cannot be, therefore, as straightforwardly clear and controlled as "rationality" frequently functions in *Blessed Rage for Order*. I still believe in the self-correcting power of reason (as Bernard Lonergan nicely names it). However, I am not as sure as I once was that modern reason can produce so unproblematically the kind of uncomplicated metaphysical and transcendental arguments needed for a fundamental theology.[21]

This turn to a more explicitly hermeneutical approach, however, does not mean that Tracy is turning his back on the public character of theology. A public theology, for Tracy, is "available, in principle, to all intelligent, reasonable, responsible persons."[22] If there is any question as to whether Tracy has moved toward a more confessional and less public theological position, the following comment from a later work, *Plurality and Ambiguity* (1987), should clear this up:

---

[19] See William Placher, *Unapologetic Theology: A Christian Voice in a Pluralistic Conversation* (Louisville KY: Westminster/John Knox Press, 1989) 155.

[20] Tracy, *Blessed Rage for Order*, xiv.

[21] Ibid.

[22] Ibid., xiii.

When challenged on an interpretation, do I have any evidence that my conversation partner could accept? Can we find those common places that constituted the right places for discussing our differences? Can we find common places on what constitutes arguments itself? Or shall I simply retreat into announcements arising from my intuitive sense? I may be right, but no one else, in principle, will ever know it. I have become the Delphic oracle. I am reduced to solipsism, which is the enemy of conversation.[23]

The theologian who offers an interpretation of life is also responsible for setting forth public reasons for this interpretation. Tracy understands a public realm as a "shared rational space where all participants, whatever their other particular differences, can meet to discuss any claim that is rationally redeemable."[24] We should not run back into our confessional communities and avoid public discussions. While our apologetic efforts may not be universally convincing or totally validated, they can further a cultural conversation and demonstrate that Christianity is hardly irrelevant to the discussion at hand.

Public vs. Confessional Approaches

In the past several decades of Christian theology, particularly in the United States, a division has emerged concerning how "public" and how "confessional" theology should be. At the risk of overgeneralization, this American theological debate has been represented by two excellent centers of theological education, the University of Chicago and Yale University. Browning, of course, along with Tracy, Langdon Gilkey, James Gustafson, and others have consistently represented the apologetic side of theology as it has emphasized the public character of theology. Yale, on the other hand, has been the center of "postliberal" theology. It has been shaped by individuals such as Hans Frei and George Lindbeck and includes

---

[23] Tracy, *Plurality and Ambiguity*, 25.

[24] David Tracy, "Theology, Critical Social Theory, and the Public Realm," in Don S. Browning and Francis Schussler Fiorenza, eds., *Habermas, Modernity, and Public Theology* (New York: Crossroad, 1992) 19.

such well known Yale-influenced figures as Stanley Hauerwas and William Placher. *Browning believes it is possible to combine the best of the Chicago revisionist and the Yale postliberal approaches*, but before we examine how he attempts this, it is important to see the primary differences between these two theological methods.

The confessional, postliberal theology of Yale is rooted firmly in Karl Barth's warning against trying to win epistemological approval from non-Christian sources. In other words, theology, in its eagerness to make Christianity plausible to a secular audience, has too frequently been willing to sacrifice its own unique message and turn the gospel into something the non-Christian world can digest. These intellectual points of contact, for Barth, are dangerous and do not recognize that the Word of God establishes its own epistemological assurance. John Thiel provides a helpful summation of Barth's position:

> By accepting human knowledge as the criterion for divine revelation, the "Modernist" or "Cartesian" theologian mistakenly concedes that the Word of God stands in need before the claims of noetic expectations, ready to be shaped to the ever-shifting lines of relevance. "God's revelation," Barth asserts, "is a ground which has no higher or deeper ground above or below it but is an absolute ground in itself, and therefore for man a court from which there can be no possible appeal to a higher court." And precisely because revelation has "its reality and truth wholly and in every respect…within itself," the dogmatic task of expounding its promise in faith and for the church proceeds properly only by respecting the integrity of its proclamation.[25]

As Thiel goes on to suggest, while the concept of natural theology has been traditionally understood as metaphysical speculation based on natural reason, Barth redefines it as a preoccupation with methodology and prolegomena to doing theology. This preoccupation is based on a perpetual attempt to find a shared epistemological starting point with modernity.

---

[25] John E. Thiel, *Nonfoundationalism* (Minneapolis: Fortress Press, 1994) 50.

Like the nonfoundational philosophers, Barth presents his own position as a cure for a disciplinary malady diagnosed as the pretentious search for immediate and certain truth in some dimension of human subjectivity. Like the nonfoundationalist philosophers, Barth understands the modern preoccupation with methodological first principles as a formal way of making exaggerated claims for the capacities of human knowledge. And like the nonfoundational philosophers, Barth objectifies these errors as particularly modern, as part and parcel of a corrupt epistemic tradition worthy only of rejection.[26]

The public theology advocated by the University of Chicago, and particularly by Tracy's revisionist, critical correlational model, insists that we must come out of a strictly confessional context and engage culture in an effort to show the relevance of the Christian message. Tracy puts it like this:

In short, the revisionist theologian is committed to what seems clearly to be the central task of contemporary Christian theology: the dramatic confrontation, the mutual illuminations and corrections, the possible basic reconciliation between the principle values, cognitive claims, and existential faiths of both a reinterpreted post-Christian consciousness and a reinterpreted Christianity.[27]

Christian theology involves a philosophical reflection on the meanings present in common human experience, as well as the symbols and meanings within the Christian tradition. It is not enough for Christians to appeal simply to the Bible or tradition; instead, they must provide reasons and explanations that address a wider audience. Again, the theologian must engage in a cultural conversation that critically reflects upon the claims of faith. As such, these theological claims must be open to all reasonable persons. As Tracy puts it, "The central subject matter of theology, the reality of God, demands by the very universality of its claims to meaning an

---

[26] Ibid., 51.
[27] Tracy, *Blessed Rage for Order*, 32.

truth a public explication of such claims."[28] Again, the theologian cannot simply retreat back into a confessional community.

It must be strongly emphasized that Tracy is *not* a foundationalist. It is very important to read Tracy's early works in light of his progressive involvement in hermeneutical theory. He does not believe that we can, through the use of objective, neutral rationality, demonstrate the truth claims of any position. He is not trying to get rid of tradition in order to make room for a "pure rationality." Thus, *Blessed Rage for Order* can be best understood when read along with *The Analogical Imagination* and *Plurality and Ambiguity*. The hermeneutical turn becomes very obvious.

As we have seen, for Tracy, classic texts have already influenced us before we begin to interpret them. This influence is not strictly personal; instead it has been socially and culturally formed. In this sense, Tracy recognizes the significance of language in shaping the way we see the world. Our experience is mediated through language. It is not as if we have all sorts of prelinguistic experience and then shop for a language that can adequately express it. Instead, our experience only makes sense through a language. Tracy sounds almost like a postliberal in the following comment:

> We do not first experience or understand some reality and then find words to name that understanding. We understand in and through the languages available to us, including the historical languages of the sciences.... We understand in and through language. We do not invent our own private languages and then find a way to translate our communications to others. We find ourselves understanding in and through particular languages. No historical language is strictly necessary, but none is private, either. I think my best and worst thoughts, I understand my most intense pleasures and pains, I make my most considered and most rash judgments, I reach my most responsible and irresponsible decisions in and through the languages available to me. These languages are social and historical: particular languages of pleasure and pain, of judiciousness and

---

[28] Tracy, *The Analogical Imagination*, 62.

argument, of shame and honor, of responsibility and guilt. I interpret my experience by understanding it through language.[29]

Interpretation, once again, always involves an interaction and dialogue between the interpreter and the text. This dialogue between interpreter and text is crucial for the work of Tracy *and has deeply influenced Browning.* It involves the simple but profound word, "conversation." As Tracy puts it, "Just as there is no purely autonomous text, so there is no purely passive reader. There is only that interaction named conversation."[30]

Tracy identifies two important but opposing schools of thought—positivism and romanticism—which do not adequately understand the manner in which we are shaped by language. These two perspectives see language as merely instrumental. For instance, the positivist sees language as the means by which to express a prelinguistic fact of experience. They are "reporting facts" and not making interpretations. Science is a nonhermeneutical effort to report the facts that are floating around "out there." The romanticist, by contrast, sees language as the tool for expressing some deeper, internal, prelinguistic truth about the self. The romantic understanding of personal truth is that it stands independent of language. Language attempts to describe it, but the truth is beyond language. For Tracy, both these approaches forget that we would not understand anything if not for language. We are steeped in it. As he puts it, "I belong to my language far more than it belongs to me."[31]

To understand that our thinking is "language-saturated" is to also understand that it is historically and socially located. There is no timeless language and there is no timeless understanding of the world. Each of our interpretations is profoundly embedded in a social and historical matrix. Whether we like it or not, we all fall prey to cognitive finitude. No one speaks from an unchanging, ahistorical, culture-free perspective. Our thinking is no more timeless than we

[29] Tracy, *Plurality and Ambiguity*, 48–49.
[30] Ibid., 19.
[31] Ibid., 50.

are. As Tracy suggests, "Any theorist is tempted to make her or his theory the one innocent, free, precontextual hope for emancipation and enlightenment."[32] Yet this will never work. Our specific social, historical, and psychological context inevitably influences the "eternal" truth we claim to speak.

The Best of Two Worlds?

Why does Browning follow Tracy's basic methodology? Because he believes that Tracy's work "combines the best of the cultural-linguistic and the apologetic approaches."[33] While it is public and apologetic, it not based on a naïve foundationalism. Tracy clearly sees that religious classics already *shape us* before we attempt to *interpret them*. Browning further applauds Tracy's insistence that all thought is historically and socially embedded before it becomes conscious. Browning also realizes that contemporary pluralistic societies have a variety of confessional starting points and that there are no unambiguous traditions. This pluralism "out there" has also become internalized as part of our own thinking. We don't simply live in a world that is "intertextual," or involves competing definitions of reality; instead, this intertextuality has become part of consciousness itself.

While Browning agrees with the postliberal notion that all conceptual claims *begin* with faith assumptions, he also believes that if these claims are to be taken seriously they must move out of a strictly confessional community and into the public realm. In other words, the fact that all thought begins in faith is not to say that it should simply appeal to faith and refuse the apologetic task. A confessional approach argues that the church should simply exist as an alternative community in the world, a community that becomes its own apologetic by its way of life. Or as James A. K. Smith puts it,

---

[32] Ibid., 80.

[33] Don S. Browning, *A Fundamental Practical Theology: Descriptive and Strategic Proposals* (Minneapolis: Fortress Press, 1991) 45.

"The church doesn't *have* an apologetic; it *is* an apologetic."[34] Yet Browning argues that the church expresses particular claims to the world, claims that need arguments if they are to be taken seriously. These arguments will not be universally accepted and immediately embraced. Nevertheless, if the church is to move out of a hopeless fideism, then it must advance reasons for its beliefs and actions, reasons that can make sense even to those who do not share all the church's presuppositions.[35] The church must not refuse this discussion or it will be seen as sectarian and irrelevant.

Again, this is *not* a return to foundationalism. While Browning has been influenced by Jürgen Habermas, who is often considered a champion of the Enlightenment, Browning's approach is more modest. Browning recognizes the dangers of appealing to an ahistorical and asocial, disembodied sense of reason. Browning's appreciative, but cautious, attitude toward Habermas is revealed in the following comment.

> Habermas' call for a discourse that provides for the systematic redemption of validity claims sounds foundationalist. It suggests that he believes certainty about factual perception and cognitive truth, about moral rightness, and about personal authenticity can be achieved. This search for certainty seems illusory from a pragmatic and hermeneutical point of view. Both pragmatism and hermeneutics know that all discourse is more historically situated, conditioned, and relative than foundationalist and Enlightenment views allowed. At times, Habermas' work seems like a continuum of the Enlightenment quest for certainty.[36]

It is possible, argues Browning, to recognize that while a purely objective appeal to reason is not feasible, it *is* tenable, even within tradition-saturated, historically and socially limited communities, to offer public claims of a nonfoundational nature. Put simply, we can

---

[34] James K. A. Smith, *Who's Afraid of Postmodernism?* (Grand Rapids MI: Baker Academic, 2006) 29.

[35] Browning, *A Fundamental Practical Theology*, 69.

[36] Ibid.

give *good* reasons even though they may not be *perfect* reasons. Validity claims, as Habermas frequently calls them, will not necessarily convince all parties involved in the conversation, but they help keep the conversation going. Richard Bernstein states this point very well:

> ...although all claims to truth are fallible and open to criticism, they still require validation—validation that can be realized only through offering the best reasons and arguments that can be given in support of them—reasons and arguments that are themselves embedded in the practices that have been developed in the course of history. We never escape from the obligation of seeking to validate claims to truth through argumentation and opening ourselves up to the criticisms of others.[37]

Again, the fact that the pursuit of knowledge begins in a particular tradition does not mean that we shouldn't offer reasons for our cognitive claims. All communal discourse is embedded in tradition, but we also need to take the next step of dialoguing not just within our own community but with other communities as well.

Enter Paul Ricoeur

How can Browning appeal to apologetics if he has rejected the idea of objectivity? The primary reason—and this is one of the most important aspects of Browning's thought—is that he follows Paul Ricoeur's distinction between objectivity and "distanciation."[38] Distanciation is not objectivity in a foundationalist sense; instead it is the process of critically examining our own theoretical and historically shaped assumptions. It does not mean we empty all our assumptions and become neutral and objective, but it does mean that we have the capacity to reflect critically upon the cluster of assumptions, images, and symbols we have inherited. While we are each steeped in a tradition, that tradition is not the end of the story.

---

[37] Bernstein, *Beyond Objectivism and Relativism*, 153.

[38] Paul Ricoeur, *Hermeneutics and the Human Sciences*, ed. and trans. John B. Thompson (Cambridge: Cambridge University Press, 1981) esp. ch. 4.

We can both critically reflect upon that tradition and compare it with other traditions. We are not simply trapped in our own language game. We can move out of purely confessional language and offer good, even if not certain, reasons for our perspective. Human reason is not so completely corrupt that it cannot help us establish points of contact with alternative perspectives. Cognition has not been so negatively affected by self-interest that apologetics is useless.

To understand Browning's methodology, it is crucial to grasp Ricoeur's relationship to Gadamer and Habermas. Unlike Edmund Husserl, who thought human understanding involves pushing aside or bracketing all personal biases and commitments and engaging in a "pure description" of experience, Gadamer argued that this self-emptying for descriptive purposes is impossible. Our own effective history determines even the kind of questions we ask, the particular interests we hold, and the manner in which we approach life. As Dan Striver writes,

> Rather than pursuing the continual modern attempt to bracket the past, which is another way of expressing the attempt to bracket the self's preoccupations and start anew, Gadamer argues that we are formed by tradition and cannot escape it. Instead, tradition gives us questions to ask and then a foothold to grasp new ideas. It is indeed the case that presuppositions can become deformed into prejudices, but the answer is not to engage in another form of self-deception by supposing that we can rid ourselves of our past and our presuppositions. Rather, our presuppositions *enable* our understanding, as well as sometimes *disable* it. The one thing we cannot do is escape them.[39]

As we have seen, investigation can only occur because we have already been shaped by a tradition that orients us to life and makes inquiry possible. To eliminate this effective history is to eliminate any possibility of understanding. It does not matter whether we attempt to "get rid of" of our assumptive world in order to do purely

---

[39] Dan R. Striver, *Theology After Ricoeur: New Directions in Hermeneutical Theology* (Louisville: Westminster John Knox Press, 2001) 49.

empirical science or to do purely phenomenological description. The point is that we would not even attempt any form of research if we had not already been influenced by an assumptive world.

Ricoeur, however, adds an important factor to the interpretive process. While fully acknowledging the manner in which we are shaped and informed by particular traditions, Ricoeur argues that we also have the capacity to distance ourselves from these assumptions. This distancing factor will not involve complete emancipation, but it will allow a place in the interpretive process for critical reflection and corrective thinking. *And for Browning, it is this moment of critical reflection, of distanciation, in which science becomes so important*. Within the process of distanciation, the empirical findings of science can offer a corrective to assumptions that no longer seem tenable. For instance, a theological anthropology *needs* a process of critical reflection in which it allows itself to be informed by the human sciences. Just as a theology of creation cannot ignore the findings of cosmology and evolution, so a theology of the human condition cannot ignore the empirical research in psychology and other human sciences. Distanciation provides the place whereby such empirical findings can offer a critique of our inherited assumptions. If we are going to be intellectually responsible, we cannot simply affirm that these findings have nothing to do with our own particular confessional community. One reason is simply that we don't *stay* in that confessional community. We live in a highly pluralistic world, and part of that pluralism, whether we realize it or not, has already been internalized.

We need, therefore, to offer what Habermas often calls "validity claims," or rational evidence for our beliefs. For Habermas, all communication implies this capacity to offer reasons to support the claims we are making. Again, Browning's revised correlational approach accepts this obligation, as long it is not understood as a call back to the certainties of foundationalism. Just as a psychoanalyst such as Winnicott frequently talks about "good enough" parenting,[40]

---

[40] Donald W. Winnicott, *Through Pediatrics to Psychoanalysis* (New York: Basic Books, 1975).

so we can offer a "good enough" apologetic. Will it convince everyone? Of course not. But it *will* provide evidence that our claims are not defenseless. When brought into an overall hermeneutic perspective, validity claims are an important *submoment* in the process of understanding. Again, no one will be able to become tradition-free, completely neutral and objective, but that should not mean that we cannot find a critical and reflective process within the overall process of understanding.

The point is to have conversation. And conversation cannot occur when we retreat into the privacy of a language game so unique to our confessional community that we refuse engaging the culture around us. Is there a danger of losing the uniqueness of our religious understanding in this cultural dialogue? Of course. But does that mean that we should quit talking to the larger community? Hardly. The wisdom of the postliberal approach is that it reminds us that all communal discourse begins in faith assumptions that are embedded within a particular tradition. It is confessional. This is not the end of the story; this faith assumption needs to provide reasons for its commitment—reasons that will never contain foundational certainty but that are nevertheless set forth for the general public. Browning nicely summarizes his indebtedness to Gadamer and Ricoeur:

> Both Gadamer and Ricoeur believe that human understanding is primarily a historically situated dialogue or conversation exhibiting the features of question and answer. To describe is first to understand the situated dialogue in which one is already embedded—the dialogue that also already makes up the self. Hence, description, even social-science description, is not primarily an objective process of standing outside one's historically located dialogue. Rather, it is first a matter of accounting for what already has shaped us in the unfolding situation we are attempting to describe. Both Gadamer and Ricoeur believe that the prejudgments or prejudices, shaped by our cultural inheritance from the past and therefore implicit in our questions, are crucial for the understanding process. They are shaped by the continuing presence in our experience of the "effective history" of the past, especially the classic texts and monuments that have shaped our

civilization. These prejudgments must be brought to life as referents in relation to which we understand new experience.[41]

It is fair to say, then, of both Browning and Ricoeur, that they fall between the thinking of Gadamer and Habermas. The critical Frankfurt school represented by Habermas has a legitimate place within the broader act of interpretation. Science is very important within a larger hermeneutical approach.

Five Levels of Investigation

These validity claims should deal explicitly with five levels of all practical thinking that Browning begins to introduce into his writing in the mid 1980s and early 1990s. The first level is the visional level that invariably makes metaphysical claims about the ultimate context of our lives. This metaphysical level is often not officially stated, but instead assumed. It is important to smoke out these assumptions and directly talk about them. This, as I have already mentioned, is perhaps the guiding theme of Browning's career. While some may claim to be metaphysically disinclined, a closer look at underlying assumptions will reveal an assumptive world about the ultimate context of our lives. There is always an underlying vision about the nature of life in general. Even to claim that metaphysical speculation is a waste of time *is itself* a metaphysical assumption.

Investigating this level of thought will necessitate a search for deep metaphors. For Browning, following Ricoeur, we start thinking about our world in metaphors and symbols long before we entertain specific propositions. As George Lakoff and Mark Johnson put it, "The essence of metaphor is understanding and experiencing one kind of thing in terms of another."[42] Browning puts it this way: "When it comes to speaking about the most ultimate (in the sense of most determinative) aspect of our experience, we do it in

---

[41] Don S. Browning, *Christian Ethics and the Moral Psychologies* (Grand Rapids MI: Eerdmans, 2006) 88.

[42] George Lakoff and Mark Johnson, *Metaphors We Live By* (Chicago: University of Chicago Press, 1980) 5.

metaphorical language. None of us knows directly the ultimate context of experience; therefore we take more familiar and tangible aspects of experience and apply them metaphorically to the intangible and mysterious ultimate features of experience."[43] Again, because this ultimate context is beyond what can be described with ordinary language, we are "stuck" with metaphors. This is the nature of human finitude. We do not have direct access to the deepest levels of reality.

A crucial aspect of the metaphors we adopt is that they orient and direct our basic response to the universe. Is ultimate reality cold and indifferent, warm and friendly, responsive to our needs, or indifferent to our deepest concerns? Our metaphors about the cosmos shape our basic response to these questions. As Browning puts it, "Whatever our specific moral principles happen to be, they will function differently if our metaphors of ultimacy tell us that we live in a basically warm and providential world with an open future rather than the center of a black hole where all is collapsing and there is no tomorrow, or in a basically hostile world where the fates play fiendish tricks on defenseless mortals."[44] This larger worldview always dangles from even our most practical activities. We always work with assumptions about this larger context in which we live our lives.

The next level of our thinking is the obligational level. This is the level at which any perspective makes claims about what is ethically normative for the human condition. What ethical principles are implicitly used to guide human action? Browning has been a pioneer in reconnecting psychology to ethics. He hasn't simply reintroduced psychological theories to ethical thinking; instead, he has pointed out the ethical principles already implicit in various psychological perspectives. Frequently, he has suggested that Protestant Christianity and psychotherapy share something in common: Neither

---

[43] Don S. Browning, *Religious Ethics and Pastoral Care* (Philadelphia: Fortress Press, 1983) 58.

[44] Ibid., 60–61.

has spent enough time outlining the ethical principles that should guide the postconverted or posttherapized life. Just as many Protestant theologians have assumed that the experience of grace will simply guide the convert into ethical living, so many psychotherapists have assumed that the recipient of therapy will naturally and automatically know how to live authentically. For Browning, critical moral reflection is needed to achieve human flourishing. The first step is to become more conscious of the principles of obligation that inform us.

The next level of thinking is the tendency-need level. This involves anthropological claims about human nature, basic human needs, and a discussion of the pre-moral goods required to meet those needs. We gain our information about basic human needs from (a) our own intuitive experience, (b) our religious and cultural traditions, and (c) the human sciences. While we each have many desires, wants, and preferences, these do not necessarily constitute a human need. Sometimes, our desires and wishes conflict with each other and call into question once again the nature of our basic needs. Browning puts it this way: "But as traditions break down and personal experience becomes confused, humans begin to quarrel with one another about what their basic needs really are. This throws them into a comparative mentality whereby they attempt critically to correlate their historically inherited perceptions of value with what the sciences have discovered about the central tendencies of human beings."[45]

Human science information about our basic tendencies and needs can help us make rational, ethical decisions. As we have seen, this is a scientific submoment within a larger conversation. However, this newly acquired information will not immediately prescribe our ethical principles for us. Put another way, *there is no scientifically derived morality*. Science can be quite helpful in the larger discussion of ethics but it cannot, in itself, lay down the blueprint for a moral life.

---

[45] Ibid., 70.

The fourth and fifth levels are the environmental-social dimension and the rule-role level. The environmental-social dimension raises questions about the social-systemic and ecological constraints on our needs. The rule-role level is concerned with the concrete actions prescribed. For the purposes of this study, I will concentrate primarily on the first three levels.

For Browning, these five levels serve as a helpful guide for assessing any particular perspective. Further, they offer a chance to compare competing theoretical models. The apologetic task is unafraid to compare one's faith perspective with alternative views of reality. Each of these levels can be examined in a public discussion.

The Quasi-Religious Dimension of the Social Sciences

Browning makes the highly interesting claim that all social scientific perspectives eventually fade into a quasi-religious perspective. If we push a perspective far enough, we will see this partially religious dimension. Religion, for Browning, is "a narrative or metaphorical representation of the ultimate context of reality and its associated world view, rituals, and ethics."[46] Full-blown religions contain the following: (a) narratives and metaphors of ultimacy, (b) a worldview, (c) rituals, (d) ethics, and (e) a community that acknowledges these things. While various psychologies do not contain *all* of these elements, they are at least quasi-religious in that they hold implicit faith assumptions about the ultimate context of life, have a specific vision of the good life, and encourage a particular form of trust, devotion, and faith in human possibilities. They attempt to describe "the way things are" even beyond sense experience. They are also "diluted forms or fragments of historically inherited, and indeed sometimes competing, religious traditions—traditions to which modern psychologists still belong, however hazily or unconsciously."[47] The religious and cultural classics shape the pre-theoretical world of psychologists, and in turn, affect their final

---

[46] Browning, "Can Psychology Escape Religion? Should It?" 3.
[47] Ibid.

theorizing about the human condition. While Browning recognizes that some perspectives in psychology deny that they carry this philosophical baggage, Browning challenges this conviction.

> Some people might complain that insofar as such deep metaphors exist in these psychologies, they are an embarrassment and discredit any psychology aspiring to be a science. From another angle or vision, it can be argued that insofar as these metaphors exist and influence psychology, it can only gain credibility when it learns to acknowledge them and submit them to critical analysis. If the modern psychologies can avoid engendering such attitudes and holding such metaphors, it is clear that they have not as yet found a way to do so. The modern psychologies have not up to now found a way to escape faith, and faith, as I have argued, is an essential element of religion.[48]

But why not simply call these assumptions *metaphysical* rather than *religious*? Clearly there are metaphysical assumptions present, but are they truly semi-religious? For Browning, the key factor is that these metaphysical principles *elicit attitudes of trust, faith, hope*. The metaphors are religiously inspiring. They contain a philosophical anthropology that has already been affected by religious classics. The living religions provide the classic image of human nature and human fulfillment, images that live on—even if unconsciously—within our current experience. As Browning writes, "These classics contain symbolically expressed images of the human that inform our cultural imagination long before we distance ourselves from them sufficiently to begin critical reflection and more refined psychological research."[49] As Ricoeur frequently reminds us, these symbols give rise to thought. We build theories on the basis of these inherited images of human frailty and possibility. These images tell us about our nature, our normative images of health, our ethical obligations, and whether or not transcendence is possible. They tell us who we are within the specific world in which we live.

---

[48] Ibid., 7.
[49] Ibid., 8.

Once the implicit philosophical anthropologies of the contemporary psychologies have been brought to the surface, they can be evaluated and compared with other perspectives, including the philosophical anthropology of the Judeo-Christian tradition. Browning demonstrates how a philosophical anthropology can be abstracted from the symbols of the Jewish and Christian traditions. Both of these Western traditions emphasize that we are finite, conditioned people who are capable of self-transcendence. We are created by a trustworthy higher power and live in a basically trustworthy world. Creation is good, at least in a pre-moral sense. However, this good creation is susceptible to distortions through the misuse of freedom. While humanity is firmly rooted in nature, it also has the capacity for self-reflection and a dialogue with itself and God. Conscience does not simply represent the internalized prohibitions of society but a dialogue between the self and its transcendent Source. To truly understand our lives, we must understand them in the light of our relationship to our Creator.

An important task, then, is the comparison of these images and assumptions within a *broad* empirical framework. (Note that I say "broad" empirical framework.) Like William James and Reinhold Niebuhr, Browning wants to expand our understanding of human experience to include more than the discrete realm of observed data and laboratory testing. While these "harder" forms of empirical research are indeed important, they will never be able to provide answers to questions about responsibility, meaning, loss, and purpose. It is flatly inappropriate to "test" religious or metaphysical models on the basis of their ability to account for discrete, observed data. That is not their function.

Should the Clinical Psychologies Be
Chastised for Becoming "Religious"?

In the late 1970s, Paul Vitz wrote *Psychology as Religion: The Cult of Self-Worship*.[50] In this work, Vitz blisteringly accused certain forms of psychology (mostly the contemporary clinical psychologies) of forsaking science and fostering a kind of "religious" outlook. The religion, argues Vitz, is a religion of the self, a rather narcissistic worship of human potential. Vitz, like many other conservative Catholic and Protestant evangelical authors, faulted the clinical psychologies for masquerading as "science" when they were in fact nothing more than faith commitments. Vitz's perspective blew an important whistle and reflects a common assumption in many psychology circles—namely, that the scientific dimensions of the field need to push out the less-than-empirically verifiable clinical perspectives.

However valuable Vitz's observations, it is very important to understand that this is *not* what Browning is saying. In fact, Browning is arguing that it is *inevitable* that the clinical psychologies address these broader regions of human experience and, hence, leave the world of the laboratory. Browning is not "putting down" the clinical psychologies for this more-than-scientific stretch; he thinks it is inescapable. Further, he welcomes these new perspectives to the conversation. But the conversation occurs at the level of philosophical anthropology. Any pretension to still be speaking as a "pure" scientist must be renounced. There may be highly data-driven scientific submoments in this conversation, but the conversation will involve a much wider range of human experience than laboratory verification can possibly handle. Put another way, the questions are broad and encompassing ones. They involve human motivation, a sense of purpose and direction, and the ultimate aims of our lives. Clinical psychologies will always move in these directions.

---

[50] Paul Vitz, *Psychology as Religion: The Cult of Self-Worship* (Grand Rapids MI: Eerdmans, 1977).

To deny the emergence of these questions is to deny something fundamentally human. Browning points toward the important work of the historian of religion Mircea Eliade in exploring the universal urge humans have to find a sacred center that guides their lives; the work of Jung, who frequently commented that he didn't have a patient past the age of thirty-five whose primary crisis wasn't spiritual in nature; the work of William James, who identified a deep need to believe in a universe that responds to our passionate needs; and the work of Steven Toulmin, who argued that we convert our scientific theories into systems of meaning because of our essential insecurity. Psychology lapses into religion because it attempts to answer these insecurities, to give us generalized images of the world, to form the attitudes we take toward life and death, and to implicitly encourage a particular morality.

Should psychology be shamed when it journeys into this turf? Should it simply be called "bad science"? It might be called "bad science" from the perspective of a very neat-and-tidy laboratory study that looks at highly discrete data. But the broader study of the human condition, a study that dares to ask questions about our deepest human needs, what motivates us, and what grants our lives a sense of purpose *must move beyond these narrow empirical confines*.

Perhaps this can be stated a different way: Unfortunately, rigorously scientific forms of psychology can easily fall prey to foundationalism. In other words, these scientific approaches try to continue the Enlightenment hope of completely emptying ourselves before "objective reality." As we have seen, for Browning, this ignores the simple reality that none of us begin from "nowhere." It denies the basic principle that understanding always involves interpretation. We do not robotically find "facts" that tell us the meaning of our lives. Instead we search, we seek, and we interpret. Rigorous, controlled experimentation with highly selective data can help with the larger process of interpretation. As we have seen, it is an important submoment in the conversation. But the overall interpretation will transcend this. It is a long way from the lab to life's meaning.

Two Models of Psychology

Browning makes the interesting observation that we really need *two* models of psychology instead of one. We need a scientifically rigorous psychology to develop a fund of knowledge about the more biological dimension of psychology. Clearly this is important as many psychology departments across North America see themselves as moving closer and closer to biology. This is explanatory psychology. Yet we also need a more self-consciously critical and normative understanding of the person and society. This approach is broader in scope and includes the larger issues of human experience. It will not lend itself to the same strict methodology of the biological approaches. Laboratory measurements are less helpful here. Browning compares this descriptive psychology to the larger task of theology.

> It is clearly the task of theology to orient the believer to the broadest ranges of human experience, to describe and represent what experience testifies to be its ultimate context, and to induce the appropriate existential and ethical response. The function of scientific psychological language, by contrast, properly should be far more modest. If theology tries to interpret the widest possible range of human experience, experimental psychology, as does any rigorous science, narrows its task and tries to test its propositions "against the data." By *data* I mean a particular set or collection of sense data that are clear and distinct enough to be managed, controlled, isolated, and counted. The clinical psychologies, on the other hand, stand somewhere between experimental psychology and theology; rather than prediction and control based on the manipulation of discrete facts of sense experience, the clinical psychologies—or at least some of them—are thought to be concerned with the interpretation of basic patterns, modalities, themes, and narratives that give lives their underlying cohesion. To do this, they often proceed by correlating

internally perceived introspective knowledge with externally observed patterns, themes, and modalities.[51]

This, again, does not minimize the importance of rigorous scientific psychology. But the focus on this smaller range of observable data needs epistemic humility as it eventually leads to larger questions of interpretation, meaning, and ethics. Scientific psychology can provide a very helpful moment of distanciation within the larger process of understanding. A broader, critical psychology will then focus on exposing the philosophical matrix out of which scientific psychology operates. It will also push scientific psychology to reveal any normative claims it is making. A critical psychology will help prevent scientific psychology from trying to anchor itself in foundationalism. Or to state it more directly, it will help scientific psychology keep from becoming *scientistic* psychology. Many forms of scientific psychology that claim to have completely cut the umbilical cord from philosophy are merely reflecting another form of philosophy, and a not very informed one at that.

Browning's Turn to Ethics

In one of his most recent books, Browning clearly states the inevitable connection between psychology and ethics: "The questions pertaining to the meaning of ideas such as health, human fulfillment, and optimal development are difficult to confine to the disciplines of psychology; they venture into the field of ethics."[52] Yet even in the early 1970s, Browning began to notice that psychology, and even pastoral counseling, was paying very little attention to ethics. More specifically, the helping professions didn't spend much time thinking about the vision of life they recommended, nor the ethical principles that might guide that sense of human flourishing. In 1976, Browning blew the whistle. In his book, *The Moral Context of Pastoral Care*, he pointed out that there often seems to be very little, if any, difference

---

[51] Don S. Browning and Terry D. Cooper, *Religious Thought and the Modern Psychologies*, 2nd ed. (Minneapolis: Fortress Press, 2004) 6.

[52] Browning, *Christian Ethics and the Moral Psychologies*, 2.

between pastoral counselors and secular psychotherapists.[53] In describing a new generation of pastoral psychotherapists, he offered this challenge: "They appear to mean that they are psychotherapists who are also Christians. It appears, however, that the fact that they are Christian has nothing special to do with the fact that they are psychotherapists. Thus there is lacking anything like an adequate explanation for the creation of a new profession of specialized pastoral counselors."[54] Browning was not unappreciative of genuine insights into the human condition offered by contemporary psychotherapy. However, he insisted that these insights must be critically examined and compared with the vision and insights within the Christian tradition. The dialogue had become a one-way discussion in which clergy were too easily and uncritically accepting at face value the underlying ethical framework of the psychotherapies. Browning made it abundantly clear that this was *not* a call back to moralism, a world in which psychological dynamics were unappreciated.

In attempting to make this point, Browning drew upon the work of anthropologist Victor Turner, who was interested in the therapeutic rituals of primitive societies.[55] Turner divided these ancient rituals into three stages. The first stage is the phase of separation. Here, individuals give up or become separate from their former roles and automatic identities. The second phase is called "liminality." It is a transitional phase during which old commitments, values, and identities are temporarily abandoned. There is an aura of innocence and rebirth. This stage is never an end in itself but a time pregnant with new possibilities. The third phase is a period of reincorporation. The person moves out of the limbo of liminality and is reincorporated into the group with renewed vitality.

---

[53] Don S. Browning, *The Moral Context of Pastoral Care* (Philadelphia: Westminster Press, 1976).

[54] Ibid., 20.

[55] Victor Turner, *The Ritual Process* (Aldine Publishing Co: Piscataway NJ, 1969) 94–97, 102–107.

Talcott Parsons called this liminality phase a "sanctioned retreat."[56] William Bridges, in his book *Transitions,* discusses this phase as a limbo period.[57] For both Parsons and Bridges, the structure of the former life fades into the background as one explores new possibilities. The psychotherapist becomes a sanctioned retreat expert who helps us deal with the issues of our psychological dynamics while bracketing the immediate concerns of ethics. It is perfectly appropriate, argues Browning, to bracket moral convictions and ethical judgments *as we examine the psychological dynamics in our behavior.* If this were not the case, then judgment would prevent the possibility of new self-discovery. The former structure of morality needs to fade, at least for a while. Yet we should not encourage anyone to *stay* in this limbo period. We must be able to both leave and come back to the structure of our lives. As Browning puts it, "if there is no moral world from which to retreat and to return, then emotional and mental capacity will only be followed by moral confusion. When a person is so confused morally as not to be able to act or to choose, this in itself will end eventually in emotional incapacity."[58]

Browning also noticed that pastoral care in mainline churches, at least in the 1970s, was practiced with little interest or concern for larger socioeconomic problems. The focus tended to be intrapsychic. Browning also noticed that a great deal of "socio-ethical problems are often addressed without much knowledge of and sympathy for the more intimate and personal dimensions of human suffering."[59] Both perspectives are important. In this sense, Browning was very similar to Christopher Lasch, who offered a critique of the culture of psychotherapy but never minimized its importance.[60] For instance,

---

[56] Talcott Parsons, *Social Structure and Personality* (New York: Free Press, 1964) 274–75.

[57] William Bridges, *Transitions* (Reading MA: Addison-Wesley Publishing Co., 1980) ch. 5.

[58] Browning, *The Moral Context of Pastoral Care,* 37.

[59] Ibid., 17.

[60] Christopher Lasch, *The Culture of Narcissism* (New York: W.W. Norton, 1978).

while Lasch did not hesitate to charge much of post-Freudian therapy with a retreat from the ambiguities of social life, he believed that Edwin Schur, who offered a similar critique, failed to see how frantic social activities—even serious political involvement—could involve running away from the inner life.[61] This double appreciation of the intrapsychic and social worlds would often be lost in later works. And this leads to a central point: *While Browning's work clearly pushed pastoral counseling to look beyond the mere intrapsychic realm to the larger issues of social and ethical concerns, he should not, in my estimation, be considered a pioneer of a new trend in pastoral care and counseling that has practically eradicated the personal in its preoccupation with sociopolitical reality and public policy.* I have been critical of this recent trend in pastoral care and counseling primarily because it involves a pendulum swing too far in the direction of social and political preoccupation at the expense of attending to the psychodynamics of individual lives.[62] It does not simply correct the hyper-individualism of psychology; instead, it is often antipsychological. But repenting from previous excess in psychotherapy should not mean an end of interest in psychotherapy. Training in public policy analysis will not eliminate the need for deep and attentive listening to the inner world of another. Yet unfortunately, for some in mainline pastoral counseling, this so-called inner world has been completely replaced by a socially and politically constructed "self."

I believe that Browning, even as an astute critic of psycho-therapy, never lost his appreciation for psychotherapy. Psycho-therapy is a very useful enterprise. It needs, however, to be critiqued. And it further needs to be brought into the realm of ethical discourse. And this is especially true of pastoral counseling.

---

[61] Edward Schur, *The Awareness Trap: Self-absorption Instead of Social Change* (New York: McGraw Hill, 1976); Lasch, *The Culture of Narcissism*, 25–27.

[62] Terry D. Cooper, "Inner Issues and Outer Realities: Balancing Psychotherapy and Social Justice," *Journal of Psychology and Christianity* 25/2 (2006): 177–85; Cooper, *Paul Tillich and Psychology*, 208–14; Cooper, *Dimensions of Evil: Contemporary Perspectives* (Minneapolis: Fortress Press, 2007) 238–41.

When pastoral care relinquishes the attempt to reestablish at the level of the individual a sense for normative values that might be shared by a general public, it is furthering the process of privatism and pietism. An ethos which suggests that moral values are to be bracketed and relegated to the private tastes of the individuals involved makes one more contribution to the general idea that there is no shared or public moral universe. In that sense, secular individualism becomes the predominant style of the day.[63]

Browning further points out that in any "ideology of liberation," there is always the temptation to simply throw over the dysfunctional structures of the past without thinking through the standards for a new situation. Eradicating injustice is an important goal, but something must replace the unjust scheme. This requires constructive thinking. Too often, the assumption is made that sheer liberation is an end in itself. Neither Freud nor Rogers spent much time thinking about the ethics of a "posttherapy" life. Their perspectives are somewhat reminiscent of the Protestant assumption that grace and forgiveness will automatically "tell us how to live." For Freud, the elimination of neurosis will naturally place one in a position of ethical living. For Rogers, once the energies of self-actualization have been tapped, ethical issues will take care of themselves. Rogers and other humanistic psychologists would no doubt say that when human beings are freed from the demanding voices of external control, they can be deeply trusted to connect with a natural, constructive inclination. When values are not imposed and individuals are allowed to find their own deepest sense of direction, that direction will be friendly, cooperative, and socially constructive. Put another way, ethical living will occur *naturally*. This conviction seems similar to Plato's classic notion that if we really know the right thing to do, we will always do it. Self-actualizing people exhibit similar value orientations because self-actualization has a universal dynamic that produces a particular life-orientation. As we shall see more fully in chapter 2, however, Browning's critique of humanistic psychology—

---

[63] Browning, *The Moral Context of Pastoral Care*, 27.

and it is a brilliant critique—is that it completely assumes a preestablished harmony in which everyone can simultaneously self-actualize without conflict.[64] Yet this ignores the very real dilemma of one person's self-actualization blocking the actualization of another. In those situations, which actualization is privileged? On what basis do we determine whose fulfillment is most important in this situation?

Again, this critique has not been an effort to undermine the value of humanistic psychology or launch a campaign of "Rogers-bashing." Forgetting how much Rogers shaped many directions in earlier pastoral counseling, some contemporary therapists have little good to say about Rogers, period. Even the well-received book by Philip Cushman, a book that attempts a cultural history of psychotherapy in America, completely ignores the enormous impact of Carl Rogers on twentieth-century psychotherapy.[65] Whatever attitudes one might *currently* hold about Rogers, it is historically irresponsible to leave out of the record a man who fundamentally shaped counselor education programs across the American landscape.

Liberation and Its Limits

Browning believes that Protestant Christianity has often been too disconnected from its Jewish roots in the law. While being faithful to this Jewish heritage does not necessarily mean practicing all the specifics of the Jewish law, it *does* mean appreciating the need for moral rules, even if those rules must be flexible enough to deal with a rapidly changing society. Describing many Protestant churches, Browning argues that "in trying to avoid what would appear as moralism, they have in general maintained a low profile on a wide range of practical moral issues, taking no position and offering no real guidance."[66] Effective pastoral counseling must swing back and

---

[64] See Browning and Cooper, *Religious Thought and the Modern Psychologies*, 57–85.

[65] Philip Cushman, *Constructing the Self, Constructing America: A Cultural History of Psychotherapy* (Cambridge MA: Perseus Publishing, 1995).

[66] Browning, *The Moral Context of Pastoral Care*, 129.

forth between practical moral thinking about normative patterns and the forgiveness, grace, and freedom from guilt that makes such thinking possible in the first place. Browning states this directly: "We cannot understand the meaning of forgiveness unless we first throw ourselves into a radical concern about the nature of right moral action. We cannot be delivered from the curse of the law unless first of all we know, contemplate, and strive to keep the law."[67] Thus, there is a huge difference between a temporary suspension of moral judgment and a *permanent* suspension. If, and only if, a person comes out of a particular moral outlook can he or she temporarily suspend it for the purposes of working on clinical issues and psychological exploration. If, however, this backdrop is not operative, then the grace of the suspension may not be adequately appreciated. One may wonder why, exactly, one even needs to be forgiven. Grace may be meaningless in such a context because one has not felt the sting of failure. It is because this moral context is taken for granted that the bracketing of such standards, for purposes of psychological exploration, is appropriate.

> I take the position that it is precisely because the minister is working in the context of the church community, which is always attempting to clarify its value commitments, that on many occasions the pastor indeed would have the privilege of temporarily bracketing the moral issues in his care. This does not mean that moral issues are irrelevant to the counseling process, or that love and acceptance conquer all. Rather, it means that the minister can afford, by virtue of the charity of his moral context, to bracket moral issues temporarily for the sake of concentrating more specifically on dynamic, motivational, and emotional issues.[68]

In a somewhat humorous comment, Browning questions even veteran pastoral counselor Howard Clinebell for not being more specific about the ethical guidelines that should guide care. Clinebell

---

[67] Ibid., 125.
[68] Ibid., 78–79.

argues that we should increase a person's capacity to establish mutually need-satisfying relationships and to demonstrate love for both God and neighbor.[69] Yet for Browning, we need a more specific discussion of the nature of both human need and the marks of love. As he puts it, admittedly with tongue somewhat in cheek, "Hence, we do not know whether love means giving another person a massage, sleeping with his wife, inviting him to a cocktail party, joining him for a potluck dinner, or what."[70] Those who help people with marital problems need the benefit of a practical theology of marriage. Counselors who help people with sexual problems must rely on a practical theology of human sexuality. Neither pastoral nor secular counseling will be of much value unless the counselor has a background of ethical principles on which to draw. A normative set of value symbols—not too vague and diffuse—is required. Again, in an effort to escape moralism, some have lost sight of the very normative moral claims that give life purpose. Yes, a central task of the church is to create, maintain, and revise normative value systems. In fact, *if we don't have this fund of normative meanings, then we will also not have the luxury of bracketing them for the purpose of psychotherapy.* Further, confusion about the nature of what is "good" will itself create psychological disturbance.

Often assuming that mental health is the goal of the church, we miss the deeper point that establishing a moral universe is a key ingredient in mental health. As Browning puts it, "To minimize value confusion, to clarify the objects and values worthy of people's loyalty, is to contribute to their emotional and mental well being."[71] Healthy action and moral action are not synonymous. Healthy action simply refers to the capacity to act without internal conflict. Moral action moves beyond this as it seeks to act in responsible ways that will contribute to the enrichment of values for self and others. The greater

---

[69] Howard Clinebell, *The Mental Health Ministry of the Local Church* (Nashville: Abingdon Press, 1972).

[70] Ibid., 79.

[71] Ibid., 99.

the clarity about our moral commitments, the greater the possibility of healthy living.

The church is not simply the local place to debate moral issues. This would make it indistinguishable from a good course on ethics in a philosophy department. Instead, the church attempts to embody these value commitments. Browning describes this task of the church:

> It attempts to make these meanings seem real, concrete, alive, attractive, and commanding. This is the function of ritual repetition. Through dramatic repetition, ritual attempts to deepen within the worshipping community a sense for solidarity of the value systems it has come to believe are important…. Ritual tries to create a world of meaning and give it a sense of permanence through repetition. In the relative isolation of the worshipping situation, the congregation attempts to reenact the essential features of how the world should be. In this way, it further convinces its members of the validity of this vision and deepens their sense for the possibility of it becoming reality.[72]

The church both critically reflects on ethical concerns and embodies as a community its vision of the good life.

The relationship between forgiveness and the moral life can be put this way: Forgiveness makes moral life possible, but forgiveness would mean very little without an attempt to live a moral life. Forgiveness would then lose its power. Defeat precedes grace. We only prize acceptance when we first have felt rejection.

Freedom to Do What?

Browning points out that psychotherapy frequently helps people get "untangled" and experience greater freedom, but the question becomes *Freedom to do what?* Freedom, in itself, is not the ultimate goal. It is here that Browning is in agreement with longtime colleague Langdon Gilkey, who puts the issue pointedly:

---

[72] Ibid., 101.

It is the *corruption* of freedom in ourselves, not the enslavement of our freedom to others, that represents the most basic issue of history. Thus the "freeing of freedom" in human society, even if it were to be achieved, and however valid a political and Christian goal it may be, would by no means represent the final redemption of mankind or of history: for it is in freedom that we all sin. The freeing of freedom, liberation, achieves the conquest of the *consequences* of human sin in history (i.e., fate) and so—let us repeat—is an essential aspect of Christian concern for action. Nevertheless, it does not represent the conquest of sin itself out which fate and fatedness continually arise. Only a new relation of mankind to God, to self and to the neighbor can achieve that goal, an achievement far beyond the range of political activity…. By the same token, no level of political achievement, no "freeing of freedom," could prevent the reappearance of injustice, the domination and the oppression which follow from it, because the latter follow precisely from freedom, albeit a freedom misused. In the long run, warped social structures are *consequences,* not causes, of human greed, insecurity and self-concern which in turn flow from the exercise of freedom, not its oppression.[73]

This insight, so well spoken by Gilkey and so well developed in Reinhold Niebuhr, is one of the reasons that Browning has taken an appreciative (but less than enthusiastic) view of liberation theology. The liberation of freedom is extremely important; however, it hardly guarantees that today's liberated will not become tomorrow's oppressors. Browning, like Gilkey, has drunk deeply from the Niebuhrian well.

Distinguishing Pastoral Counseling from Secular Psychotherapy

For Browning, there are two senses in which the pastoral counselor can be distinguished from the secular therapist. The first is that the pastoral counselor is conscious of the transcendent dimension of what he or she is doing. The therapeutic context is "read" theologically as an arena of horizontal grace. Second, the

---

[73] Langdon Gilkey, *Reaping the Whirlwind: A Christian Interpretation of History* (Eugene OR: Wipf and Stock Publishers, 2000) 236.

pastoral counselor works out of a specific moral context that should be visible to the public even though the work may occur outside an official church setting. While the specialized pastoral counselor should be able to count on the sanction of the larger church, this counselor should be grounded in the values represented by the larger church. Again, this does not mean that the pastoral counselor cannot bracket this moral universe for the purposes of understanding the deep world of psychological dynamics. A promiscuous man or woman, for instance, can suspend judgment on his or her behavior as he or she explores the inner landscape of source relationships, the craving for love, and the inappropriate attempts to get it. This does not mean that the client or patient is left in limbo without any help in molding behavior around person-affirming standards of sexual activity. Again, one cannot take a "retreat" from normative standards unless those normative standards are already present. In an interesting example of how a theory of moral obligation operates beneath all perspectives, Browning reports the following conversation.

> One of my scholarly friends accused me of using this model to subordinate psychology to theology. He was, in fact, a professional psychologist and valued the autonomy of psychology as a scientific discipline. He did not want theology telling moral psychologists what to think. I responded that I was not so much trying to subordinate psychology and social sciences to theology as I was trying to locate both disciplines—psychology and theological ethics—within a larger theory of experience and praxis. I hold that the effective history of a tradition—that is, its memory of the resolution of past moral crises and hence its possible wisdom—is always needed to make moral sense of the discrete facts of scientific discovery. A moral tradition should not dictate to the scientist what the facts really are, even though a tradition may provide the psychologist some good, testable hypotheses about the facts. But science alone cannot establish the

broader theory of experience and praxis required to give the more discrete facts of science their full meaning.[74]

Tracking down a person's sense of moral guilt is not the task of psychotherapy. Psychotherapy instead brackets those questions so that psychological diagnoses can be made. But the person needs to re-enter a moral universe informed by a tradition. One may critique that tradition but one first has to know it.

Psychology, Community, and Moral Tradition

In his 2006 book *Christian Ethics and the Moral Psychologies*, Browning turns his attention to how the moral psychologies might be able to help both moral philosophy and Christian ethics. Can these new psychologies be trusted as a guide for ethical thinking? Browning's answer to this question is that moral psychology can indeed contribute to developing Christian ethics, but it must have competent prescientific and preempirical understandings of morality.[75] In other words, moral psychology cannot be completely autonomous. Instead, it must be developed with a clear understanding of its own preempirical, philosophical, and even quasi-theological assumptions. This brings moral psychology into the same situation that other forms of psychology face. As we have seen, in an attempt to be scientific, psychology has sometimes bought into a foundationalist understanding of the development of knowledge. This understanding insists on beginning with an absolutely sure foundation, a starting point that is beyond doubt. The mind must be emptied of its previous assumptions and objectively "take in" the facts. This passive view of science does not adequately acknowledge the interpretive process that is always involved in scientific discovery. Browning asks the following question of scientific psychology:

---

[74] Browning, *Christian Ethics and the Moral Psychologies*, 10.
[75] Ibid., 2.

51

> Psychology aspires to be a science. But what does that mean? Does it mean that in order to be objective and advance publicly replicable knowledge about human behavior it must forget the history of the human race, wipe it away from the minds of psychologists, who must study behavior as though they had never learned anything from the past? Some psychologists think that is what objectivity means…. I don't hold that view. I argue that moral psychology must build its empirical work on pre-empirical philosophical and even theological assumptions.[76]

Foundationalism, in its perennial attempt to start from scratch with a neutral perspective, attempts to wipe out the very effective history that makes research meaningful in the first place. But who can arrive at a totally neutral starting point? As Browning points out, many non-foundationalists argue that this form of objectivity is both culturally nihilistic and arrogant.[77]

> Think what it would mean to start from a neutral foundation in raising children. Parents and teachers would be saying, in effect, that our community and the human race have nothing to learn from our history about the good and the right and that we must discover it all over again—a very confusing experience, I would think for a two-year-old. The foundationalist attitude…alienates us from the wisdom of the tradition, assumes that our ancestors never learned anything that was true or valid, and assumes that to learn how to design a society or live a good life, we literally must invent the world anew.[78]

Agreeing with many aspects of the study *Hardwired to Connect: The New Scientific Case for Authoritative Communities*,[79] Browning argues that we do not need an uncritical return to *authoritarian* communities but instead a return to *authoritative* communities. There is a significant difference between these two terms. Authoritarian

---

[76] Ibid., 6.

[77] Ibid., 7.

[78] Ibid.

[79] *Hardwired to Connect: The New Scientific Case for Authoritative Communities* (New York: Institute for American Values, 2003). This study was also sponsored by Dartmouth Medical School and the YMCA of the USA.

communities applaud tradition and authority *but have no critical principle by which to test these ideas.* Authoritative communities contain this critical component. Authoritative communities respect the wisdom of the past and do not try to eliminate it. However, they *are prepared* to examine this wisdom critically and carefully; it is not simply accepted without question. We *both* learn from and critique our traditions. There must be a critical moment in the middle of the interpretive process, and this critical moment needs to involve conversations with others. One cannot do this in isolation. Our need for support and feedback also has a cognitive component.

As Christopher Lasch pointed out in *The Culture of Narcissism*, psychology can easily fall into an ahistorical, overly individualistic, and egocentric mode.[80] Moral psychology, also, can fall prey to this minimization of wisdom of the past. As in all aspects of life, we begin thinking about moral issues *after having already been shaped by communities and classics that have shaped our image of human goodness.* These influences are there whether we recognize them or not. In fact, this ethical assumptions will sneak into our theoretical formulations in highly subtle ways. Thus, as this chapter's beginning quotation suggests, the choice is not between tradition *or* critique. Instead both need to be present. Thus, Browning puts his critical hermeneutical approach this way: "We first come to know our moral and premoral goods by interpreting a tradition; science can then play a secondary diagnostic role in helping us to clarify goods and threats to them when conflict and obscurities within our cultural and religious traditions require additional testing.[81]

A Summary of Browning's Methodology

Theology must move in the same direction that *all* thought moves—from practice, to theory, and back to practice. Unlike Barth, who believed the theological community should empty itself of its usual attempts to verify its experience and simply conform to the

---

[80] Lasch, *The Culture of Narcissism*.
[81] Browning, *Christian Ethics and the Moral Psychologies*, 14.

Word of God as it is revealed in Scripture, Browning argues that we already approach Scripture with an implicit cluster of assumptions we can never completely eradicate. We may distance ourselves from those assumptions, but we cannot step outside of them any more than we can cease to have a history. We never really move from theory to practice, even though it may seem that we do. As Browning puts it, "When theory seems to stand alone it is only because we have abstracted it from its practical context. We have become mentally blind to the practical activities that both precede and follow it."[82] Practical reason attempts to reconstruct a picture of the world, as well as our concrete practices in that world, when our inherited assumptions are in crisis.

For Browning, we must look backward before we can look forward. In other words, we are already steeped in a tradition. We cannot be a citizen of a culture without also being a recipient of a tradition. This tradition presents its own classics which have already shaped our consciousness before we begin our formal theorizing. Something has already become normative for us before we go searching for normative claims. We have already digested many assumptions before we begin our conceptual constructions.

As we have seen, this nonfoundational perspective does not mean that we cannot have a submoment of critical reflection and distanciation from those assumptions. This will *not* involve the total objectivity of foundationalism, but it *will* involve a place for crucial role of critique. This critical submoment is always a part of the overall interpretive process even when it involves an attempt to step outside ourselves and examine our own assumptions. It is here, during this important stage of self-critique, that science plays such a crucial role. Browning's dependence on Ricoeur's notion of distanciation sets him at odds with a confessional community that backs away from providing public reasons for its perspective. Again, Browning argues that we all *begin* in confessional communities and that faith is the necessary prerequisite to all knowledge. But we also need to meet

---

[82] Browning, *A Fundamental Practical Theology*, 9.

others in a public discussion, a conversation that attempts to put forward our perspectives in a reasonable fashion. Part of this discussion will necessitate the stretching of the word "empirical" to include broader ranges of human experience. If one uses a narrow definition of "empirical" as simply that which can be replicated and tested in the laboratory, we will miss much insight that a broader understanding of experience entails. Following both William James and Reinhold Niebuhr, Browning wants to move away from strict, laboratory-controlled definitions of human experience. Niebuhr, for instance, could say that the Christian understanding of sin can be empirically validated even though it cannot be demonstrated in the classroom. This empirical examination of sin as excessive self-regard in the face of anxiety needs the additional insight of Christian revelation, but the fruits of sin can be seen all around us.

Critics of this approach might well say that Browning is still looking for some form of objective or neutral reason by which we can compare our positions. It is precisely this kind of shared episte-mological standard they reject. Each faith community has its own epistemology and we would only be speaking "past each other" in conversation. There is no point in appealing to reason to solve our differences because "reason" is already controlled by our presup-positional frameworks. If we attempt to justify our perspectives according to some form of publicly agreed upon and neutral reason, we are already a captive of modern thinking. For confessional theologians, the primary witness to the world is not a justification to the world of its rational claims but instead the depth of its model of a redeemed community. The quality of life represented by the church is its only apologetic. It can speak until it is exhausted about the rational qualities of its convictions, but it will be assuming once again a neutral reason "out there" that can determine the truthfulness of faith. Such a standard does not exist.

For Browning, our reason is not so corrupted by self-centeredness that we cannot evaluate the plausibility of our claims. In describing Reinhold Niebuhr's view of reason, Browning also describes his own:

> In spite of sin's corruption of reason, Niebuhr believed that we retain sufficient moral reason to make universal and just ethical judgments. This means that even as sinners, we have the moral capacity to view moral conflicts from the perspective of our neighbor's interests and to imagine universally generalizable solutions. According to Niebuhr, sin does not destroy our moral-cognitive capacity to make such reasoned judgments. *Instead, sin simply impairs our capacity to fulfill them in action.*[83]

This is not to say that our perspective does not go beyond reason, but it does say that our perspective should not contradict or oppose empirical evidence, coherence, or consistency. While all perspectives have a narrative, we should be able to compare and contrast those narratives. How do they stack up with what we know about the world? Do they need to be adjusted based on new information? Without this self-critical moment of distanciation, we might very well continue embracing some aspects of a narrative that has outlived its usefulness. Perhaps the most obvious example of this might be our theory of how the world came into existence. Many creationists refuse to submit their thinking to a critical submoment in which evidence from paleontology, archaeology, and biology make important contributions. Their avoidance of these scientific contributions pushes their conceptions toward enormous incredulity as they argue, in some cases, that these bones were somehow put in the ground to "test" our faith. Any conceptual scheme, if it wants to survive, ought to pay attention to scientific discoveries. This is not to say, however, that the implicit philosophical assumptions of science should not be critiqued. As I have already suggested, science can quickly become scientism. A naturalistic methodology can easily turn into a naturalistic ontology. Philosophical assumptions can be smuggled into so-called scientific investigations, investigations that

---

[83] Browning, *Christian Ethics and the Moral Psychologies*, 30.

try to prove the validity of the philosophical starting point while ignoring contradictory evidence. For example, some "scientists" argue that we will soon be "over" our need for religion and that this primitive impulse will be replaced by science. This shallow view of religion ignores the reality that there has probably never been a culture throughout human history for which religion was not a primary factor. Quite frankly, this secular tale about the irrelevance and obsolescence of religion has been stated repeatedly since the Enlightenment and always proves to be shortsighted.

So where does Browning's critical hermeneutical approach fit into the battle between modernity and postmodernity? Basically, it affirms the frequent postmodern conviction that all thought begins in a historically located tradition. Our thinking bears the stamp of our own historical and linguistic situations. A horizon of assumptions and implicit values is always a part of even our scientific thinking. No one begins from complete neutrality. Browning, though, carries a modernist submoment within a postmodern view of interpretation. This distancing factor, as we have seen, is precisely the place where science can be so helpful. Further, Browning also follows the modernist impulse to compare and critique various worldviews. While he does not believe that this critique can involve the radical objectivity of the Enlightenment, he *does* believe that it is an important process of the overall hermeneutical process. Many postmodernists would argue that it is impossible to perform this type of comparative analysis to see which perspective matches the multi-dimensional level of our experience. We are stuck within the narrative of our own circumstances, and critical reason will not help us. Why? Because reason is already shaped and controlled by our assumptive worlds. Browning disagrees with this rejection of the role of reason and argues that while foundationalism is out, critical distance from our assumptions is not. We do not need total objectivity to ensure a submoment of critical reason.

This, then, is an overview of Browning's critical hermeneutical approach to psychology. Both the words "critical" and "hermeneutical" are extremely important because his view of interpretation makes room for the crucial submoment of distanciation in which science plays such an important role. The deeper claims and hidden assumptions of psychology must be named, critically evaluated, and brought into a larger discussion of philosophical anthropology. The theologian is not doing his or her job if these psychologies are allowed unquestioningly to come forth as "science," while neglecting the underworld of assumptions beneath their own practices.

2

Basic Instinct(s): Human Nature and Culture

"Perhaps more than any other feature, psychology in the twentieth century has been marked by an awareness of the role of instincts in the mental life of humanity. What is the nature of human beings? More than any other question that people ask, this is the most important." —Don Browning

There are few things more controversial on college and university campuses than the issue of whether we can speak of a "human nature," and what role the instincts play in such a "nature." The battle lines are often drawn around biologically inclined and social-constructionist-inclined persons speaking about the human condition. Some believe that the outdated issue of discussing a universal human nature needs to be given up as another misguided Enlightenment hope. Others argue that the denial of such a nature is precisely what is wrong with the human and social sciences. Still others argue that whether we admit it or not, we are always working with a background picture, a normative image, of human nature. Some postmodernists insist that we must stop imposing a singular definition of humanity on the multiplicity of human life we encounter. Some feminists insist that when we speak of human nature, we are typically speaking from the standpoint of privileged, white, typically Euro-American males. The old and familiar battleground between psychologists and sociologists over whether we truly have "instincts" has been expanded and turned into a discussion about normative images of humanity. If one thought the debates between an evolutionary and social constructionist perspective died out in the 1970s war over sociobiology, then one has not witnessed the current heat generated by discussions between evolutionary psychologists and social constructionists. In fact, some of the intensity of these debates make older controversies over theological dogma look pretty tame.[1]

Some of Don Browning's best work is his investigation into the place of instincts in the modern psychologies. More specifically, Browning is concerned with the relationship between instincts and culture, between basic human inclinations and ethics. In this chapter, an admittedly long one, I will examine Browning's exploration of Freud's dual instinct model, the single instinct perspective of humanistic psychology, the near no-instinct model of radical behaviorism, the current instinctual views of evolutionary psychology, and the instinctual pluralism of William James. Controversy over the relationship between instinct and culture pushes this chapter toward a wider analysis than any of the other chapters. But this multifaceted exploration is necessary because the controversy surrounding culture and instincts is so crucial to psychological theory.

Freud and the Double-Instinct Model

Freud defined instinct as an inherent biological drive to restore an earlier state of equilibrium and thereby reduce the tension present in one's present life. During an early period in Freud's life, he believed that we have only one basic instinct—sexuality. Working with sexually repressed individuals, Freud believed that the key to resolving psychological problems *is* the overthrow of rigid sexual restraints. These sexual taboos *chained* us to constant conflict. Repression was the enemy and liberation was the cure.

Unfortunately, this is the only Freud many people know. Many individuals do not grasp Freud's later, sober realization that a life of unrestrained sexual liberation would make civilization impossible.

---

[1] David M. Buss and Neil Malamuth, *Sex, Power, Conflict: Evolutionary and Feminist Perspectives* (New York: Oxford University Press, 1996).

Restraint is needed if we are to live cooperatively with each other. Over the years, Freud's position came closer and closer to that of pessimistic social philosopher Thomas Hobbes (1588–1679). In fact, remarkable parallels can be drawn between Hobbes and Freud. They both (a) were materialists who argued that all mental life can ultimately be reduced to biological processes; (b) believed that the same laws that govern physics can be used to study psychology; (c) were profoundly interested in tracing the law of cause-and-effect in human behavior; (d) believed that human beings have a natural inclination to be excessively self-interested; (e) believed that society would not be possible unless individuals give up some of their freedoms and submit to a larger rule of law; (f) believed that religion is founded on the basis of fear; (g) believed our desires are by-products of physiological activity; (h) were highly suspicious of any hint of true altruism in human behavior; (i) believed that the primary motivations of human life are pleasure and pain; and (j) were pessimistic about human possibilities. For Hobbes, we are basically barbarians in dire need of social restraint. If one reads Freud's seasoned thought in *Civilization and Its Discontents*, one gets nearly the same conclusion.[2]

Freud's developing focus on aggression led him to believe that it was not simply a byproduct of sexual frustration. Instead, aggression had its own line of development. In *Civilization and Its Discontents*, Freud stated, "I can no longer understand how we can have overlooked the ubiquity of non-erotic aggressivity and destructiveness and can have failed to give it its due place in the interpretation of life."[3] Again, he now considered this an autonomous drive, an instinct separate from sexuality. This was not an easy point for him to admit: "I remember my own defensive attitude when the idea of an instinct of destruction first emerged in psychoanalytic literature, and how long it took before I became receptive to it. That others should

---

[2] Sigmund Freud, *Civilization and Its Discontents*, trans. James Strachey (New York: W. W. Norton, 1961).

[3] Freud, *Civilization and Its Discontents*, 67.

have shown, and still show, the same attitude of rejection surprises me less. For little children do not like it when there is talk of the inborn inclination toward badness, to aggressiveness and destructiveness, and so to cruelty as well."[4]

Beginning in 1920, Freud's view of the human condition became much more pessimistic.[5] Repression was no longer the great enemy to be overthrown. In fact, like Hobbes, he believed that it was necessary for survival. Stephen Mitchell and Margaret Black describe Freud's later position: "Ideal mental life does not entail an absence of repression, but the maintenance of a modulated repression that allows gratification while at the same time preventing primitive sexual and aggressive impulses from taking over. The turn toward a darker vision of instincts brought a more appreciative attitude toward social controls, which he now regarded as necessary to save people from themselves."[6]

Freud eventually moved to the position that our lives are dominated by *two* dominant instincts—sex and aggression. While they often overlap, they have distinct, biological roots. The notion of "drive theory" is typically associated with this classical Freudian view. Destructiveness is innate. It doesn't result simply from being wounded, hurt, or deprived. It is a natural outgrowth of our biology. Drives, themselves, can be destructive.

Freud eventually conceived of these tendencies toward sex and aggression as larger instincts he called *eros*, the life instinct, and *thanatos*, the death instinct. Human beings are locked in an ongoing internal conflict between the two. The death instinct rarely expresses itself directly. Instead, it emerges as hatred of others, aggression toward others, aggression toward oneself (moral masochism), and a rather uncanny desire to return to the inorganic realm. This ultimate

---

[4] Ibid.

[5] For a more developed view of Freud's gradual turn to the death instinct, see my *Dimensions of Evil: Contemporary Perspectives* (Minneapolis: Fortress Press, 2007) 102–117.

[6] Stephen A. Mitchell and Margaret J. Black, *Freud and Beyond: A History of Modern Psychoanalytic Thought* (New York: Basic Books, 1995) 19.

resignation is also part of the death wish. It reveals a passive, "giving up" attitude toward life. Since Freud assumed that the major goal of life is tension reduction, it is natural to seek the ultimate reduction of all tension—namely, death. The life instinct always attempts to push the aggression of the death instinct outward and away from oneself. Aggression must be externalized for survival to be possible. Otherwise, it will destroy us. A common example of this is the inability to express anger, a tendency which then makes one depressed. The aggression is turned back on oneself and depletes the self of vital energy.

Even though the death instinct and life instinct have autonomous sources, they often travel together. We rarely see "pure" forms of either of them. As Freud put it, "The two kinds of instinct seldom—perhaps never—appear in isolation from each other, but are alloyed with each other in varying and different proportions and so become unrecognizable to our judgment."[7]

This biologically rooted aggressive instinct is the major threat to civilization. As Freud put it, "I adopt the standpoint, therefore, that the inclination to aggressiveness is an original, self-subsisting instinctual disposition in man, and I return to my view that it constitutes the greatest impediment to civilization."[8] The life and death instincts are locked into a cosmic battle. Freud describes what seems like an eternal dualism: "This struggle is what all life essentially consists of, and the evolution of civilization may therefore be simply described as the struggle for life of the human species. And it is the battle of the giants that our nurse-maids try to appease with their lullaby about heaven."[9]

Browning has pointed out that in taking this intrapsychic battle between life instincts and death instincts into a larger view of life, Freud has turned metaphysician. Freud makes a clear connection between his view of biological instincts and his entire cultural vision.

---

[7] Freud, *Civilization and Its Discontents*, 66.
[8] Ibid., 69.
[9] Ibid.

His psychological observations have turned into something very similar to Zoroastrianism, a Persian religion that emphasizes a cosmic battle between the forces of light and darkness. As Browning puts it, "When Freud's increasing affirmation of his two instincts of life and death combines with his scientific naturalism and positivism, the net result is to make these instincts more than humble working hypotheses designed to order discrete areas of observed data, but instead they are elevated into a cosmology and inflated into metaphors which represent the ultimate context of experience."[10] These forces no longer simply occupy the human mind; instead, they have taken on a cosmic dimension. They now apply to *all* biological life. Freud has thus developed a kind of quasi-religious outlook. His religious creed of naturalism and positivism elicits a kind of faith in the ultimate nature of things. But Browning wants to understand how Freud "knows" we live in a strictly material world and that there is nothing beyond his naturalistic ontology. In reality, Freud doesn't "know" these things, particularly as he speaks as a scientist. He has turned an interesting hypothesis that helps him observe clinical data into a much larger worldview with two cosmological principles in conflict. Freud would no doubt deny that he is speaking "religiously" here; nevertheless, when he insists that the naturalistic dimension is the only dimension within the universe and that his psychological claims can provide an ultimate explanation for *all* of life, he is indeed speaking from a quasi-religious perspective. This is Freudian *faith*. Again, Freud, like everyone else, is stuck with the epistemological problem of not knowing, in an empirical way, the ultimate context of human experience. He claims to know, though, sometimes with a dogma as pronounced as any theological perspective. Browning doesn't fault him for moving his perspective beyond a strict empiricism; however, he should be conscious of what he is doing and not claim to be acting as a scientist.

---

[10] Don S. Browning and Terry D. Cooper, *Religious Thought and the Modern Psychologies*, 2nd ed. (Minneapolis: Fortress Press, 2004) 42–43.

In examining Freud's view of the instincts, it is crucial to understand the cultural context in which he made his discoveries. At the risk of generalization, Freud began his investigations in a social context that emphasized the Enlightenment ideal of human progress through rationality. Reason can emancipate us from the ignorance of the past. On a steady path of both scientific and moral progress, humanity can eventually eliminate its own evil. The world is becoming better, people are becoming more reasonable, and the future is looking more positive.

In such an optimistic context, Freud's views represented an astounding alarm against notions of human progress. Freud relentlessly insisted that our "pure" reason is frequently governed by sources completely outside our awareness. Our sexual "purity" is a self-conjured delusion. The conscious ego, to use Freud's language, does not enjoy the control of the psyche it imagines. Unconscious factors are always at work. For Freud, the unconscious is never pretty. Freud has been frequently dubbed a "master of suspicion" precisely because he does not take many things at face value. Reason is hardly as noble as we may think. In fact, it is deeply influenced by underlying urges we would rather not face—but Freud pushed us to face them.

This is the Freudian picture of the human psyche: Our instincts have a deep grip on our intellect and behavior. There are two basic instincts Freud developed into enlarged metaphors describing all of reality. It's not just that the individual psyche is riddled with conflict; reality itself is troubled by a cosmic conflict. This conflict will never be completely healed or resolved. It is built into the very structures of life. Conflict is an ontological reality. We learn to tame our instincts and act in fairly constructive ways, but both actions necessitate a great deal of work. Our instinctual life will *always* be pushing for expression. The dark forces of destructiveness will forever attempt to ambush the constructive dimensions of life.

Perhaps Freud's convictions should be stated this way: Human healing can never occur as a result of returning to a previous innocence, a life before some sort of psychological "fall." Our very nature itself is part of the problem. Our destructiveness doesn't simply result from "what's been done to us," but from the very biological core of our being. Our own innate drives—even apart from abuse, neglect, or wounding—will create problems for us. Put another way, we are constitutionally destructive. There never was a "psychological Eden." While early relationships are important, we would have psychological conflict even if we were raised by perfect parents. The problem, again, is endogenous. It can certainly be exacerbated by our emotional environment, but bad parenting, poor schools, or various forms of abuse are not the only causes of our human ills. This, again, is the backbone of drive theory in psychoanalysis. Neither the individual nor the social world will ever be healed by historical progress. And further, as Browning points out quite well, Freud sees this conflict as so deeply embedded in life itself that it actually becomes a kind of faith, a conviction about the nature of reality. It hardly needs to be said that this belief extends beyond the tidy world of empirical verification.

This point is crucial in Freud because we will later see some humanistic psychologists calling for a return to lost innocence, a time in which the healthy child had not been negatively affected by the psychological pollution of society. This "return to nature" will become the model of health. Somehow we must get back to what has been lost, but for Freud, this so-called innocence was never there. It hardly offers an unambiguous source of goodness. We will not be able to retreat into our early psychological past and find an uncomplicated, "pure" self. As Thomas Finger reminds us, for Freud, "The self is not nearly so much discovered as created and recreated amid conflicting pressures."[11]

It is at this point that Browning builds on the work of Reinhold Niebuhr and, to a lesser degree, the work of Paul Tillich to evaluate Freud's instinctual claims. While Tillich is quickly associated with

---

[11] Thomas Finger, *Self, Earth, and Society* (Downers Grove IL: Intervarsity Press, 1997) 38.

psychology, and particularly psychotherapy, the thought of Reinhold Niebuhr, because he is usually understood as a social ethicist and political thinker, is not so clearly connected with the helping professions. Yet it is Browning's conviction that Niebuhr has a great deal to say to psychologists.[12] In a nutshell, both Tillich and Niebuhr applaud Freud's realistic picture of the human condition but think he was wrong in calling human destructiveness our "essential" or "ontological" condition. While Niebuhr and Tillich differed in their assumptions on the nature of what theologians have called "the Fall," they both agreed that Freud located the problem too much in our basic nature.[13] Tillich argued that Freud confused our "estranged" nature with our "essential" nature.[14] In other words, Freud took our distorted condition and argued that this is our essential condition. It "has to be this way." For Tillich, in our essence, we are not estranged, neurotic, or self-destructive. Because Freud held the view that our essence, itself, is distorted, his portrait of humanity was very gloomy. Thus, Tillich says of Freud, "His dismay of culture shows that he is very consistent in his negative judgments about man as existentially distorted. Now if you see man only from the point of existence and not from the point of view of essence, only from the point of estrangement and not from the view of essential goodness, then this consequence is unavoidable."[15]

---

[12] My own book, *Reinhold Niebuhr and Psychology: The Ambiguities of the Self* (Macon GA: Mercer University Press, 2009), is deeply influenced by Browning's use of Niebuhr in interpreting contemporary psychology. We both share a conviction that Niebuhr's theological anthropology holds a great deal of promise for understanding the human sciences.

[13] This disagreement between Tillich and Niebuhr on the nature of "the Fall" is a complex issue and beyond the purposes of this book. The reader might be helped by examining Langdon Gilkey's attempt to resolve this dispute in *Gilkey on Tillich* (New York: Crossroad, 1990) 114–37; I also discuss this issue in *Paul Tillich and Psychology* (Macon GA: Mercer University Press, 2006) 69–75.

[14] Paul Tillich, "The Theological Significance of Existentialism and Psychoanalysis," in Perry LeFevre, ed., *The Meaning of Health* (Chicago: Exploration Press, 1984) 81–95.

[15] Ibid., 88–89.

Tillich frequently used the traditional Christian concept of "concupiscence," or inordinate desire, to illustrate the difference between our created and distorted natures. Our basic desires are not innately out of control. Our desires only become excessive when we have lost our essential connection to our Ground and Source, God. When that fundamental relationship has become distorted, it is then, and only then, that our desires become excessive and destructive. We become idolatrous as we try to turn the object of our desires into a "god" that will rescue us from the dilemmas of life. We deify the objects of our desires and treat them as if they are pivotal for our entire lives. But this elevation of a finite object quickly throws our lives out of balance, makes us insatiable, and turns us away from the true Source of our contentment. We've lost our rootedness in the ultimate and turned limited goods into the all-important givers of life. We are pushing these things to be more than they are designed to be. Again, there is nothing in our essential nature which demands this process.

Thus, while Tillich believed Freudian psychology could greatly benefit theologians as they examine estranged existence, Freud was wrong about the origin and necessity of our estrangement. He rooted our problem of "sin" in biology. Freud offers a brilliant diagnosis of our problem; however, his etiology is flawed.

While appreciating many aspects of Tillich's anthropology, Browning uses Niebuhr much more frequently than he uses Tillich. Part of this may be because of his shared belief with Niebuhr that Tillich's understanding of an "ontological Fall" comes dangerously close to an inescapable fate which ultimately threatens the notion of human responsibility. Like Tillich, Niebuhr finds enormous insight in the work of Freud and thinks Freud realistically described human existence. Niebuhr is particularly fond of Freud's challenge to pretentious, Enlightenment reason. Throughout his classic work, *The Nature and Destiny of Man*, Niebuhr sounds quite Freudian as he resurrects the older doctrine of "original sin" and describes the capacity of human beings to focus excessively on their own security at the expense of others.[16] Niebuhr puts it this way: "Reason is never completely emancipated from the particular and parochial interests of the individual and collective particularity."[17] Niebuhr, also, was a master of suspicion in his own right, arguing passionately that human beings are capable of enormously complex and intricate self-deception.

Niebuhr's theological anthropology closely follows that of Søren Kierkegaard. For Niebuhr, as for Kierkegaard, human beings are born into a state of anxiety. This anxiety is a natural part of the human condition because human beings are both embedded in nature and have a self-transcending capacity. This capacity for self-transcendence simply means that we can rise above human existence and reflect upon the meaning and purpose of our lives. We have a capability that other species don't seem to share: We realize that we are finite, limited creatures who are going to die. Thus, we have one foot squarely planted in biological existence and another foot planted in this capacity to think about our mortality and human limitations. Niebuhr frequently refers to this as a combination of nature and spirit. This combination of nature and spirit produces anxiety. Again, this anxiety is an essential part of the human condition. In other words, it doesn't happen simply because we distort our experience. *When we see the world realistically, we will be anxious.* This anxiety cannot be completely "therapized" away. We cannot get rid of it by taking Valium or any other antianxiety medication. It is "part of the package" of being human. It is both inevitable and unavoidable.

A crucial point, however, is that this anxiety does not necessitate destructive action. While it may be the "precondition" or "breeding ground" of destructive action, there is nothing about the anxiety that demands estrangement. Put simply, anxiety is not the cause of human sin. For Niebuhr, we always have the possibility of trusting God as the Ground and Source of our lives and thus finding a sense

---

[16] Reinhold Niebuhr, *The Nature and Destiny of Man*, 2 vols. (New York: Charles Scribners, 1964).

[17] Ibid., 1:268.

of internal peace amidst life's anxiety. But when insecurity sets in, we are powerfully tempted to distrust God and instead place our confidence in our own ability to manage our own lives. Sometimes this confidence takes a very bold and self-assertive form as we attempt to deny our finitude and master our own lives. This is a form of pride which has an obvious egocentric quality. It is full of itself, arrogant, self-inflated. This form of pride was brilliantly exposed throughout Niebuhr's writings. However, pride does not always take this form. For Niebuhr, pride is completely connected to the issue of distrust. Any time we distrust God, we inevitably fall into pride because pride refers primarily to *self-preoccupation.* This undue focus on self is the root of the problem. It may take on a very arrogant posture or it may appear to be worried about its competence. Regardless of the expression it takes, *it always involves an undue self-preoccupation*. Thus, distrust in God and excessive focus on self are two sides of the same coin. Without a trust in the providence of God, anxiety will often push us into a frantic concern with our own security. This self-preoccupation keeps us from caring for others and living fully.

Browning's work is loaded with Niebuhrian insight. He also shows how Niebuhr has often been misunderstood. For one thing, Niebuhr's well-known preoccupation with the issue of human self-regard is frequently treated as an offense to the importance of self-esteem. But when Niebuhr discusses self-regard he is always referring to *excessive self-regard*, and not a healthy level of self-esteem. Niebuhr provides a comprehensive picture of excessive self-preoccupation (due to mishandled anxiety) and should not be seen as an enemy of self-esteem. Self-care is as important in Niebuhr as it is to any psychologist. However, because of the nature of anxiety, self-care can turn into a self-preoccupying focus that exploits and uses others for our own sense of security.

Browning also tirelessly points out that this Niebuhrian anxiety is not simply a result of faulty interpersonal processes. If that were the case, this anxiety could be "cleaned up" and humans could flourish in an uncomplicated manner. As Browning puts it, "Even the most emotionally and interpersonally secure of us become anxious in response to the indeterminacy of our decisions, choices, and the freedom that they imply."[18] But there is no such utopia in Niebuhr (or Tillich) because our anxiety problem goes to the very heart of our being. We are "situated" between nature and spirit and this situation invariably brings forth anxiety. This anxiety is not simply an "outside-in" process which results from clumsy interpersonal treatment. It emanates from the very nature of our existence. Psychotherapists, social planners, or religious leaders who think they can eliminate our anxiety need to take another look. To be human is to feel anxious. Of course there are forms of neurotic anxiety that can be treated clinically, but the core ontological anxiety we each share requires much more than what psychologists can offer.

Browning also uses Niebuhr to make the important point that this combination of nature and spirit (self-transcendence) can never be eliminated. In other words, no matter how much our lives are governed by our biological instincts, we still carry the capacity to rise above them and imagine other directions for ourselves. A person utterly consumed with bodily pleasure does not lose the capacity for self-reflection or a spiritual quality of self-transcendence. The ability to step outside ourselves and review our own lives is always present. Similarly, we never become so "spiritual" or self-transcendent that our biological lives no longer affect us. To do so would deny that we are embodied creatures. Thus, no one is ever "just a drunk" or "just a prostitute"; at the same time, no one is ever "just a saint" or "purely spiritual." A non-bodily spiritual existence is as impossible as a non-spiritual, strictly bodily existence. We have the capacity to orient our bodies in one direction or the other, but we certainly don't have the ability to be completely unaffected by our bodies. The refusal to recognize this simple truth has led countless religious individuals into profound and unnecessary internal conflict and guilt. Any view of spirituality that suggests we can be emancipated from the body is

---

[18] Browning and Cooper, *Religious Thought and the Modern Psychologies*, 52.

wrongheaded; similarly, any form of hedonism that suggests we can be free of the spiritual dimension is equally fallacious.

Perhaps this issue can be stated more psychologically: Browning argues that *the spiritual dimension of our condition has its own vital energies and vitalities and is not simply a transformation of biological drives*. Browning puts this very well:

> Nature and spirit are distinguishable but never separate; for Niebuhr, they interpenetrate and mutually qualify one another. We never experience our sexuality or our hunger, our procreative impulses or our drive to survive, our fear of our natural aggressivity, as raw, mechanistic, and totally determined natural forces. They are always in humans qualified by freedom and imagination.[19]

It is not as if we have unruly instincts that desperately need spirit to order and tame them into milder expressions. Our instincts are not, contrary to Freud, intrinsically destructive or excessive. If the Judeo-Christian tradition is right in proclaiming that all creation is good, this must also include the instincts. These tendencies are not without some degree of self-regulation and order. They are not naturally "out of control." Similarly, our sense of spirituality is not simply the "drained off" energies of libido. The energy of our self-transcendence is not merely a sublimation of more basic, biological energies. Instead, this spiritual capacity has its own source of energy and vitality. The body does not need to get its entire sense of order and self-regulation from the spiritual dimension, and the spiritual dimension does not have to derive all its energy from the body. We are much more complicated than that. At the risk of excessive quotations, I must include Browning's statement on this issue:

> There is hardly any single point in Niebuhr that is any more important and yet so easy to overlook. It means first that when we speak of our animal natures (our bodies and their instinctual tendencies), we should not think of them totally as energy, impulse, appetite, and formless wants and wishes without any boundaries,

---

[19] Ibid.

order, or self-limitations. Instead, Niebuhr believes that both Judaism and early Christianity want us to think that in its created and undistorted condition, our animal and instinctual nature does have some internal regulating capacities and is not ordered simply by impositions from reason and culture. In addition, Niebuhr believes that this religious tradition does not understand spirit simply as order, rationality, and the container of abstract possibility. Instead, this tradition wants to see spirit as both infused with the vitalities of nature and having its own intrinsic vitalities, imaginal yearnings and higher possibilities. Hence, human beings are *motivated* by both nature and spirit and *ordered* by both. Spirit does indeed add refinements to the ordering capacities of nature, but it can also, when distorted, add wild and chaotic embellishments—greed, pride, and the most hideous and uncontrollable disorders, crimes, and destructions. Such is the ambiguity of human creativity.[20]

The conviction of both Browning and Niebuhr that human nature is not essentially or biologically out of control runs counter to a more literal understanding of inherited sin often put forward by Christian conservatives. Yet a nonliteral account accents the universal human tendency to experience anxiety, distrust God, and turn toward self as the solution to life's predicament. But if one pushes it to mean that we actually receive, by way of transmission, a "sin gene." then it seems to lose its vitality. The majority of liberal and neo-orthodox theologies have realized this for several decades, but in some conservative circles, the literal interpretation is still pushed. This theology is not simply expressed among a few obscure, backwoods places. Instead, it is often proclaimed from the pulpits of very large, urban megachurches.

Freud and Detachment

For Freud, then, the instincts are primary, and any potential "self" is created out of our struggle with instincts. As Phillip Rieff describes Freud, "He conceives of the self not as an abstract entity,

---

[20] Ibid., 26.

uniting experience and cognition, but as the subject of a struggle between two objective forces—unregenerate instincts and overbearing culture."[21] There is no "hidden self" or "buried self" waiting to be discovered. Again, there is no return to a "pure" self which has been lost along the way. Just as humanity cannot look backward to a superior Adam in its past, so the individual cannot look back to an innocent self. To once again quote Thomas Finger:

> ...for Freud, human existence consists originally not of individual selves—not even primitive, undifferentiated ones—but of diverse instinctual drives. These are not really directed toward objects—toward people or things in the world—but toward internally experienced satisfactions. The sense of being a self, of being a person whose desires are organized within a body distinct from other entities, arises only in order that these drives may find satisfaction. In the Freudian paradigm, it is not selves involved in a world of others that come first. The instinctual drives come first and gradually become organized as selves in order to achieve instinctual satisfactions.[22]

What is Freud's solution to our instinctual situation? The answer, argues Browning, can be seen in the word "detachment." It is necessary to detach oneself from *both* the raw instincts and the cultural authorities that form the superego. Without such a detachment, one is a puppet in one direction or the other: If one blindly obeys the instincts, civilization will not be possible; if one blindly follows the rules of social authorities, one will be lost in a hopeless conformity which forbids the forging of one's own identity. Neither the instincts nor the superego can be completely trusted. Again, if we depend on external authority figures for our guidance, and consequently develop an overactive superego, we may be depleted of the very libidinal energy we need for love and work. The goal is the development of a strong, rational, detached ego which can

---

[21] Phillip Rieff, *Freud: The Mind of the Moralist* (Chicago: University of Chicago Press, 1959/1979) 28.

[22] Finger, *Self, Earth, and Society*, 36.

calculate one's situation and not be governed by the instincts of the body or the dictates of cultural repression. This is why Browning frequently calls Freud's perspective part of the "culture of detachment." Detachment is the way out of our dilemma. But again, this dilemma will never be resolved, only managed. Psychologically speaking, there is no "salvation" in Freud. Instead, there is only a modest but important attempt to balance selfish desires with the demands of culture, demands which become internalized in the individual and form the superego. Without detachment, we cannot achieve such a balance.

For Freud, healthy people have a cautious attitude toward their own instincts and superegos, as well as the instincts and superegos of others. This has definite implications for his ethics. Allowing the superego to dictate moral demands that are impossible to fulfill does not lead to better ethics; instead it leads to destructive internal conflict. While we should not "give into" our instincts or culture, we had better have a sober realization of what is humanly possible. For instance, Freud argued that the Judeo-Christian notion of "loving the neighbor as oneself" (Matt. 22:39) is quite unrealistic. To Freud, this seemed like a demand that produced more self-contempt than loving behavior. It's hard enough to restrain our aggression toward others without expecting ourselves to dredge up the same level of affection for them that we have for ourselves. Perhaps this is the key to Freud's attitude toward this standard: He understood "love for neighbor" to involve deep affection and warm kindness. This point is argued very well by Ernest Wallwork in his excellent study of psychoanalysis and ethics.[23] Wallwork states that Freud ends up arguing for a kind of mutual respect and reciprocity toward others. For Freud, the expectation to love one's neighbor as oneself produces neurotics, not ethical people. Freud argued that if the neighbor treats one with respect and consideration, it is possible to return such an attitude.[24]

---

[23] Ernest Wallwork, *Psychoanalysis and Ethics* (New Haven: Yale University Press, 1991).

[24] Freud, *Civilization and Its Discontents*, 56–63.

Browning, however, argues that "Freud's deep metaphors are compatible with either ethical egoism or cautious views of reciprocity and respect, and he probably oscillated between them."[25]

Freud's deep suspicion about "neighbor-love" would seem to place him at odds with Reinhold Niebuhr's emphasis on the importance of self-sacrificial love. Yet the appearance of total disagreement may fade some as we remember what Freud meant by neighbor-love (deep affection) and what Niebuhr believed to be empirically possible. Browning, in bringing Niebuhr and Freud into dialogue, offers significant insights into exactly how far apart these two men were in their ethical convictions. Niebuhr, Browning tells us, would agree with Freud that on a consistent, predictive basis, mutuality and respect are all we can expect from human beings. This may at first seem contradictory to Niebuhr's emphasis on *agape*, or self-sacrificial love as the goal of life. Niebuhr *does* insist that *agape* can break into historical existence (as it did decisively in Jesus Christ) and that it is utterly transformational. Self-sacrificial love is an ideal possibility, a worthwhile pursuit, even though it can never be completely realized under the conditions of historical existence. It can be a deeply meaningful goal without being a consistent, empirical actuality. Further, Browning argues that Niebuhr never declares that *agape* somehow pushes *eros* out of the way. Instead, it builds upon it. As Browning puts it, "It is clear that agape builds on, transforms, and enlarges these natural energies, rather than burying, repressing, or disconnecting them."[26] Self-sacrificial love and self-concern are not arch enemies. Self-sacrificial love is only the enemy of excessive self-regard.

Are Freud and Niebuhr in agreement on this difficult issue of self-regard and neighbor-love? Not quite. Browning offers a very important summary:

---

[25] Browning and Cooper, *Religious Thought and the Modern Psychologies*, 49.
[26] Ibid., 54.

Clearly, Freud's careful reciprocity has a different quality to it than Niebuhr's understanding of mutuality. In ways that Wallwork does not fully admit, Freud's image of reciprocity clearly expects the others to take the first step; as we saw, Freud said that he would accept the love commandment if it meant "Love thy neighbor as thy neighbor loves thee." Niebuhr's mutuality calls for genuinely equal initiative; Freud's reciprocity is cooler, hesitant, unequal with regard to the first step.[27]

This relationship between self-sacrificial care or altruism and our basic instinctual nature has emerged again in recent discussions of evolutionary psychology and ethics, a discussion we will explore shortly. In this discussion we will see Browning argue that *agape* does not so much eliminate our natural instincts but instead builds upon them. Before we entertain this evolutionary psychology discussion, it is important to examine another significant perspective on human instincts, the twentieth-century emergence of humanistic psychology.

One Basic Instinct: Self-Actualization

One of the great ironies about twentieth-century psychology is that the two thinkers who probably influenced counseling and psychotherapy more than any others (Freud and Rogers) could not be further from each other in their basic views of human nature. As we have seen, Freud was the great dualist—first of the psyche, and then of the cosmos in general. As long as there is life, there will be struggle between these two conflicting forces. This struggle is not simply an intrapsychic problem; it applies to all of life.

Rogers, on the other hand, rigorously believes in the trustworthiness of a singular instinct within human beings—the actualizing tendency. Rogers defines the actualizing tendency as "the inherent tendency of the organism to develop all its capacities in ways which serve to maintain or enhance the organism."[28] Note that this instinct is

---

[27] Ibid., 53.

[28] Carl Rogers, "A Theory of Therapy, Personality, and Interpersonal Relationships as Developed in the Client-Centered Framework," in S. Koch, ed., *Psychology: A Study*

biological in origin, a basic part of the human condition. This is the master-motive of human life, a singular movement toward growth and health. It may at first seem foreign to associate humanistic psychology with the idea of instinct, but this organic understanding of human growth is basic to Rogers and Maslow. Destructiveness comes when (and only when) this singular, positive instinct toward self-actualization has been frustrated. Need deprivation and conditions of worth push individuals away from their instinctual natures and create an incongruent, false self. Rogers has always been very clear about this: "The organism has one basic tendency and striving—to actualize, maintain, and enhance the experiencing organism."[29] This conviction is based on a huge assumption that individuals, provided that they experience a healthy emotional environment, will grow naturally and progressively into fuller selves. There is no need to direct or coerce this process; it is a profoundly natural one. Further, if one acts in accordance with this natural inclination, one will do not only what is in one's own best interest but also what is in the best interest of the social community as well.

This Rousseau-like belief in the natural goodness of humanity is completely at odds with Freud's emphasis on a natural state of conflict between life and death instincts. The child, for Rogers, is an image of mental health. The child naturally and spontaneously follows his or her own self-direction and experiencing process until that experience is met with "conditions of worth" from the emotional environment. Further, the child has a basic, biologically driven approach to values. The infant prefers some experiences to others, and throughout all Rogers' writings, he argued that the infant seeks these experiences that actualize his being. The infant's approach to values is flexible and changing rather than rigid. The locus of this valuing process is within the infant:

---

of Science, Vol. 3: Formations of the Person and the Social Context (New York: McGraw-Hill, 1959) 196.

[29] Carl Rogers, *Client-Centered Therapy* (Boston: Houghton-Mifflin, 1951) 487.

Unlike many of us, he *knows* what he likes and dislikes, and the origin of these value choices lies strictly within himself. He is the center of the valuing process, the evidence for his choices being supplied by his own senses. He is not at this point influenced by what his parents think he should prefer, or by the persuasive talents of an advertising firm. It is from within his own experiencing that his organism is saying in non-verbal terms, "This is good for me." "That is bad for me." "I strongly dislike that." He would laugh at our concern over values, if he could understand it. How could anyone fail to know what he liked and disliked, what was good for him and what was not?[30]

Gradually, however, infants learn that certain actions bring condemning judgments from others. These "conditions of worth" push the infant to serve up an acceptable self rather than a genuine self. Instead of paying attention to their own valuing process, children then begin to absorb values from others, regardless of whether or not those values match their experiences. They begin to force their experience to match what they are *supposed to* think, feel, and perceive. Their own sense of inner trust in their own direction is lost in an attempt to please others. This is the emergence of incongruence, the state of being estranged from our own experiencing process. Incongruence is "unnatural" and not part of our original biological process. We thus "fall" from an Eden of organismic valuing into a world of distorted and confused strivings.[31] An external standard replaces the internal, natural inclination. Rogers describes the implications:

...in an attempt to gain or hold love, approval, esteem, the individual relinquishes the locus of evaluation, which was his in

---

[30] Carl Rogers, "Toward a Modern Approach to Values: The Valuing Process in the Mature Person," in Rogers and Barry Stevens, *Person to Person* (New York: Pocket Books, 1971) 8.

[31] For an elaboration of this point, see Thomas C. Oden, *Kerygma and Counseling* (Philadelphia: Westminster Press) ch. 3; Oden, *The Structure of Awareness* (Nashville: Abingdon Press, 1969) ch. 7.

infancy, and places it in others. He learns to have a basic *distrust* for his own experiencing as a guide to his behavior. He learns from others a large number of conceived values, and adopts them as his own, even though they may be widely discrepant from what he is experiencing. Because these concepts are not based on his own valuing, they tend to be fixed and rigid, rather than fluid and changing.[32]

This path leads toward an inward alienation and a divided self. Operating contrary to the innate actualizing tendency, we act incongruently, and hence, destructively. We act against both our own best interests and those of society as well.

Rogers spent most of his life outlining the significance of empathy, unconditional positive regard, and congruence as the therapeutic ingredients necessary to help someone reconnect with the actualizing tendency. This reconnection with the natural, biological tendency toward growth is always the primary goal of psycho-therapy. The therapeutic situation offers someone a nonthreatening reversal of those conditions of worth that got one in trouble. As the client experiences the deep acceptance and empathic affirmation of the therapist, he or she can reconnect with this natural process. The return of the prodigal son, therapeutically speaking, is really a return to our own trustworthy inclination toward growth. Rogers did not think, however, that one could simply "decide" to accept oneself. Once the conditions of incongruence have set in, there is a definite need for an accepting other who can reflect back one's own acceptability.

Browning was interested for a long time in analyzing Rogers. His first book, *Atonement and Psychotherapy*, drew analogies between the Rogerian experience of acceptance and the Christian understanding of grace.[33] More specifically, Browning and colleague Thomas Oden almost simultaneously demonstrated how there is an implicit assumption of ontological acceptance built within the

---

[32] Rogers, "Toward a Modern Approach to Values," 9.

[33] Don S. Browning, *Atonement and Psychotherapy* (Philadelphia: Westminster Press, 1966).

Rogerian framework.[34] Later, Browning was influenced by the important work of David Norton (*Personal Destinies: A Philosophy of Ethical Individualism*[35]), and by the time he wrote *Pluralism and Personality* (1980), and particularly the first edition of *Religious Thought and the Modern Psychologies* (1987), he had developed a highly nuanced and insightful critique of Rogers, Maslow, and Perls. Browning points out that Rogers assumes a metaphysical world of perfect harmony in which all living creatures can simultaneously self-actualize without conflict, negotiation, or struggle. This pre-established view of harmony, argues Browning, simply does not match our daily experience of realizing that our own actualization must be balanced with those around us. Rogers doesn't offer us any help in making difficult value choices concerning who gets to actualize and when. He merely assumes that we can all live in a self-blossoming world that does not create tension as we follow our own directions.

Browning also points out, following his mentors on anxiety—Kierkegaard and Niebuhr—that Rogers minimizes the problem of ontological anxiety. While Rogers is quite aware of interpersonal anxiety that occurs when our own inclinations clash with those of others, he does not adequately grasp what Tillich and other thinkers mean by ontological anxiety. This is the anxiety that arises all on its own, even without any external help. As we have already seen, this is the anxiety of being self-conscious persons who realize that our choices often define our future and that we are not nearly as secure as

---

[34] Thomas Oden's book, *Kerygma and Counseling*, relied on Barth's analogy of faith and suggested that the Christian story can help us see more vividly what is happening in the interpersonal healing process. Browning believed the analogy can work both ways: Just as the theologian can help the psychotherapist see the ultimate context of healing, so the psychotherapist can sharpen the theologian's own understanding of the nature of Divine experience. They differed on whether or not the analogy could work both from the human to the Divine as well as the Divine to the human. From this early stage onward, one can clearly see Browning's movement away from Barth, who was pivotal for Oden.

[35] David L. Norton, *Personal Destinies: A Philosophy of Ethical Individualism* (Princeton: Princeton University Press, 1976).

we'd like to be. This anxiety is the precondition of sin, the fertile ground of self-preoccupied and destructive behavior. Rogers leaves us with the view that if we can only live in a therapeutic atmosphere, our problems with anxiety will all be over.

Thus, we come back to the deeply instinctual nature of Rogers's singular drive theory. Radically unlike Freud, Rogers believed that this single, powerful urge toward actualization can be completely trusted. It has no competitor. We do not have a second instinct toward destruction, as Freud believed. We don't even have an inward problem of facing ontological anxiety. If we simply return to the natural, the organic, then the riddles of our existence will be resolved.

Browning's turn to Gadamer's and Ricoeur's approach to critical hermeneutics (outlined in chapter 1) also brings us to another problem he has with Rogers's understanding of ethics and the valuing process. Rogers's deep trust in our own individual, biological resources for decision-making minimizes the value of our effective history, the classics contained in that history, and the wisdom which past generations offer us. Experience itself, for Rogers, becomes a quasi-omniscient source of direction which holds little appreciation for the accumulated wisdom from the past. Put simply, Rogers doesn't offer much of a place for tradition. In fact, he comes close to encouraging a near-paranoia about tradition. Tradition, cultural standards, and the collective past are the threats to true autonomy and self-direction. Browning sees this as a clear obstacle to utilizing past resources in our ethical struggles to balance our lives.

For Browning, Rogers makes ethical decision-making look a little too natural and too easy. In fact, it is subsumed under a biological inclination toward self-actualization. This perspective also gives us no insight into how we can actualize together, particularly when one person's fulfillment gets in the way of another's. Rogers simply assumes a preestablished ontological harmony that allows growth to occur spontaneously. For Browning, this doesn't match our life experience.

The Irrelevance of Instincts: B. F. Skinner and Radical Behaviorism

Few psychologists have worked harder than B. F. Skinner to make psychology scientific. While Skinner refines and develops the radical behaviorist position, J. B. Watson is considered the founder of behaviorism because he coined the term and developed its most basic theories. Watson accepted Pavlov's theory of classical conditioning and declared that if psychology really wants to be a science, it must be based on that which can be observed and measured. External behavior is the only facet of human life open to such analysis. We obviously cannot observe mental states, so they are off-limits. We certainly cannot observe the unconscious, so it is irrelevant. Psychology must be a *strictly empirical, observable, public, repeatable science*. We must completely cut the umbilical cord with the humanities and focus on the only thing we can truly be scientific about—observable, measurable behavior. And most of this observable behavior involved rats and pigeons rather than human beings.

Watson famously made the claim that through conditioning, he could turn any average baby into anything the mother might want him/her to be. Thus, behaviorism always asks, "Which conditions will most effectively lead to desirable changes in behavior? In many respects, behaviorism reduces personality theory to learning theory. Education, as defined by behaviorists, is a change in behavior resulting from some aspect of experience. If instruction affects learners in such a way that their behavior after instruction is observably different from before instruction, we can infer that learning has taken place. Behaviorism is concerned about the conditions that promote certain kinds of behavior or responses (stimuli) and the behavior that those stimuli prompt (responses). Hence, the stimulus-response theory. Stated differently, behaviorism is concerned with studying the rules for conditioning.

Watson and Skinner want to get rid of concepts such as "sensations," "feelings," "consciousness," and "mind" because they are unscientific concepts, even mythological notions that psychology must leave behind. Whatever is not open to repeatable, public observation should not be part of psychology. Only behavior can be observed.

B. F. Skinner spent most of his career at Harvard and died in 1990. Skinner was committed to a nontheoretical description and science of human behavior, a nontheoretical science of behavior, much like engineering. Skinner was very "lean" in his terminology. He didn't make use of a lot of theoretical concepts. He argued that we can only observe the *externals* of human behavior. All the questions about motives, intentions, or underlying thought processes are irrelevant and should not be a part of psychology.

While Skinner spent an enormous amount of time studying rats and pigeons in small boxes, he attempted to extend his findings to human beings and argued that we must go "beyond freedom and dignity" and engineer a society that reinforces particular types of behavior. For Skinner, the language of freedom, autonomy, and human dignity push us back to earlier periods of superstition, religion, and mythology. Should we control behavior? For Skinner, all behavior is controlled anyway, so why not engineer a better society? All social problems are in reality behavioral problems. Skinner argued that the determinants of behavior are always *outside* of us. We decide nothing freely. The autonomy, freedom, and personal responsibility prized by the humanistic psychologies are based on a complete misconception. Our behavior does not emerge from internal decisions. As a consequence, we have no moral grounds for blaming anyone for their behavior. Put simply, there are no "bad" people, only "bad" environments. Once we give up our habit of making moral judgments about people, we can turn our attention to the real problem, the environment.

The essential fact of human life is the same as animal life: Adaptive behavior is designed to meet the demands and challenges of the external world. We are conditioned toward adaptive behavior. In spite of its denial of freedom, Skinnerian behaviorism appealed to some Americans because of its focus on equality. It is not our instincts or heredity that shapes us. It is instead our experience. We are born as blank slates, and our experience defines us. The environment is the author of our lives. It determines our story. Innate abilities, instinctual patterns, inherent "archetypes," or so-called inclinations toward wholeness are simply not relevant to understanding human beings. Thus, even though some Americans may like the emphasis on equality in Skinner's thought, his ideas do indeed fly in the face of another American value—personal freedom to define our own futures.

For Skinner, the laboratory alone can tell us what we need to know about ourselves. The famous "Skinner box" is a small, enclosed environment in which an animal such as a rat or pigeon is placed. It is like a cage with sophisticated gadgetry, a controlled environment. The box is constructed in such a way that it will provide the researcher with responses that he or she would like to find out about. It allows the researcher to determine the rewards or punishments, hence, the opportunity to understand the conditioning process. For instance, if a rat hits a lever and a food pellet is produced, this action forms a definite association for the rat between the lever and the food. Skinner wants to *generalize from the simple behavior of a rat or pigeon to the complex behavior of a person.*

For Skinner, there are two types of reinforcement: positive or negative. Positive reinforcement conditions behavior by rewarding certain things. Something pleasant is then *associated* with doing a particular activity. Examples of positive reinforcement in the classroom are teachers smiling at students, praising students in front of their peers, or affirming them in front of their parents. Good grades are another obvious positive reinforcement. Negative reinforcement shapes behavior by removing unpleasant things when a person behaves in a particular way. For instance, if all the students do extremely well on an exam, they do not have to write a paper. It is important to note that this is *not* punishment. Keeping students after class, giving them a poor grade, or making them write on the board one hundred times are examples of punishment. Negative reinforcement removes something unwanted, motivating the child to do well in an effort to escape something unpleasant. Punishment focuses on the bad or undesirable behavior. Negative reinforcement focuses on the desired or good behavior, behavior which will help us dodge unpleasantness. Skinner is categorically against any form of punishment. Positive reinforcement might include a teacher buying pizza for students who have excelled. For Skinner, pleasure appears to be a much more powerful tool for shaping behavior than pain is for stamping it out. Punishment does not illustrate or emphasize desirable action but usually just draws attention to undesirable behavior. It is thus not very useful for learning purposes. Another objection to punishment is that it is usually accompanied by undesirable emotional side effects that can be associated with the *punisher* rather than the *behavior* being punished.

Punishment often leads not to the *extinction* of particular behavior but only to a temporary *avoidance* of it. Instead, Skinner wanted to extinguish certain negative behaviors by not reinforcing them. By withdrawing reinforcements, the behavior will eventually fade away.

Perhaps at this point it is important to discourage an unfair stereotype. It is very easy, particularly for those of us coming out of a humanistic tradition, to view Skinner as a less-than-human, malevolent controller of people. We may think he lived in a world devoid of feelings as he robotically *reacted* to his surroundings and wanted to engineer lifeless individuals. The truth is that Skinner *was* a humanitarian. He *was* deeply bothered by human suffering, and because he believed human behavior is environmentally controlled anyway, he wanted to set up a society in which everyone, not just a select few, can achieve a greater degree of happiness. Even if we fault him for his radical determinism, we should not see him as a heartless scientist. Clearly he was not. Just as theologians have for centuries struggled with the question as to how a loving God can allow horrendous human suffering, Skinner wanted to know how a so-called just society can allow so many of its citizens to live desperate and unhappy lives. For Skinner, of course, the appeal must be made to social engineers and not to anything transpersonal. Skinner's psychology didn't allow for the possibility of human transcendence, much less take seriously any notion of a transcendent realm to which we might appeal.

Skinner's perspective, then, places virtually no weight on instincts or inherent tendencies within us. We are blank tablets waiting the environmental scribe. Our dreams, aspirations, sense of meaning, internal motivation, anxiety, despair, and every other existential inclination result from what is *done to us* by the environment. One should be careful not to take credit or accept blame. We are products, nothing more. Our interiority is an illusion, at least in determining any aspect of our lives. The sense of inner freedom we may think we have is actually a hangover of a scientifically unsophisticated age. Any sense of personal freedom is an illusion. Do we think we "picked" our partner? Nonsense. Did we "choose" which school to attend? Hardly. If one could know all the variables in our past, our decisions would be wholly predictable.

Browning on Skinner and Ethics

Browning points out that while the humanistic psychologies are primarily interested in individual fulfillment, Skinner was more concerned with social cooperation and the benefit of the larger society. In fact, Skinner was so completely preoccupied with the technologies of behavior formation that he was quite unaware of the philosophical and quasi-theological assumptions he brought to his program of behavioral engineering. Skinner made no bones about it: He wanted to predict and control human behavior. We simply *must* give up the illusory but stubborn, notion that we are free. Again, the concept of reinforcement became for him the all-consuming explanation of reality. As Browning describes it, Skinner

arrived at a dogmatic, radical, and metaphysical behaviorism that denies that there are any internal mentalistic phenomena—thought, emotions, feelings, motivations, or intensions—that shape behavior independently of the schedule of environmental reinforcements and rewards that ultimately control our behavior.... The environment and the reinforcements that it mediates to our responses constitute the sum total of psychological realities.[36]

Skinner, in a sense, backed himself into a corner. To keep psychology scientific, he had to insist that behavior is its only focus. Since the world of thoughts, emotions, intentions, and motivations get in the way of a strictly external focus, those aspects of life must be ignored. Skinner's science forced him to deny his own inner life. Yet this clearly seems more like "scientism" than science. It is a method of behavior observation turned into a whole worldview with positivistic assumptions dangling from it. The study of behavior, for Skinner, *must* tell the whole story. Science demands it! I would suggest that "science" demands no such thing; it is Skinner's materialistic scientism uttering this claim.

Ironically, Browning argues that in many respects Skinner limited what supposedly "controls" human beings. He focused exclusively on the specific patterns of positive and negative reinforcements that determine our lives. Instead, argues Browning, Skinner should have expanded his understanding of influencing factors to include our "effective history," which includes the cultural classics and images that have infiltrated human consciousness. Skinner's understanding of what influences behavior is both too limited and too strong. It concludes that specific reinforcements completely dictate our actions; consequently, it misses the larger cultural meanings which shape our activity. Nevertheless, argues Browning, an astute hermeneutical philosophy (which is broader than Skinner's philosophy) should take Skinner's insight concerning the power of reinforcements into its own framework. In this way, Skinner's work can be appreciated without making it into the end-all philosophy about what controls behavior. It would then become a much softer determinism as it recognizes the limited, but significant, possibility of self-transcendence.

---

[36] Browning and Cooper, *Religious Thought and the Modern Psychologies*, 88.

Niebuhr, again, is Browning's mentor here. Niebuhr deeply understood the conditionedness, context, and limitations of human life and thought. He realized that finitude has a cognitive impact. Yet he also emphasized our capacity to step outside our situation and reflect on it. This self-transcendence, as we have seen, is the source of anxiety.

Browning points out that Skinner saw his perspective as a form of Darwinism. Sprinkled throughout Skinner's writings are comparisons between his environmental reinforcements and Darwin's natural selection. "A culture," argues Skinner, "like a species, is selected by its adaptation to an environment."[37] Yet, as Skinner argues, cultural accomplishment must be transmitted and learned.

Browning asserts that Skinner truly believed he was bringing into psychology the scientific dimensions of Darwinian evolution. Further, Skinner escalated his understanding of natural selection into an ultimate metaphor. There is "nothing but" natural selection. In other words, it accounts for the full range of human experience. Browning argues that Darwin himself never intended this.

The image of "husbandry" is crucial for Skinner. He borrowed Darwin's image of how a farmer selects animals with particular characteristics for breeding. Similarly, argues Skinner, the environment selects and "husbands" those species with survival characteristics. Browning insightfully points out the limits of this parallel:

> When applied to the farmer, it refers to his *intentional* and free manipulation of desired animal characteristics through breeding. As a scientific model for explaining evolutionary change in species, the selection of the environment becomes blind; the environment has no intention or purposes. When applied as a metaphor once again to account exhaustively for the ultimate determinants of all experience, selection is still blind; it implies, however, that at the very depths of life there are only random selective determinants, that they are

---

[37] B. F. Skinner, *Beyond Freedom and Dignity* (New York: Bantam, 1972) 123.

capricious, mechanical, and without humanly intelligible purposes, and that finally they control all aspects of life and the world.[38]

Again, this philosophical declaration that natural selection or behavior reinforcement explains *all* life clearly goes beyond Darwin's own understanding, though it is sometimes embraced by some contemporary Darwinians who turn the scientific findings of evolution into a full-scale, naturalistic worldview.

Also, Darwinian anthropology, as we shall see, would never endorse Skinner's blank slate theory of mind. For evolutionary psychology our minds are hardly neutral tablets; instincts are alive and well. Steven Pinker, evolutionary and cognitive psychologist, has written a best-selling book that argues against this blank slate notion.[39] Skinner is in fact a strange bedfellow with radical social constructionists, who argue that we enter the world with very few, if any, inherent biological inclinations.

As Browning points out, while humanistic psychologies over-value nature and tend to see it as offering an uncomplicated source of constant growth, both Freud and Skinner, in different ways, either disregard nature or think it is in desperate need of being tamed. This is a deeply insightful point. Nature, for Freud, is out of control. Without the regulation from reason, nature itself has no form of self-regulation. Yet, as we have seen Browning argues that the instincts are not naturally or essentially out of control. They can easily *get* out of control, fixated, and indulgent. But that occurs from the dual dangers of anxious self-concern and an anxiety-dodging plunge into sensuality. Nature is not the enemy—this is the perennial message of Browning's Christian anthropology.

> The acknowledgment of the reality of freedom and self-transcendence, no matter how small, leads to the acknowledgment of the inevitable appearance of anxiety in the imagination of human beings. The presence of anxiety, no matter how elementary, leads to

---

[38] Browning and Cooper, *Religious Thought and the Modern Psychologies*, 91.
[39] Steven Pinker, *The Blank Slate: The Modern Denial of Human Nature* (New York: Penguin, 2002).

the prideful or sensuous grasping after an idolatrous security based on the created values and actualities of this world. This idolatrous effort to secure oneself against the contingencies of this world is the essence of original sin as Kierkegaard and Niebuhr so forcefully have argued. And it is this original sin that distorts our natural self-regard into an inordinate self-regard that has motivated much of the injustice, exploitation, and overt violence that has characterized the human scene throughout its long history.[40]

Skinner's noble effort to erect a society engineered in such a way that only humanitarian beliefs would be reinforced misses a couple of key points: (a) Who is "free enough" to make such a decision, a decision which obviously affects everyone? and (b) How could we trust that the self-interests of this decision-making board would not eventually infiltrate and affect its own planning? This is precisely what is meant by the Christian notion of "original sin." Consequently, we must have a system by which planners and social engineers can be "checked." As Browning puts it, "Skinner's goodhearted planners and managers, unchecked by the people they shape, reinforce, and reward, would invariably drift toward the unjust and inordinately self-seeking use of this power."[41]

Instincts, Altruism, and Evolutionary Psychology

As I indicated at the beginning of this chapter, there is a controversial debate about whether human beings have an inherited "nature," and the role that instincts play in that nature. More specifically, this intellectual conflict is driven by two often antagonistic perspectives: evolutionary psychology and social constructionism. While many find themselves somewhere between two extremes on this issue, others argue that the opposite perspective will be the demise of the human sciences. Evolutionary psychology typically sees itself as extending to human personality Darwin's great biological discoveries. We are hardwired to replicate ourselves, to see

---

[40] Browning and Cooper, *Religious Thought and the Modern Psychologies*, 102.
[41] Ibid.

survival as the ultimate goal of our lives. We do this by extending our own genes into the future. Powerful biological tendencies cannot be ignored in personality theory. Dating and courtship, family life, group attitudes, child rearing, and a host of other issues can be better explained in the light of natural selection. Evolutionary psychologists, like psychoanalysts, are profoundly interested in our past. However, evolutionary psychology is interested in our collective past as an entire species, and not simply our individual psychological development. This is the distinction between phylogenetic factors (history of our entire species) and ontogenetic factors (history of our individual personhood). Much of our current behavior exists precisely because it was advantageous to the survival of our ancestors. Though much of our behavior is unconscious, the unconscious inclinations do not result simply from early relationships and individual drives; instead, we inherit a cluster of inclinations that have gradually developed as a result of our evolutionary survival. While evolutionary psychologists readily acknowledge that there are a variety of cultural differences, they emphasize common human tendencies that bind us together as a species. Evolutionary psychologist David Barash asserts this view:

> Human beings are, after all, still human beings, and as such, there is a certain range within which their behavior will fall. They may develop distinctive customs of dress and adornment, perhaps parrot feathers in one place, strange patterns of head shaving in another, the ritual carving of deep scars on cheeks and foreheads in yet another, but some pattern of dress and adornment is always found. Similarly marriage in one place might be sanctified by a ceremonial sharing of food, or maybe by the union of menstrual blood with semen, or by the payment tokens from one partner to the other or by signing a document and uttering officially approved words, but some ritualized sanctioning of male-female association seems almost always to take place.... While it is true that culture makes people, people also make

cultures, and there is much to gain by looking at what remains the same about people underneath their customs and habits.[42]

Again, for evolutionary psychologists, human beings have inherited universal structures beneath their behavior. Psychology can be grounded in a much larger evolutionary theory. While there are *proximate* causes of human behavior such as environmental factors, level of motivation, and previous experience, we human beings are also pushed along by *ultimate* causes of our behavior. These ultimate causes reflect a much larger portrait of our evolutionary survival. Perhaps an example would be helpful. It is certainly true that parents love their children for proximate causes such as their children needing them. They are cute, they make their parents feel good, and they are helpless. Yet, on the other hand, parents also love their children because their kids guarantee the survival of their genes. We are "programmed" to like what is in our survival interest. Thus, while our behavior may be socially influenced, it is *not* socially constructed. In fact, our natural instincts often push culture in specific directions. Some of our important social institutions have their roots in our genetic inclinations.

Social constructionism usually rejects evolutionary psychology. While this position, like evolutionary psychology, holds a range of positions about the importance of how culture shapes and regulates our lives, some forms of social constructionism flatly deny that biological factors have any important role in our lives. Our basic inclinations, our so-called instincts, and our behavior in general are nothing more than a cultural product. Contemporary social constructionists would tend to agree with the words of Ellsworth Faris in 1927: "Instincts do not create customs; customs create instincts for the putative instincts of human being are always learned and never native."[43] Ashley Montagu reflects the same sentiment: "Man is man because he has no instincts, because everything he is and has become has been learned, acquired from his culture, from the

---

[42] David Barash, *The Whisperings Within* (New York: Penguin, 1981) 4–5.

[43] Quoted in Pinker, *Blank Slate*, 24.

man-made part of the environment, from other human beings."[44] Our "natures" are socially generated and do not arise from biology. For instance, we do not enter this world with natural gender inclinations or even a basic human nature. Discussions of "human nature," for social constructionists, inevitably deny the diversity of people by focusing on genes rather than culture. In fact, for many social constructionists, we can only talk about "human *natures*" rather than human nature. In other words, what so easily passes as our *essential humanity* is nothing more than what our culture has created and instilled in us. Hence, social constructionists frequently place themselves as arch enemies of any form of essentialism, the view that human nature is more "given" than constructed. We are completely and exclusively shaped by our experience; there are no innate dispositions or inherent tendencies. Thus, thinkers as far apart as Jean Paul Sartre and B. F. Skinner can both affirm that human beings do not have a basic nature. And thinkers as far apart as Steven Pinker and Paul Tillich, albeit for different reasons, argue that we do indeed have a nature. In fact, for both Pinker and Tillich, it is impossible to say much of anything without some sort of belief in human nature. As Tillich puts it, "There is no existentialist description of the negativities of the human predicament without an underlying image of what man essentially is and therefore ought to be."[45]

Social constructionism is typically embedded in a larger, postmodern perspective which makes it highly distrustful of all "universal" language about our so-called human condition. There is no "one-size-fits-all" metanarrative that defines our basic humanity. Instead, a plurality of narratives bumps into each other. Any attempt to establish a universal perspective will inevitably threaten, oppress, and attempt to dominate minority voices. "Big stories" about human identity minimize differences, and worse still, function to conquer

---

[44] Ashley Montagu, *Man and Aggression* (New York: Oxford University Press, 1973) 9.

[45] Paul Tillich, "Existentialism and Psychotherapy," *The Meaning of Health*, ed. Perry LeFevre, 154.

alternative perspectives. Put another way, metanarratives about human nature are violent, intrusive, and nonrespecting of alternative viewpoints. A quest for a "unity of truth" can easily crush the varieties of cultural expression. The problem in the past is that the most powerful groups have been allowed to define everyone else. In other words, narratives about the human condition are more often based on dominance and power rather than on evidence. Besides, all "evidence" is read in terms of a specific cultural interpretation anyway. We cannot get away from this cognitive limitation and speak from some universal position. No one has direct access to reality, so we are left only with our intellectual constructions. For social constructionists, this search for a universal human nature is a hangover of the false hopes of the Enlightenment. They believe evolutionary psychology, especially, offers false claims about the universality of our instincts. Worse still, it threatens to undermine human diversity and allow a dominant (usually male) perspective to eliminate all counterdefinitions of reality. For instance, social constructionists frequently hold a deep suspicion that evolutionary psychology will reinforce the status quo of society by arguing that differences such as gender are biologically rooted and inevitable. Once one postulates an "essential" quality to men and women, for instance, their differences can be interpreted as simply "the way things are." For social constructionists, evolutionary psychology constantly confuses the "way things are" with what has been socially created. This promotes a highly conservative estimation of what can be changed. After all, our behavior is simply "natural." For social constructionists, it is precisely because human beings are so malleable and without basic instincts that social change is possible. Put differently, to hold an optimistic view about social change, we must, of necessity, see the human condition as a flexible existence void of natural instincts. A hope for a better tomorrow is not compatible with an essentialist view of human nature. A science of human nature threatens the possibility of social change. Thus, many social constructionists believe that evolutionary psychology is doing far more than describing human beings; instead, it is reinforcing a particular political perspective. In the words of the Sociobiology Group Statement at Harvard, including Stephen Jay Gould, Richard Lewontin, and Steven Rose:

> The reason for the survival of these recurrent determinist theories is that they consistently tend to provide a genetic justification for the *status quo* and of existing privileges for certain groups according to class, race, or sex.... These theories provided an important basis for the enactment of sterilization laws and restrictive immigration laws by the United States between 1910 and 1930 and also for the eugenics policies which led to the establishment of gas chambers in Nazi Germany.... What Wilson's book illustrates to us is the enormous difficulty in separating out not only the effects of environment (e.g., cultural transmission) but also the personal and social class prejudices of the researcher. Wilson joins the long parade of biological determinists whose work has served to buttress the institutions of their society by exonerating them from responsibility for social problems.[46]

It is particularly interesting to note that among three of these antisociobiology voices (Gould, Lewontin, and Rose) that while they are quick to see an underlying political agenda and ideology in evolutionary psychology, they don't seem to raise the possibility that they are viewing the evidence through a Marxist agenda. Put even more strongly, many Marxists tend to be excellent at pointing toward the ideological contaminants in others' theories but are quite slow to see how their own political assumptions guide their work as well. In this scenario, what's good for the goose seems off limits to the gander.

Evolutionary psychologists, on the other hand, argue that social constructionists often stand in the way of advancing a scientific understanding of human nature. However, this social constructionism is hardly new. It shares deep affinities with previous

---

[46] Elizabeth Allen, Barbara Beckwith, Jon Beckwith, et al., "Against 'Sociobiology,'" *New York Review of Books,* AUGUST 7, 1975, 22, 43.

forms of extreme empiricism, starting with Locke's *tabula rasa*. From this standpoint, we each come into this world with a "blank slate" and await experience to paint its story onto an empty canvas. We have no inherent tendencies, dispositions, or inclinations. The influential evolutionary psychologist David Buss describes this way of thinking:

> This old paradigm holds that we have no essential nature when we are born, aside from a general capacity to learn. The content of our character gets written onto this blank slate as we develop. Our "nature" is shaped by outside influences: parents, teachers, peers, society, the media, and culture.... Evolutionary psychology, by contrast, contends that we come into the world factory-made— equipped with a mind that is designed to solve a range of adaptive problems our ancestors grappled with throughout human history. This psychological equipment helps us to handle challenges of survival and reproduction—the adaptive problems that have confronted generations of predecessors going back into deep time. People do not spring from the womb, of course, with these adaptations fully formed. Men are not born with fully developed beards and women are not born with fully developed breasts. They develop later on to help solve problems during the reproductive phase of our lifespan. Similarly, our psychological adaptations appear at the appropriate time over the course of our development.[47]

Buss does not think that the study of human nature is a "dangerous" thing. Such a study does not necessarily lead to reinforcing systems of dominance. The greater danger is that by forsaking a scientific study of humanity we remain hopelessly adrift in an extreme relativism which insists that all voices be heard equally. For Buss and other evolutionary psychologists, having a voice is not enough; one needs evidence to support that voice. For social constructions, however, there is no universal bar of evidence to which we can appeal. Even the way we define "evidence" is socially

---

[47] David M. Buss, *The Murderer Next Door: Why the Mind Is Designed to Kill* (New York: Penguin Press, 2005) 35.

constructed. At that point, evolutionary psychologists fear that a unified body of knowledge will be lost if we truly take radical social constructionism seriously.

The current battle over evolutionary psychology still reflects much of the tension in the older, 1970s controversy over "socio-biology." Clearly one of the most influential voices in the current debate is that of Harvard psychologist Steven Pinker. Pinker, a formidable intellect, is also a very good writer. As a result, his books have been read by people both in and out of the academic community. The title of his book *The Blank Slate: The Modern Denial of Human Nature* signals the reader to the argument he makes—and makes very well—throughout this book. As Pinker writes, "My goal...is not to argue that genes are everything and culture is nothing—no one believes that—but to explore why the extreme position (that culture is everything) is moderate, and that the moderate position is seen as extreme."[48] Pinker further describes how an evolutionary psychology position has been associated with social conservatism:

> When it comes to explaining human thought and behavior, the possibility that heredity plays any role at all still has the power to shock. To acknowledge human nature, many think, is to endorse racism, sexism, war, greed, genocide, nihilism, reactionary politics, and neglect of children and the disadvantaged. Any claim that the mind has an innate organization strikes people not as a hypothesis that might be incorrect but as a thought that is immoral to think.[49]

For Pinker, acknowledging the existence of human nature does *not* necessarily mean that we will reject feminism, become racist, or start voting to reinforce the status quo. Further, he believes that *not* acknowledging human nature distorts science and ends very fruitful public discussions. Pinker is tired of political smears and personal

---

[48] Pinker, *The Blank Slate*, ix.
[49] Ibid., viii.

attacks, which distort or ignore the evidence pointing toward human nature[50] He doesn't spare words:

> I first had the idea of writing this book when I started a collection of astonishing claims from pundits of social critics about the malleability of the human psyche: that little boys quarrel and fight because they are encouraged to do so; that children enjoy sweets because their parents use them as a reward for eating vegetables; that teenagers get the idea to compete in looks and fashion from spelling bees and academic prizes; that men think the goal of sex is an orgasm because of the way they were socialized. The problem is not just that these claims are preposterous but that the writers did not acknowledge they were saying things that common sense might call into question. This is the mentality of a cult, in which fantastical beliefs are flaunted as proof of one's piety.[51]

Pinker and other evolutionary psychologists believe their approach has been dismissed too easily without any appeal to evidence. Instead of a deliberate discussion, a reaction of panic and judgmentalism has been created as evolutionary psychology is associated with Nazi Germany or the eugenics movement. The "criticism of the new sciences of human nature went well beyond ordinary scholarly debate. It turned into harassment, misrepresentations, doctored quotations, and, most recently, blood libel."[52]

This charge, as many will remember, arose in connection to the work of noted sociobiologist E. O. Wilson at Harvard University. As Pinker writes, "The accusation that Wilson (a lifelong liberal democrat) was led by personal prejudice to defend racism, sexism, inequality, slavery, and genocide was especially unfair—and irresponsible, because Wilson became a target of vilification and harassment by people who read the manifesto but not the book."[53] All

---

[50] Ibid., x.
[51] Ibid.
[52] Ibid., 119.
[53] Ibid., 110.

this came to a boil in the 1978 meeting of the American Association for the Advancement of Science in Washington, DC:

> Once they staked themselves to the lazy argument that racism, sexism, war, and political inequality were factually incorrect because there is no such thing as human nature (as opposed to being despicable regardless of the details of human nature), every discovery about human nature was, by their own reasoning, tantamount to saying that those scourges were not so bad after all. That made it all the more pressing to discredit the heretics making the discoveries. If ordinary standards of scientific argumentation were not doing the trick, other tactics could be brought in, because a greater good was at stake.[54]

Again, Pinker believes that an evolutionary psychology perspective doesn't need to rule out the significance of cultural influence. For instance, the particular language we speak is obviously a cultural factor. However, *the fact that we speak a language*, argues Pinker, is largely biological. We begin our lives with a language-acquiring mechanism. The brain seems hardwired for it; we "grow" into a language as much as "learn" it.

Pinker further offers an interesting commentary on why we are afraid of the idea of having a human nature. First, he says, is a fear of inequality. Yet for Pinker, the issue is not the possibility that people may differ from each other, but with the question as to what we will *do* with those differences. It is a far cry from saying that people are different to saying that it is therefore acceptable to discriminate *because of those differences*. Nazi and Marxist biological and psychological ideologies are very different, argues Pinker, but *both* have led to mass slaughter and oppression.[55] Mass killing can come from an anti-innatist as well as an innatist theory. The warfare in Hitler is between races; the warfare in Marx is between classes. Both postulated that the human condition can only be purified by the conquest of the opposing group. Whether we call it "social

---

[54] Ibid., 119–20.
[55] Ibid., 156–57.

Darwinism" or "class struggle," the conflict is there. Marx may use the softer word "struggle," but violence is implicit.

A second fear Pinker discusses is the fear of imperfectability. This fear is based on a conviction that if we have a human nature, then that "unchanging" quality could get in the way of true reform. If something is "fixed and permanent" about the human condition, then hopes for change are greatly reduced. We are simply stuck with life as we see it. Further, there is a basic tendency to want to see nature as good. Pinker writes, "According to the worry, if scientists suggest it is 'natural'—part of human nature—to be adulterous, violent, ethnocentric, and selfish, they would be implying that these traits are *good*, not just unavoidable."[56] Without a view of unlimited human plasticity, it is very difficult, argue social constructionists, to argue for the genuine possibility of social change. It is far more comforting to simply believe that our destructiveness is simply socially formed than to say that it arises from within each of us. If our problems always come from outside of us, we can do something about that. But programs for social change reach a screeching halt when we believe that our dilemmas are at least partly created by our basic inclinations. Put theologically, to say that much of our sin arises from within us is to say that sin may always be with us. The fear is that this conviction produces passivity and even resignation. Why try to change the world if we will simply spin out new and different forms of destruction?

This quarrel is part of the tension between Reinhold Niebuhr and liberation theology. Niebuhr's Christian realism is often seen as far too negative in its assessment of the human condition. Liberation theology sometimes takes on many of the older qualities of the social gospel movement, which Niebuhr appreciated but ultimately rejected as naïve. Today's oppressed will become tomorrow's oppressors— this was the mantra Niebuhr regularly maintained. While Niebuhr was enormously involved in helping change the world, he equally insisted that we will never be able to clean it up completely. Though

---

[56] Ibid., 159.

he held a disdain for a nonsocially focused religious piety, he also utterly rejected any position that argued our central problem is *external* to our own freedom. As long as we experience the human condition—finite, anxious creatures with the capacity for transcendence—we will sometimes, in an attempt to anchor our own security, choose destructive forms of behavior. For instance, while Niebuhr remained very attentive to issues of social injustice, he never believed, as did Marx, that once things are divided fairly, we will have no "sin" problem. Rather than this realistic assessment of the human condition leading us to despair and cynicism, Niebuhr believed it will actually help us. How? Because the most devastating forms of despair come from the crushing of our optimistic hopes to eradicate all inhumanity and injustice. Exaggerated claims about human possibility set us up for a demoralized crash when those hopes are dashed. This did not make Niebuhr a self-hater or a voice for total human depravity in the sense that we are as bad as we can possibly be, but he was a voice who pointed out that, in spite of our very best efforts, excessive self-regard can creep into any aspect of our lives.

Pinker, like Browning and William James, argues for an instinctual pluralism. Note how utterly similar the following statement is to Browning's own position:

> Peaceful co-existence, then, does not have to come from pounding selfish desires out of people. It can come from pitting some desires— the desire for safety, the benefits of cooperation, the ability to formulate and recognize universal codes of behavior—against the desire for immediate gain. These are just a few ways in which moral and social progress can ratchet upwards, not in spite of a fixed human nature but because of it.[57]

Thus, for Pinker, a science of human nature can coexist with social change. We can accent one particular instinct over against another. Acknowledging human nature does not condemn us to ongoing

---

[57] Ibid., 169.

oppression, violence, or greed. We move forward by turning some internal tendencies against others and cooperating to bring about a better world.

Pinker and Feminist Theory

As a general rule, many feminists have been against the sciences of human nature because they believe those sciences argue that the minds of the sexes differ at birth. Unfortunately, this has often led to the unequal treatment of women. Pinker, however, argues that this does not have to be the case:

> There is, in fact, no incompatibility between the principles of feminism and the possibility that men and women are not psychologically identical. To repeat: equality is not the empirical claim that all groups of humans are interchangeable; it is the moral principle that individuals should not be judged or constrained by the average properties of their group. In the case of gender, the barely defeated Equal Rights Amendment put it succinctly: 'Equality of Rights under the law shall not be denied or abridged by the United States or any state on account of sex.' If we recognize this principle, no one has to spin myths about the indistinguishability of the sexes to justify equality. Nor should anyone invoke sex differences to justify discriminatory policies or to hector women into doing what they don't want to do.... Despite these principles, many feminists vehemently attack research on sexuality and sex differences. The politics of gender is a major reason that the application of evolution, genetics, and neuroscience to the human mind is bitterly resisted in modern intellectual life. But unlike other human divisions such as race and ethnicity, where any biological differences are minor at most and scientifically interesting, gender cannot possibly be ignored in the science of human beings.[58]

Pinker applauds Christina Hoff-Summers in her controversial book, *Who Stole Feminism?*[59] One of the central themes in Hoff-

---

[58] Ibid., 340.

[59] Christina Hoff-Summers, *Who Stole Feminism* (New York: Simon and Schuster, 1995).

Summers's book is a distinction between "equity feminism" and "gender feminism." Equity feminism opposes discrimination and the unfair treatment of women, grows out of the classic liberal tradition, and holds a moral doctrine about the equal treatment of women which makes no claims about empirical issues in psychology and biology. Gender feminism, on the other hand, holds that "women continue to be enslaved by patriarchy in which 'bi-sexual infants are transformed into male and female gender personalities, the one destined to command, the other to obey'."[60] It is typically allied with Marxism, postmodernism, and social constructionism. It argues that differences between men and women have nothing to do with biology but are entirely socially manufactured. It often assumes that the master motive in human life is power, so social life can be best interpreted in terms of power distributions. Human interactions stem not from human beings individually interacting, but from larger groups interacting (male and female power systems). Gender feminism often seems to be a combination of women's studies and postmodern sociology. This group of feminists are sometimes less prone to draw people from the discipline of psychology precisely because they tend to minimize psychological factors in favor of systemic ones. A much larger force of patriarchy looms in the background of decisions we think we're making on our own. The focus, of necessity, is on systemic analysis.

> In embracing these doctrines, the genderists are handcuffing feminism to railroad tracks on which a train is bearing down. As we shall see, neuroscience, genetics, psychology, and ethnography are documenting sex differences that almost certainly originate in human biology. And evolutionary psychology is documenting a web of motives other than group-against-group dominance (such as love, sex, family, and beauty) that entangle us in many conflicts and confluences of interest with members of the same sex and of the opposite sex. Gender feminists want either to derail the train or to have other women join them in martyrdom, but the other women are not

---

[60] Quoted in ibid., 22.

cooperating. Despite their visibility, gender feminists do not speak for all feminists, let alone for all women.[61]

Pinker's question is a bold one: If feminism attaches itself so rigorously to a social constructionist view which denies all biological differences between the sexes, will it be unnecessarily damaged by new evidence regarding difference between the sexes? Will it be necessary to deny all counterevidence in maintaining an outworn view of social constructionism? Pinker, who considers himself a supporter of equity feminism, believes that feminism must not root itself in such a scientifically antagonistic and hopeless paradigm as the radical social constructionist view. He writes, "To say that women and men do not have interchangeable minds, that people have desires other than power, and that motives belong to individual people and not just entire genders is not to attack feminism or to compromise the interests of women, despite the misconception that gender feminism speaks in their name."[62]

Browning and Evolutionary Psychology

Browning, in many ways, can be found between the perspectives of evolutionary psychology and social constructionism. Relying on a critical hermeneutical model, he would see many forms of evolutionary psychology as too rooted in a foundationalism which seeks to strip us of our interpretive framework and simply gather the "facts" of human nature. But those "facts" are already approached from a particular orientation. In that sense, science cannot simply "tell us who we are." We bring an effective history to our scientific work. Scientific foundationalism, whether it appears in evolutionary psychology or any other form, must be rejected.

However, unlike social constructionists, Browning believes that evolutionary psychology offers important data about the human condition, particularly as we attempt to distance ourselves from our orienting assumptions in a critically reflective submoment of

---

[61] Pinker, *The Blank Slate*, 341–42.
[62] Ibid., 343.

understanding. As Stephen Pope's helpful article on Browning and evolutionary psychology suggests, "Don Browning is one of only a few scholars who draw from evolutionary psychology in the development of a constructive theological position."[63] For Browning, evolutionary psychology can be appreciated and informative without believing it provides the *total* picture of who we are. Take, for instance, the frequent argument made by evolutionary psychology concerning kin altruism. Put simply, there is a natural inclination to help those to whom we are genetically related. This is part of inclusive fitness, which recognizes that the best ways to perpetuate our own genes is to help our relatives. Browning argues that an evolutionary psychology perspective can actually be seen, at least implicitly, in the work of Aquinas, and even earlier in the philosophical writings of Aristotle.[64] Aquinas directly recognizes a natural inclination to show greater preference for those children to whom one is biologically related. While there are some exceptions, these exceptions do not negate the general rule that we offer our own offspring preferential treatment and more invested care. Because human infants need far more time and investment than many other species, an intense tie is often created with the mother. A large factor in whether the father joins this mother/child union is the assurance that this child is indeed his offspring. Aquinas says, "Man naturally desires to be assured of his offspring and this assurance would be altogether nullified in the case of promiscuous copulation. Therefore the union of the man with the woman comes from a natural

---

[63] Stephen J. Pope, "The Place of Evolutionary Psychology in a Practical Theological Ethics of Families," in James Witte, Jr., M. Christian Green, and Amy Wheeler, eds., *The Equal-Regard Family and Its Friendly Critics* (Grand Rapids MI: Eerdmans, 2007) 56.

[64] Don S. Browning, *Marriage and Modernization* (Grand Rapids MI: Eerdmans, 2003) 84–117; Browning, Bonnie Miller-McLemore, Pamela Couture, et al., *From Culture Wars to Common Ground: Religion and the American Family Debate* (Louisville KY: Westminster John Knox Press, 1997) 113–18.

instinct."[65] Mutual assistance and regular sexual exchange may also be motives for joining this dyad.

Before we turn Aquinas into an early representative of evolutionary psychology, argues Browning, some caution is in order. Browning believes that Aquinas probably overemphasizes the natural instinct of the male to join the female, a pattern which is often not seen among other mammals. Browning would prefer to state the thesis as follows: "Among conflicting male tendencies, there are some which, when faced with the dependency of an infant that a human male recognizes as his, can be channeled into enduring male-female family arrangements for the purpose of caring for the infant."[66] This natural inclination does not completely assure that the male will join the female. Conflicting tendencies remain. As Pope suggests, "Browning accepts the basic outline of 'kin altruism' without reducing every component of family life to the logic of natural selection. He understands that evolution has shaped our emotional capacities and needs, but not in a way that makes culture and personality of little significance. Both culture and biology can make the family a place of unbalanced power and unhealthy cooperation."[67] As we shall see in fuller detail, Browning clearly prefers William James's understanding of a plurality of instincts rather than any notion that we are driven by a singular master instinct or in constant conflict with dualism. Also, Browning is quick to point out that this natural impulse in Aquinas needs the additional reinforcement of ethical arguments to further establish the goodness of marriage. Nature, alone, will not guarantee a family unit. But the point is that *the arguments in favor of marriage and family life can build upon a natural inclination outlined by evolutionary psychology*. Again, is the natural inclination itself enough? No. This biological inclination needs the further reinforcements of cultural values, symbols, and narratives. Nevertheless, evolutionary

---

[65] Thomas Aquinas, *Summa Contra Gentiles* (London: Burns, Oates, and Washbourne, 1928) 3, ii, 118.

[66] Browning, *Marriage and Modernization*, 87–88.

[67] Pope, "The Place of Evolutionary Psychology in a Practical Theological Ethics of Families," 59.

psychology does indeed provide some important information for us to use and build upon in our views of marriage. Of course, a theological perspective will move beyond this kin altruism and offer images of all other children as children of God. We are therefore called to act lovingly toward all children whether we are related to them or not. But this larger theological vision does not cancel out the significant contributions of evolutionary psychology, contributions that like all science, can be very important in the time of critical reflection or "distanciation" in which we question and challenge our own thinking. Browning once again wants to use science as a means of clarifying and perhaps modifying our assumptions in the larger task of interpretation. Thus, Browning can use the findings of evolutionary psychology within a larger theological framework which employs evolutionary science to help clarify and sharpen a theological view of the human condition.

However, Browning is very aware of how science easily turns into scientism. As we have seen, this is one of his major critiques of the contemporary psychologies. In this sense, he would applaud the "nose" of many social-constructionists who may smell something more than science in the perspectives of evolutionary psychology. Pinker himself seems to reveal this. For instance, he says, "Religions have provided comfort, community, and moral guidance to countless people, and some biologists argue that a sophisticated deism, toward which many religions are evolving, can be made compatible with an evolutionary understanding of the bind of human nature."[68] Some, including me, might find this statement somewhat condescending. It seems to imply that biologists are giving theologians their agenda and deciding what is theologically feasible. But biologists, as biologists, cannot possibly tell theologians what is or is not ontologically plausible, at least when it comes to the ultimate context of our lives. When Pinker suggests that a "sophisticated deism" is the only option, he speaks as a theologian, not merely as a cognitive scientist or evolutionary psychologist. One might ask, "Who put evolutionary

---

[68] Pinker, *The Blank Slate*, 187.

psychology in charge of theology?" One minute Pinker is speaking against reductionism, and the next minute he is telling us what theology is "allowed" to entertain. The fear, for many, is that all discourse will be pushed onto the scientific playing field. But this actually is a philosophical discourse that goes beyond science. Again, perhaps this is one of the reasons that some worry about a creeping reductionism in evolutionary psychology. What it initially says, and what it finally allows, can sometimes be two different things. So Browning's position, in my estimation, is a very sober one: He neither accepts evolutionary psychology as the ultimate paradigm for understanding the human condition nor condemns it as right-wing propaganda. He listens to it, appreciates it, but makes sure that it stays within a submoment of a larger interpretive process. Pope agrees: "I would like to argue that Don Browning's most important contribution to the discipline of theological ethics consists in his ability to use these evolutionary sources without accepting the unwarranted reductionisms with which they are often, but unnecessarily, joined."[69]

Throughout Browning's works he has so emphasized the idea of "equal-regard marriage" that John Witte Jr., M. Christian Green, and Amy Wheeler have titled their edited responses to Browning's work on the family, *The Equal-Regard Family and Its Friendly Critics*.[70] While Browning is clearly an equity feminist, to use Summers's and Pinker's terms, he would not be considered a gender feminist. Recent mainline pastoral theology, which has been much more affected by gender feminism, might well suggest that Browning's work does not adequately emphasize liberation, particularly the liberation of oppressed women. He is too abstract, too philosophical, and not political enough for some. This discussion of Browning's perspective on gender and family is beyond the scope of this book, but the reader

---

[69] Poe, "The Place of Evolutionary Psychology in a Practical Theological Ethics of Families," 58.

[70] See note 63.

is encouraged to examine Witte's work *The Equal-Regard Family and Its Friendly Critics* for an extended focus on this issue.

William James's Instinctual Pluralism

As we have seen, Browning thinks that both Freud's instinctual dualism and Rogers's instinctual monism provide an inadequate picture of the human condition. Instead, he advocates the position of William James and Reinhold Niebuhr that we actually have a number of competing instincts. This instinctual pluralism is a more comprehensive way of understanding human life. Contrary to Freud, it is not the task of reason simply to stop an instinct; instead, *reason awakens another instinct*. Stated even more strongly, it is not the job of reason to "redeem" an instinct, but instead to favor those instincts which lead to greater adaptation to life. As Browning puts it, "Reason is not against instinct. Reason, on the basis of its assessments, grants its reinforcing attention to some impulses rather than to others."[71] A ferocious battle between culture and instincts, as Freud depicts, is, for William James, an overstatement. Culture does not simply satisfy or repress our basic instincts; instead, culture often completes, guides, and directs these instincts.[72] For human beings, instincts are always mixed with consciousness and memory. As James puts it, "Man has a far greater variety of *impulses* than any lower animal."[73] Our reason hesitates and deliberates about our decisions in large part *because we have so many instincts* and not because we are void of them.[74] While human beings have all the basic instincts that animals have, we also have more. James puts his disagreement with Freud quite directly:

> In other words, there is no material antagonism between instinct and reason. Reason, *per se*, can inhibit no impulses; the only thing that can neutralize an impulse is an impulse the other way: Reason may,

---

[71] Browning, *Pluralism and Personality* (Lewisburg PA: Bucknell University Press, 1980) 164.

[72] Ibid., 161.

[73] William James, *Principles of Psychology*, 2 vols. (New York: Dover Publications, 1950) 1:392.

[74] Browning, *Pluralism and Personality*, 164.

however, make an inference which will excite the imagination so as to set loose the impulse the other way; and thus, though the animal richest in reason might be also the animal richest in instinctive impulses too, he would never seem the fatal automaton which a *merely* instinctual animal would be.[75]

Thus, reason "casts its vote" toward some instincts over others. But the instincts are multiple and often at odds with each other. A dualistic or monistic model won't do; instead, a pluralistic model of instincts describes the human condition. Browning tells us that for James, "Fear, locomotion, vocalization, imitation, aggression, sympathy, hunting, curiosity, constructiveness, play, and sexuality all have instinctual roots."[76] Again, classifying a human being with one or two instincts is not enough; human beings are instead ambivalent in the instinctual impulses. They struggle with multiple inclinations. We are not finally governed by a singular self-actualizing tendency (Maslow) or self-realizing impulse (Jung) toward growth. Nor are we the unwitting bodies on which two forces battle it out. Master-motive theories, which portray one instinct as the final governor of the psyche, minimize our multiple instinctual tendencies. Along with recognizing the multiculturalism in our pluralistic world, we also need to understand the multi-instinctualism in our inner world. Bifurcated, all-or-nothing perspectives on the human instincts miss this vitality of options. Again, it is not so much that a detached reason arises and crushes a destructive instinct; instead, reason triggers other instincts which may help modify and redirect its competitive tendency.

As Browning points out, James calls us to a "strenuous life" in that we ethically deliberate over this instinctual pluralism and choose the path which seems most beneficial. This path will not ignore our own needs nor will it ignore the needs of others. Above all, *it is not easy*. Further, it does not come automatically or naturally. Thus, James would rigorously disagree with any position that says our problems

---

[75] James, *Principles of Psychology*, 1:393.
[76] Browning, *Pluralism and Personality*, 170.

are over once we find our actualizing tendency. He would further suggest that postanalysis will not provide an automatic blueprint for healthy striving. There is no "blossoming self," no "lost" self that only needs to be rediscovered. Who we are is always the outcome of this strenuous process of deliberation and giving the nod to one impulse over the other. An important parallel can be raised here: *Just as James rejected the social Darwinism of Spencer, which argued that social progress is inevitable, so he would reject the idea, found most notably in some of the humanistic psychologies, that personal growth is inevitable and automatic.* Whether we are talking about the individual or society, James did not share this "constant improvement" thesis. Values are hard won; they do not simply pop up out of the blue. Post-therapized individuals still have to deal with the dilemmas of ethics. Growth is more rugged, more of a struggle, than the "blossoming self" notion acknowledges.

But James goes further and suggests that our romantic attempts to find an "already fashioned" self with which we need simply to re-connect, a self somehow provided by nature, is an illusion. Our sense of self is always *negotiated,* not simply *discovered.* The way we deal with the vicissitudes of life determines our sense of self much more than some sort of discovery of a self that has been there all along. Stated more directly, nature does not provide us with a "self." It is here that James's approach seems at odds with Jung and his insistence on self-discovery. As Browning describes it, "There was no 'real' or 'true' self deeply embedded in our biological roots that only needs to be liberated and set free in order for man to discover his true identity."[77] As Browning further points out, in this regard, James was closer to Freud than to Rogers or Jung, whom we shall encounter in a later chapter. I would add that this is one of the factors that separates some forms of existentialist thought from the humanistic psycho-logies: For much of existentialism, finding authenticity requires much more of a struggle with ontological anxiety, finitude, and guilt and shame than the humanistic psychologists seem to propose.

---

[77] Ibid., 166.

Thus, one doesn't have to resort to the old Freudian dualism to counter the optimistic, mono-motivational tendencies of the humanistic psychologists. Instead, one can employ James's instinctual pluralism as a means of demonstrating that human life is not quite as "easy" as the humanistic psychologists would have us believe. Rogers does indeed acknowledge the struggle of moving out of incongruence back under the umbrella of the actualizing tendency. The problem has to do with his assumption that once the actualizing tendency is tapped, it will automatically produce behavior which is advantageous for both self and society. As Browning has demonstrated so well, this is largely because of (a) Rogers's metaphysical assumptions about a harmonious universe in which everyone can self-actualize at the same time, and (b) Rogers's refusal to acknowledge fully the problem of ontological anxiety, a problem he surprisingly missed in his reading of Kierkegaard. A growth tendency will always have to compete with the anxieties of finitude, an anxiety that will tempt us toward excessive self-regard or preoccupation. This is why Rogers's valuable contribution needs the balancing factor of Reinhold Niebuhr. Again, it is simply not the case that Rogers is in favor of self-esteem and Niebuhr is against it, which has been an unfortunately popular explanation of their differences. Instead, Niebuhr, because he fully embraced the true Kierkegaardian emphasis on ontological anxiety, knew the temptations of excessive self-regard. But one nearly always needs to add, even if it is for the umpteenth time: This excessive self-regard did not always reveal itself as arrogance, conceit, and self-inflation. Whether we exalt ourselves or are ashamed of ourselves, the point is that we are excessively involved with self, an involvement which often distracts us from the full joys of relating to others.

James sees the self as a unified pluralism of potential selves, a unification that is a hard-won struggle which takes into consideration both the plurality of instincts within us and the historical and social forces surrounding us. Gains always involve some forms of loss. As

Thomas Oden puts it, choosing one value means negating another.[78] If life were such that we only had a singular "good" to actualize at each moment, human decision would be far less complicated. But there are multiple goods and each compete for our allegiance. The self is ever changing and growing as it makes difficult decisions about which values to actualize. And these strenuous decisions are always ethical in character—that is, they call into question the relationship between our own goods and the goods of our neighbor and the larger community. A plethora of choices dangle before us. Connected with these various options are different, potential selves. James writes,

> So the seeker of his truest, strongest, deepest self must review the list carefully and pick out the one on which to stake his salvation. All other selves, thereupon become unreal, but the fortunes of the self are real. Its failures are real failures, its triumphs real triumphs, carrying shame and gladness with them…. Our thought, incessantly deciding among many things of a kind, which ones for it shall be realities, here chooses one of many possible selves or characters, and forthwith reckons it no shame to fail in any of those not adapted expressly as its own.[79]

This choosing of the self one becomes needs to be based on an attentiveness to one's own growth and development as well as the ethical consideration of how one's own existence affects others. Further, "the real necessity of the strenuous life comes from the nature of communal existence—the fact that humans with their conflicting range of wills and desires must find ways to mediate and harmonize their differences."[80] Perhaps this issue can be stated this way: Whereas the humanistic psychologies believed that the actualized self would automatically make ethical choices, James argues that we find our authentic self *precisely through those ethical quandaries and struggles to relate our own needs to those of others.* Again, a

---

[78] Thomas Oden, *The Structure of Awareness.*
[79] James, *Principles of Psychology,* 1:310.
[80] Browning, *Pluralism and Personality,* 212.

"given," almost biologically unfolding self cannot go on "autopilot" for these tough decisions. We modify and even forge a sense of self by the decisions we make. Put differently, there are a number of potential meanings for each of us to actualize; our identities emerge from those meanings we affirm. Contrary to any romantic view of returning to a natural self, James believes the struggle of identity is much more difficult. It is here that James is much closer to Erikson than to Rogers, Maslow, or Jung. We move toward wholeness, and find a sense of our identity in terms of how we order the good of our lives. When we ask who we are, we need to look at those things to which we are committed. As James suggested, sometimes the various goods we must choose are "cruel to their rivals."[81] In this sense, there is a connection between the words "homicide," "suicide," "geno-cide," and "decide." They all have to do with killing something. In the case of decision, we are forced to kill an option, a potential path with its own sense of self dangling from it. We often do not have the option of remaining undecided. We also don't have forever to decide. The choices are momentous and forced.

In what is one of Browning's best statements on the significance of William James for a discussion of human instincts, he says the following:

> Whereas contemporary humanistic psychology tends toward a sweetness-and-light view of man's biological capacities for love and growth and orthodox psychoanalysis toward a bio-metaphysics of total depravity, James's analysis is situational and pluralistic. Both our egoistic and sympathetic inclinations have their adaptive significance, but in the context of the modern environment that man has created for himself, his egoistic tendencies overreach themselves and his sympathetic inclinations fail to have the range and depth that the situation requires. Education is needed. Culture and habit must build on the fragments of altruistic impulse which nature gives us.[82]

---

[81] James, *Principles of Psychology,* 1:211.
[82] Browning, *Pluralism and Personality,* 172.

For Browning, James, in his emphasis on the "strenuous life," offers the most comprehensive insight into the relationship between instincts and culture. Put simply, we are not as "bad" as Freud says we are and we're not as "good" as Rogers and Maslow say we are. We are not void of instincts, as both radical behaviorism and extreme social constructionism insist. Nor are instincts all-determining as *some* evolutionary psychologists might be tempted to suggest. Instead, we have a plurality of instincts. There is nothing inherently destructive about our instincts though the human situation of anxiety and finitude can push them toward inordinate expression. We are also probably not as free as many humanistic and existential thinkers believe we are. And we're not as determined as Skinner believes we are. Our culture can build upon, support, and encourage instincts that promote health for ourselves and others. But no amount of natural inclination toward wholeness or self-realization can provide an automatic blueprint for tough ethical decisions. Self-regard, not excessive self-regard, must be coordinated with the needs and fulfillment of others. This process is more rugged than "blossoming." Neither instincts nor the social order are the enemy. A respect for the full force of human instinctuality can be combined with an appreciation of social influence. Our biology cannot deliver our ethics, but neither can our ethics deny our biology.

3

Identity, Self-Injury, and Generativity: Browning on Erikson and Kohut

> "There is no possibility of creating truly generative people without inducting them into a *culture* of generativity with powerful accompanying symbols and communities that carry and reinforce these symbols. Generativity is a tendency of nature, but it needs the support and completion of communities of tradition that contain generatively inspiring narratives." —Don Browning

As one reads through the various writings of Don Browning, it doesn't take long to discover that his favorite psychologist is Erik Erikson. Since his important work on Erikson in 1973, *Generative Man: Psychoanalytic Perspectives*, Browning has remained convinced that Erikson offers a more adequate normative image of the "good person" than any other psychologist. This image of human care or "generativity," for Browning, is very close to a Christian anthropology that encourages love for both self and neighbor. *Generative Man* was not a theological book, nor did it pretend to be. It also wasn't an explication of Erikson's life cycle, a study of his clinical method, or a careful delineation of Erikson from other psychoanalytic ego psychologists. While some of these things were discussed, the primary focus was Erikson's ethics. This turn to the underlying ethical assumptions of various psychologies, a turn that would direct Browning's career for the next couple of decades, largely began with this work. Here we are first introduced to the notion of a "horizon," the world of background assumptions—both metaphysical and ethical—on which various psychologies shape their observations. As we have seen, all psychologists hold an implicit image of human fulfillment. For Erikson, this fulfillment is intricately tied to caring for future generations. While this theme of generativity is more explicit in Erikson than in Heinz Kohut, it is nevertheless present in the great psychoanalytic self psychologist as well. I will first examine Browning's work on Erikson, then turn my attention to Kohut, before comparing the relevance of these two great thinkers for a Christian anthropology.

Browning is not surprised that Erikson did not make a singular, systematic statement on the generative person. Browning writes, "Commanding visions of the nature of man seldom enjoy the elegance of systematic articulation."[1] In this sense, Browning's work offers a very important service for an Eriksonian perspective— namely, it pulls together from a variety of sources the emerging themes in Erikson's vision of humanity. Browning makes explicit Erikson's implicit ethical vision.

Throughout Erikson's work, argues Browning, it is possible to see an emphasis similar to Reinhold Niebuhr: The "highs" and "lows" of humanity are both necessary for the human condition to flourish. In other words, both Niebuhr and Erikson argue that it is not the task of a "higher" self to beat down and submit the "lower" instincts to a lofty cultural ideal. Both Niebuhr and Erikson balk at any notion that human instincts are inherently destructive. The so-called "problem" of the instincts cannot be escaped through spiritual progress. That is, our basic drives are not the enemy. Biological incli-nations are an inevitable part of self-transcendence. Browning explains,

> ...for Erikson the high in man must not exclude the low, just as the civilized must not exclude the primitive, the mature become dissociated from the infantile, or man's progressive advance become estranged from his more regressive renewals.... This is the fruit of the *epigenetic principle*. According to this principle, all advances to the

[1] Browning, *Generative Man: Psychoanalytic Perspectives* (Philadelphia: Westminster Press, 1973) 23.

higher and later stages of development—toward independence, responsibility, maturity—must include and carry forward, while restating, a lower level of development. For Erikson, the so-called lower in man—the animal, the primitive, the child (never, of course, to be considered as simply equivalent to each other)—contains important regulatory and organizing powers essential for the maintenance and restoration of man's ecological integrity. Yet the lower in man never functions with the precision and specificity that instinct does in the animal world. Hence, the lower in man must always be restated in the context of man's more progressive capacities for autonomy, conscious reflection, responsibility, and purposeful activity. It can be said that in Erikson's concept of generative man we have restored to us much of what is both truly animal and truly human, much that is both childlike and adult, and perhaps a great deal that is both primitive and civilized.[2]

As we saw in the last chapter, our instinctuality does not necessarily challenge a civilized existence. We are instinctual creatures even in our loftiest endeavors; no amount of culture can eradicate these instincts. They are very real biological tendencies even though they may be interpreted differently in each situation. They are neither raw, destructive forces, nor are they singularly directed toward self-fulfillment. Again, throughout Browning's work, he comes back over and over to this crucial point: *Perspectives that push a single motivation in human nature do not adequately account for human life as it is actually experienced.* Human beings are too complex, too multifaceted, to be reduced to a single or even a dual instinctual theory.

Before we look directly at Erikson's vision of human flourishing, it is important to understand how his thought is influenced by the development of ego psychology.

---

[2] Ibid., 22.

Erikson in Context: The Emergence of Ego Psychology

It is commonly recognized that Freud used the term "ego" rather loosely before his publication of *The Ego and the Id* in 1923. Prior to this work, the ego was simply a cluster of conscious ideas from which the more massive part of the mind—the unconscious—was cut off. Most college students are introduced to Freud's famous image of the iceberg in which consciousness represents the tip of the iceberg while the bulk of the structure exists beneath the surface of the water. In 1923, however, Freud signaled an important movement toward a *structural* theory of the mind, a shift that pointed toward a conflict between the id, the ego, and the superego. The ego's primary task is to represent reality, a perspective quite different from the pleasure-seeking id and the frequently oppressive and shaming superego. The goal is to develop a solid ego to mediate between the tugs of the id and the superego's sense of "oughts" and "shoulds." The id can be reckless, and the superego can be excessively punitive; therefore, the ego's job is to find balance in this war between instinct and culture, a culture internalized in the form of the superego. Unrepentant urges are in constant battle against their own prohibitions. The ego has a tough task of refereeing and mediating this conflict. Part of this job involves raising defenses against the direct expression of the id and rechanneling this energy into socially acceptable activities. The ego is in charge of sublimation, a job absolutely necessary if civilization is to survive. Thus, the tripartite, structural model, from 1923 on, argued that neurosis results from ongoing compromise. As Steven Mitchell and Marjorie Black write:

> Displaying some sympathy for the id, the ego works out a strategy that allows a certain amount of instinctual gratification but channels this gratification through a complex system of clever defenses. The ego disguises the appearance of the id's impulses, thereby both preventing social censure and keeping the impulses under careful regulation. For the neurotic person, these compromises between forbidden impulses and defenses result in complex, uncomfortable

symptoms and a constriction of functioning (often involving sexual inhibitions or an inability to work and compete successfully).[3]

Freud's daughter, Anna, began to reflect on her father's change to a structural model and asked a very important question: Since the battle is no longer simply between the unconscious id and the conscious ego, are some of the ego's defense strategies also unconscious? Perhaps the ego defends itself *unconsciously*. Maybe the defense mechanisms are far more subtle than previously recognized. Further, perhaps the ego has a vested interest in keeping its practices unconscious. In other words, while the id has every reason to have its urges and desires directly known (so that they can be expressed), the ego has nothing to gain by exposing its own defensive strategies. To expose the less-than-lovely nature of the ego's defenses would be painful rather than liberating. The id has no interest in "saving face" or leaving a positive impression on others; it only wants release. But the ego would suffer greatly if it were "found out." Thus, while Freud had worked so hard to unearth the secrets of the psyche, his daughter, Anna, turned her attention to the mechanisms by which those secrets were kept outside the range of consciousness. As Mitchell and Black put it, "The ego, charged with the daunting task of keeping peace between warring internal parties and ensuring socially acceptable functioning, works more effectively if it works undercover."[4] Freud was primarily interested in discovering the monsters within our depths; Anna was interested in how we keep those monsters *out of our view*. The unconscious defense processes of the ego must be brought out into the open. In other words, it is not enough to simply go after *what* is buried; we must understand how we unconsciously *keep it buried*. While this clearly seemed the direction her father was headed, she took this concern and developed it well. Thus, in 1936, three years before her father's death, she

---

[3] Stephen A. Mitchell and Margaret J. Black, *Freud and Beyond: A History of Modern Psychoanalytic Thought* (New York: Perseus Books, 1995) 26.

[4] Ibid.

published *The Ego and the Mechanisms of Defense*.[5] It became utterly pivotal for the emerging tradition of ego psychology. In this work, Anna Freud outlined the classic unconscious defense mechanisms of the ego. Freud had earlier used the term "defense," but had not offered the specific and elaborate meaning that Anna gave it. This changed the course of psychoanalysis.

> The shift from id psychology to ego psychology signaled a shift in the way the fundamental project of psychoanalysis was conceived. In broad strokes, id psychology was the exploration of the implications of the Darwinian revolution for the study of the human psyche; ego psychology became an avenue for the study of the ways individuals develop a distinct and secure sense of themselves. But ego psychology itself never abandoned drive theory.[6]

This retention of drive theory in ego psychology represents an important difference with the later psychoanalytic perspectives of object relations theory and Kohutian self-psychology.

Ego psychology emphasizes that unconscious ego defenses emerge even when a patient free-associates in a relaxed, nonjudgmental atmosphere. Even in the presence of a highly permissive emotional environment, the unconscious ego defenses are at work. At first, the *very existence* of these unconscious defense mechanisms has to be inferred. Anxiety is always generated when the defenses are pointed out. Thus, again, the realm of the unconscious is not simply occupied by the id; instead, there are unconscious elements in all three units of the personality—the id, ego, and superego. The analyst's task is now more complicated. Attention must be paid to all three dimensions of personhood as the search for unconscious material continues. Here is the math of ego psychology: The impulse plus the defense equals the symptom. Even though the defenses have a self-protective function, they occur automatically, without fore-

---

[5] Anna Freud, *The Ego and the Mechanisms of Defense* (1936; reprint, New York: International Universities Press, 1946).

[6] Mitchell and Black, *Freud and Beyond*, 140–41.

thought. This is why they are called defense "mechanisms"—they happen in an automatic, mechanical manner.

Along with Anna Freud, the other highly significant contributor to ego psychology was Heinz Hartmann (1894–1970). Hartmann greatly broadened the scope of psychoanalysis from a preoccupation with psychopathology to a more general theory of human development. As Mitchell and Black explain it, "One cannot understand a country by studying only its wars. And with that seemingly simple shift in focus, Hartmann powerfully affected the course of psychoanalysis, opening up a crucial investigation of the key processes and vicissitudes of normal development."[7] Hartmann was interested in understanding the nonpathological ways in which the ego adapts to changing circumstances.

Throughout his shift in focus, however, Hartmann was never "outside" the circle of psychoanalysis. As we shall see, this would not be true of Erikson. Freud had taken from Darwin the connection of human beings to other animal species and emphasized the instinctual force of our motivations. In other words, we are not as distinguishable from other species as we might have hoped. This was a common assumption in nineteenth-century medicine. Human beings are driven by both self-preservation and the preservation of the species. Our basic drives are rooted in the body. This Darwinian view was a reaction against vitalism, a perspective that had argued that human beings are animated by a rather mysterious, hard-to-pinpoint energy such as "will" or "purpose." A materialist, mechanistic view sees all energy as emerging purely from the body. The body works only on the basis of chemistry and physics, not some "vital force" that somehow empowers it. We should be exploring the electrical impulses of the neurons, not chasing some vague and speculative energy that propels us. Under this new model, all action is a discharge of energy. The build-up of energy becomes progressively uncontrollable until it is discharged. Profoundly influenced by this mechanistic model, Freud believed the id to be a

---

[7] Ibid., 34–35.

kind of horse and the ego a rider. The ego has no energy or motivation *on its own*; instead, it relies on the id for its energy. The ego tames this energy by redirecting it. The ego is thus a guide for the vitalities of the id.

Hartmann, like Freud, also focused on our evolutionary development. However, he concentrated more on the evolutionary principle of adaptation to a changing environment. He believed we are born with a natural capacity for ego adaptation. Language, perception, object comprehension, and thinking are all natural endowments that emerge at the appropriate time. In fact, even the ego's defenses are adaptive.

It may be recalled that Freud had argued that the process of sublimation redirects the primary drives of sex and aggression into socially acceptable activity. The major point, for Freud, is that this basic energy, while redirected, is not changed. Even great works of art, for instance, use the primitive energies of the id. For Hartmann, these basic energies are not simply redirected; instead, *they are changed or altered*. While Freud believed that it was the old, primitive energies of the id that produce great cultural artifacts, Hartmann argues instead that these primitive energies are *neutralized* and changed, rather than merely redirected. The next question quickly became this: Are there aspects of a child's psychological environment that help the child tone down or neutralize the urgent push of the drives?

It is very important to notice that Hartmann is *not* rejecting drive theory. In fact, as Mitchell and Black remind us, "What distinguishes the ego psychology approach from other lines of thought is the careful preservation of Freud's drive theory that underlines it."[8] For Hartmann, the drives still push us biologically and are the source of our psychic energy. Yet Hartmann was deeply interested in environmental aids to this process of neutralization. That is, he grew to emphasize the crucial importance of the early emotional environment in making drives productive rather than destructive.

[8] Ibid., 24.

The environment did not simply help us redirect these drives; instead, it helped us *change* them.

Probably no single study reveals this crucial aspect of the child's emotional environment more than Rene Spitz's classic and painful work.[9] Spitz's research focused on children who had been left from birth in orphanages. While the children's basic physical needs had been met, their emotional needs had been profoundly neglected. These children, lacking the emotional nutrients so important to their environment, had become despondent, depressed, withdrawn, and even physically sick. There was not a bridge, bond, or attachment between themselves and another person. Shockingly, by the end of several years, one-third of the children had died. Among those who did not die, few could walk or talk. This emotional deprivation had certainly *not* stimulated ego development; instead, it pushed children into a harsh reality, a reality they were not emotionally equipped to handle. There was nothing in the emotional environment that offered any support. While struggles and even emotional deprivation might develop character *in later life*, it was devastating to the children's early experience. The child desperately needs connection, support, affection, and affirmation. Without it, the child wastes away. The utterly tragic findings of this hospital argued for the importance of early emotional caretaking more dramatically than any words could convey. Reading about these children is extremely painful; seeing pictures is even worse. This hospital stands as a deeply disturbing reminder of the crucial role of a nurturing environment in early child care. As Mitchell and Black write, "It left no doubt that whatever inborn psychological potential humans may have, its realization is doomed in the absence of emotional connectedness with another person."[10]

This study was very important for Hartmann's work because he had argued that a supportive emotional environment is necessary for the natural capacities and future possibilities of the child's ego to

---

[9] For a review of this important work, see ibid., 38–45
[10] Ibid., 38.

emerge. The child's ego potential is directly linked to environmental support. Spitz spent the rest of his life carefully studying the relationship between an infant and his or her caregivers. This involved a direct, systematic, controlled observation of infants and their mothers. His work helped lead to a new development in psychoanalysis—"baby watching." Thus, while Freud largely "resurrected" early experience through adult comments, other psychoanalysts turned to a direct study of infants themselves. It was believed that infant study would not contradict Freud's reconstruction of childhood experience through adult commentary.

How did the ego psychologists view neurosis? Neurosis involved two things: (a) the return of repressed feelings and thought, and (b) the defenses against this return of the repressed. These defenses create symptoms that bring the person into analysis. The defenses have a self-protective function and occur automatically without forethought. These defenses themselves, and not just the unconscious material beneath them, need to be analyzed.

The great rivalry in 1970s' psychoanalytic circles was between ego psychology and the developing "object relations theory" in the work of Fairbairne and Winnicott. While there were many overlaps, the object-relations representatives felt no need to remain loyal to drive theory as the ego psychologists had done. They flatly stated that the primary point of a drive is not satisfaction but relationship; not gratification so much as connection. Thus, a child is not reaching out merely to have his or her hunger satisfied. Instead, the child is reaching out for connection. The child desperately seeks emotional responsiveness. Libido is not primarily pleasure-seeking but object-seeking. *Attachment and connection are goals in themselves*. Thus, infants are "wired" for attachment. This early bonding experience has enormous impact on later relationships. In fact, this strong need for attachment explains, in part, the repetition compulsion. Rather than assuming that the repetition compulsion demonstrates that people unconsciously seek pain or wish to die, the child will seek out even painful experiences if they are associated with bonding. This also offers an explanation as to why abused children sometimes continue to seek out abusive relationships. The abuse is what they tragically associate with connection. They may so identify feelings of threat with "love" that they deliberately move toward turbulent relationships. Most of us have seen this at work. In some cases, treating the person "well" can even be interpreted as boring or abandoning. Without a volatile threat, these individuals often do not see the possibility of love.

Also, when early childhood needs are not met, the child may turn toward a world of internal fantasy objects. For instance, the child may imagine caretakers having characteristics they do not really possess. Even if a father has not seen a child for several years, the child may carry a fantasy bond with him.[11]

While, as Winnicott understood, we enter this world as a "potential" person, we are not born that way. Personhood necessitates relationship. This is why Winnicott could frequently and famously say, "There is no such thing as a baby."[12] In other words, there is only the baby-mother connection. The psychological birth of the person is not the same as the child's physical birth. This is a process and not a given, and as a process, it can go wrong. The mother's primary task is to provide the baby with a "holding environment." She reflects back to the baby the sense that he or she is a unified person rather than a disconnected cluster of experiences. The mother is the medium for the child's growth. Or to state it differently, she brings the world to the child.

Later in life, the person may need a psychotherapist to create this "holding environment." Genuineness and spontaneity must be allowed. Many individuals have conformed to external expectations out of anxiety. They have developed "radar" for quickly detecting the feelings and behaviors others want and so they serve up those

---

[11] For an elaboration of this bond, see Robert W. Firestone, *The Fantasy Bond: Effects of Psychological Defenses on Interpersonal Relations* (New York: Human Sciences Press, 1987).

[12] Donald W. Winnicott, *The Child, the Family, and the Outside World* (New York: Pelican, 1964) 88.

feelings and behaviors. Therapy offers an opportunity to move out of this. However, this newfound freedom can also be frightening because it offers no direct clues as to how one should act. In other words, the very undemanding nature of therapy can at first escalate anxiety because the old pattern of picking up clues from the environment and then acting appropriately is not there.

While interpretation is still important, one must first have a healing, holding environment. Here we see psychoanalysts moving closer to humanistic psychologists, especially Carl Rogers, who emphasized that creating a nonthreatening, empathic environment is the most important thing a therapist can do.[13] Winnicott, like Rogers, believes that there is a "core" in every person that wants to come forward.

Thus, throughout the 1970s, there were three forms of psychoanalysis: classical drive theory; ego psychology, which had been born in Vienna and gravitated largely to the United States; and object-relations theory, which was located primarily in Great Britain. How did Erikson fit into this evolution of psychoanalytic thought?

Erikson, the Individual, and Culture

Erikson's central focus is on contextualizing identity in its historical and social location. By contrast, as we shall later see, Kohut offers a phenomenology of selfhood. Erikson's approach, for Kohut, is too experience-distant because it relies too heavily on the social sciences for its view of the self. For Kohutian psychoanalysis, the self can only be known through the process of empathic immersion into the patient's subjective experience, a process Kohut believed to be quite scientific.

Erikson's emphasis on the social dimensions of identity brought him many readers outside of the psychoanalytic community. On the other hand, it probably brought him fewer readers within that community. Outside of psychoanalytic circles, Erikson has probably been the most widely read psychoanalytic thinker. As I have already

---

[13] Carl Rogers, *On Becoming a Person* (Boston: Houghton-Mifflin, 1961).

indicated, his ideas have been employed in a variety of disciplines. Within the psychoanalytic community, however, Erikson is not always welcome. While Erikson, himself, saw his work as an extension of Freud's ego psychology, many psychoanalysts disagreed that Erikson extended Freud's thought. As Mitchell and Black remind us, these analysts had difficulty connecting a traditional psychoanalytic focus on instinctual conflict with the notion that identity is also shaped by the surrounding culture.[14] For Erikson, we must never abstract human beings from their cultural and historical location because we are deeply influenced by that cultural situation. This emphasis led some to consider Erikson more as a sociologist than a true psychoanalyst. His focus on the social dimensions of development pushed him to turn away from an exclusive focus on the intrapsychic world. As Mitchell and Black state, "The central theme throughout his theorizing is that interpenetrability of the individual and culture: the individual psyche is generated and shaped within the requirements, values, and sensibilities of a particular cultural context; cultural and historical change are effected by individuals struggling to find meaning and continuity in their lives."[15] Erikson's underlying criticism of strict Freudian psychology was apparent: Freud's theory, however brilliant, was too ahistorical and asocial. Psychobiology alone was not enough. One must move toward a psychosocial theory of human development. As Erikson explains,

> Instead of emphasizing what the pressures of social organization are apt to deny the child, we wish to clarify what the social order may first grant to the infant as it keeps him alive and as, in administering to his needs in specific ways, it introduces him to a particular cultural style. Instead of accepting such instinctual "givens" as the Oedipus trinity as an irreducible schema for man's irrational conduct, we are

---

[14] Mitchell and Black, *Freud and Beyond*, 141.
[15] Ibid., 143.

exploring the way in which social forms codetermine the structure of the family.[16]

For Erikson, then, there is a dialectical relationship between the individual and culture. Cultural influences are not reducible to biological forces. They have their own source of influence.

> In the same way that Freud came to see that *both* sex and aggression are two separate sources of drive energy, so Erikson came to see that *both* the intrapsychic world *and* the social world help shape human development. Again, for some traditional psychoanalysts, this was a rejection of the true psychoanalytic framework. For Erikson, this was an important corrective for a discipline that had become too narrowly focused. For Freud, social reality is the realm in which the drives are gratified or frustrated; for Erikson, social reality is a realm that shapes the drives in a culturally distinct fashion. In Freud's framework, the individual is pushed by the drives; in Erikson's framework, the individual is pushed by the drives and pulled by social institutions.[17]

This expansion pushed Erikson to rely on multiple disciplines. In emphasizing cultural factors, however, Erikson spent less time focusing on the specific nature of the child/caretaker relationship. This focus, so strongly developed in Fairbairne, Winnicott, and Kohut, is not a major part of Eriksonian theory. Because Erikson did not develop a detailed exploration into the mother/child dyad, his work is less helpful to clinicians than the work of many object-relations theorists. Again, academics tend to find Erikson more useful than do clinicians.

In discussing the limitations of traditional psychoanalysis to conceptualize the importance of the internalized environment, then, Erikson makes the following somewhat controversial statement:

> The traditional psychoanalytic method, on the other hand, cannot quite grasp identity because it has not developed terms to concept-

---

[16] Erikson, *Identity: Youth and Crisis* (New York: W.W. Norton, 1968) 47.

[17] Mitchell and Black, *Freud and Beyond*, 148.

ualize the environment. Certain habits of psychoanalytic theorizing, habits of designing the environment as "outer world" or "objective world," cannot take account of the environment as a pervasive actuality. The German ethologists introduced the word "*Umwelt*" to denote not merely an environment which surrounds you, but which is also in you. And indeed, from the point of view of development, "former" environments are forever in us; and since we live in a continuous process of making the present "former" we never—not even as a newborn—meet any environment as a person who never had an environment. One methodological precondition, then, for grasping identity would be a psychoanalysis sophisticated enough to include the environment; the other would be a social psychology which is psychoanalytically sophisticated; together they would obviously institute a new field which would have to create its own historical sophistication.[18]

In Erikson's statement, note first the hermeneutical nature of his comment. Erikson insists that we never meet a new environment as a person "who has never had an environment." In other words, in every act of experience and understanding, we bring the experiential and conceptual past with us. We are always introduced to a "new" environment from the vantage point of a previous environment. Clearly, this is Erikson's way of describing what we have previously referred to as Gadamer's "effective history."

In summary, Erikson never stopped believing that a Freudian interpretation tells an important story about many aspects of life; however, he did not believe it tells the *whole* story. One must also look to social, political, and economic factors for a comprehensive grasp of the human condition. Without these added resources, a psychoanalytic perspective alone will not be enough. This growing conviction set him at odds with many psychoanalysts who believed that these "other" methodologies and epistemologies brought contamination to their work. One such individual, as we shall soon see, was Heinz Kohut.

---

[18] Erik H. Erikson, *Identity: Youth and Crisis*, 24.

Generativity

According to Browning, generative people make a god out of neither innovation nor tradition. They realize that innovation needs to draw upon the wisdom of the past. There is no movement "higher" without taking in the "lower." Advancement does not cut us off from the past; instead, it incorporates that past. In the same way that Murray Bowen frequently talks about the dangers of "emotional cut-off" from one's family of origin, so Browning describes the danger of innovations that try to disconnect themselves completely from their past.[19] This point was also explored by Christopher Lasch in *The Culture of Narcissism*.[20] Lasch describes those who seem to believe that "all history begins with me" or my experience, and hence lose a sense of historical continuity with the past.[21] Whether we are discussing how our individual past informs our future or our collective past influences our collective future, our histories are always "with us."

Erikson does not derive his image of generativity from science alone. He bases this normative view of humanity on his own clinical work as well as his own life experience. Erikson seems well aware that a normative image of human fulfillment needs to match the findings of science. However, he also realizes that this image will go beyond what science can demonstrate concretely. In his own informal kind of hermeneutical thinking, Erikson understands that we draw upon our own effective history as we begin the theorizing process. As Erikson describes, "The 'psychoanalytic situation' is a Western and modern contribution to man's age-old attempts at systematic introspection."[22] Yet—and here is an example of Ricoeur's distanciation—Erikson uses scientific data from experimental psychology, ethnology, ethology, and other sciences to inform and

---

[19] Murray Bowen and Michael Kerr, *Family Evaluation: An Approach Based on Bowen Theory* (New York: Norton, 1988).

[20] Christopher Lasch, *The Culture of Narcissism* (New York: W.W. Norton, 1978).

[21] Ibid., 3–30.

[22] Erik H. Erikson, "Sex Differences in the Play Configurations of Preadolescents," *American Journal of Orthopsychiatry* 21 (October 1951): 424.

modify this understanding. We can state it this way: *It would be a huge mistake to say that Erikson's generative person is simply the result of scientific investigation. But his vision, informed by multiple disciplines, is certainly consistent with his scientific investigations.* Stated differently, while science is in no position to "dictate" a normative image of humanity, the normative image one builds needs to be consistent with scientific findings. Perhaps this emphasis is one of the reasons Erikson has been more widely embraced by the social sciences than any other psychoanalytic thinker. He is quite willing to use multiple epistemologies. Indeed, his work comes up in education, psychiatry, child care, psychology, human development, nursing, and a host of other disciplines.

For Erikson, generativity is *both* instinctual and cultural. In other words, it both arises out of a natural inclination and is a cultural force propelling us to build a better tomorrow. Browning states it this way:

> Generativity, for Erikson, is a process that stretches from man's most archaic and unconscious biological tendencies to the highest cultural products of his imagination and his reason. "Generativity" is the only word that expresses what Erikson has in mind. No other fashionable term, such as "creativity" or "productivity," seems to me to convey the necessary idea. Only the word "generativity" conveys that Erikson has in mind not only results of man's "genitality and genes" but also the results of his "works and ideas," as well as the continuity between the two.... Generativity sums up in man that which is most basic and most primitive. But it also points toward that which is the end and goal of existence. If all of man's instincts propel him toward biological generativity, man's capacity for imagination, reason, and conscience make it possible and necessary for him to elevate this generativity to higher cultural, ethical, and religious levels. Generativity is not only the instinctive source behind biological procreation and care; it is also the ground for man's higher attempts to create a total environment ecologically supportive of the general health—not only of family and tribe, but of the entire human species.[23]

---

[23] Browning, *Generative Man*, 145–46.

Clearly, generativity is the backbone of Erikson's understanding of life and the human condition. It is grounded in our so-called lower life of instinct, and a part of our loftiest cultural ideals. It is a vision of human wholeness and ethical obligation. The point of life moves beyond individual self-fulfillment and is concerned with tomorrow's generation. As is typical of Erikson, however, this very process involves mutuality, for it is precisely in caring for the next generation that we find our own fulfillment. Stated another way, when we obsessively narrow our focus to our own fulfillment, we do not achieve it, but as we allow ourselves to care for the young, we experience this fulfillment. The college professor who is exclusively concerned with her own publication record does not achieve the fulfillment of nurturing students into the academic life. This is Erikson's version of an old truth: We truly find our lives by giving them away.

If this is a deep need for both youth and their mentors, then what is the problem? The problem is that we live in a world in which this mutual need is often unrecognized. Put more directly, we live in a largely nongenerative world. This lack of investment in the future is most disturbing. In one of Browning's most potent passages, we are introduced to the dangers of creativity being disconnected from generativity:

> This is the essence of Erikson's startling interpretation of modernity. The problem of modern man is his *nongenerative mentality*—his inability to care for what he creates, what he generates…. Modern man appears to be generative because he creates so much; in reality his problem is his nongenerative mentality which is seen in the fact that he cares so poorly for that which he creates. Buildings which are made to last no more than thirty years; the acres of urban rubble which witness to his unsteady creativity and impatient destructiveness; his reckless tendency to produce more children than he can either educate or provide for; his unwitting habit of building cities that are uninhabitable for families and children; his penchant for pursuing careers at breakneck speed without regard to their effect upon his offspring; his knack for constructing societies so specialized

and differentiated as virtually to segregate all children and young people from adult life; and finally, his heartless capacity to conduct wars that call for no sacrifice to himself but that end in the sacrifice of his sons and daughters—all these things and many more testify to the nongenerative character of the modern mind and its strange proclivity for creating more than it can either care for or maintain.[24]

Creative explosions we deliver and quickly leave are not unlike children we bring into this world and then abandon. Intellectual integrity involves an ongoing attentiveness to what we've created. While this may involve a willingness to change our minds, it is a commitment to seeing certain projects through, cultivating them, and continuing to connect them with our current reality.

Religious Support for Generativity

Religious narratives can aid the process of generativity by providing a faith in the goodness of life or in the ultimate foundations of our existence. This Eriksonian trust that all will finally be okay is portrayed eloquently and powerfully by Peter Berger:

A child wakes up in the night, perhaps from a bad dream, and finds himself surrounded by darkness, alone, beset by nameless threats. At such a moment the contours of trusted reality are blurred or invisible, and in the terror of incipient chaos the child cries out for the mother. It is hardly an exaggeration to say that, at this moment, the mother is being invoked as a high priestess of protective order. It is she (and in many cases, she alone) who has the power to banish the chaos and to restore the benign shape of the world. And of course, any good mother will do just that. She will take the child and cradle him in the timeless gesture of the Magna Mater who became our Madonna. She will turn on a lamp, perhaps, which will encircle the scene with a warm glow of reassuring light. She will speak or sing to the child, and the content of this communication will invariably be the same—"Don't be afraid—everything is in order, everything is all right." If all goes well, the child will be reassured, his trust in reality

---

[24] Ibid.

135

recovered, and in this trust he will return to sleep…. All this, of course, belongs to the most routine experiences of life and does not depend upon any religious preconceptions. Yet this common scene raises a far from ordinary question, which immediately introduces a religious dimension: *Is the mother lying to the child?* The answer, in the most profound sense, can be "no" only if there is some truth in the religious interpretation of human existence. Conversely, if the "natural" is the only reality there is, the mother is lying to the child— lying out of love, to be sure, and obviously *not* lying to the extent that her reassurance is grounded in the fact of this love—but, in the final analysis, lying all the same. Why? *Because the reassurance, transcending the immediately present two individuals and their situation, implies a statement about reality as such.*[25]

Our own sense of generativity thus matches, at least in part, an ultimate form of generativity that guides our future toward fulfillment. Religion helps invite and confirm this trust in ultimate reality as friendly and supportive.

Religion can also help broaden our sense of kinship beyond our own families to the whole of creation. It can do this through its emphasis on the universal care of God, the dignity of each person as God's creation, and the ultimate brotherhood and sisterhood of *all* human beings.

A Summary of Browning on Generativity

Let us summarize Browning's major points concerning Erikson's development of generativity. First, generativity builds upon natural biopsychological tendencies to perpetuate our own species. While evolutionary psychology may not tell us the *whole* story about human existence, it certainly tells us *this* story. Generativity is rooted in biology. It goes beyond our natural inclinations, but it should not be disconnected from this natural inclination. Extending our understanding of generativity need not discount its foundation in our biological tendency to take care of our own.

---

[25] Peter L. Berger, *A Rumor of Angels* (New York: Doubleday, 1969) 67–68.

Second, as an instinctual pluralist, Erikson believes that we have a number of competing instinctual tendencies. If we were singularly directed toward generativity, we might need little cultural guidance, but this is not the case. We therefore need guidance and symbolic expression to reinforce our natural generativity and to give it further expansion to include others.

While these narrative communities shape and deeply influence our values and sense of virtues, they nevertheless need to include a self-critical moment in which they carefully reflect upon themselves. In other words, one needs a moment of distanciation, of critical rational reflection, to examine how the tradition "squares" with the ongoing information we are receiving from the natural and human sciences. As Browning writes, "Religious and cultural traditions may be carriers of generativity, but they often seek to apply it only to 'those like us' or only to our own kin and community. Traditions carrying powerful founding narratives also need critique."[26] Browning goes on to say that sometimes these critiques are rooted in our traditions, but sometimes they are not.

It is precisely at this point that some postliberal voices challenge the idea that any independent source of reason is available for this critique. Standing outside one community of faith means stepping into another and evaluating one's "home world" from a foreign plausibility structure. There is no "faithless reason" available for such an appraisal. There is no neutral spot for even a temporary adjudication.

As we saw in chapter 1, Browning would argue that we use critical reason even to size up and compare options that present themselves to us. Browning is not claiming to have found a neutral zone wherein complete objectivity reigns. He flatly rejects this foundationalism—so the battle is over distanciation. For some, even when we distanciate, we do so from within the tradition. For Browning, however, we can temporarily step outside that tradition

---

[26] Don S. Browning, *Christian Ethics and the Moral Psychologies* (Grand Rapids MI: Eerdmans, 2006) 163.

and offer a rational critique. Otherwise, we end up with a fideism that cannot be brought into any public discussion.

Former student of Browning and outstanding pastoral theologian in her own right, Bonnie Miller-McLemore has also offered a challenge to both Erikson's and Browning's position on generativity.[27] In an essay dealing with family concerns, she examines Erikson's original insight on the notion of generativity, Browning's elaboration of it, and a feminist perspective on the use and misuse of the word "sacrifice" in discussions of equal-regard and mutuality. While this essay is linked to Browning's involvement with family, culture, and religion issues—and therefore beyond the scope of this book—it is worth mentioning a few points. Miller-McClemore points out that Erikson has much more to say about mutuality than he does self-sacrifice. In addition to equal regard, argues Miller-McClemore, we need discussions of equal sacrifice. The specific details of sacrifice should be explicitly discussed. While a discussion of mutuality in marriage has perhaps led to less sacrifice for women, it has not necessarily led to greater sacrifice from men. Unfairness still abounds, but the way to deal with this unfairness is not to throw out the word "sacrifice" as some feminist theorists have done. Instead, "sacrifice" must be brought back into the discussion of equal regard.

Erikson, according to Miller-McClemore, discusses the issue of generativity *too late* in the lifecycle. Generative challenges occur much earlier. Part of the problem is Erikson's failure to recognize the gender differences concerning generativity. Generativity, for men, is more associated with caring for the next generation and nurturing one's own wisdom for the benefit of the future. For women, generativity refers primarily to caring for others, a *relational* generativity, which revolves around the care of the young.

Part of Erikson's blindness results from inattention to the genderized context of generativity. Generative maturity involves

---

[27] Bonnie Miller-McClemore, "Generativity, Self-Sacrifice, and the Ethics of Family Life," in James Witte, Jr., M. Christian Green, and Amy Wheeler, eds., *The Equal-Regard Family and Its Friendly Critics* (Grand Rapids MI: Eerdmans, 2007) 17–41.

mastery of two essential but all too often gender-stratified tasks—occupational or creative generativity and relational or procreative generativity. For the most part, Erikson and his followers simply accept a stark division of generative labor—what he even calls the "polarization of the two sexes": men work, women love.[28]

Clearly, Miller-McClemore believes a more serious account of gender, inequality, and sacrifice should accompany Erikson's discussion of generativity. With essay headings such as "Behind Every Generative Man Stands Sacrificing Woman," and "Equal Regard: Dry Rhetoric for a Messy Reality," it is quite clear that Miller-McClemore believes the discussion of generativity has been a male-dominated development. She states this concern as follows: "Behind the attack on selfish individualism as a key factor in family decline hides an assumption, seldom overtly voiced, that someone needs to do a little sacrificing. But who? If people do not talk openly about this, isn't sacrifice likely to fall back on the shoulders of women?"[29]

Miller-McClemore's criticism of Browning, then, is that he underestimates the importance of sacrificial love in equal regard, and further, he does not adequately identify the gender inequality in Eriksonian generativity. She believes that most men give lip service to equal regard, but when the challenges of life emerge, women do most of the sacrificing.

Browning, on the other hand, points out that it was Miller-McClemore herself who helped develop a life cycle theory of sacrifice and mutuality in *From Culture Wars to Common Ground*.[30] As Browning states, "There we argued that love as equal regard should not be interpreted to mean moment-by-moment equality of the kind that demands keeping score or adding up credits and debits in a short-term frame of reference."[31] For Browning, even parental

---

[28] Ibid., 22.

[29] Ibid., 18.

[30] Don S. Browning, Bonnie Miller-McLemore, Pamela Couture, et al., *From Culture Wars to Common Ground: Religion and the American Family Debate* (Louisville KY: Westminster John Knox Press, 1997).

[31] Browning, "Response," in *The Equal-Regard Family and Its Friendly Critics*, 253.

sacrifice for children is enveloped within a larger context of eventual mutuality. As he puts it, "Good parental care should warmly and constantly expect children to grow up and treat others and parents with equal regard—as ends in themselves deserving respect and the recognition of human needs."[32] Even God's love for humanity is not fundamentally self-sacrificial. Instead, the sacrifice is part of a larger movement for relationship and mutuality. While many classic theists might balk at such a notion, Browning, following key themes in process theology, views God's involvement with humanity as involving both vulnerability and passion: "God's sacrificial love is derived from a more fundamental thrust toward enjoyment."[33]

Perhaps Miller-McClemore believes that the discussion in *From Culture Wars to Common Ground* made mutuality look easier than she now believes it is. She may believe that there is now a stronger need to reintroduce the word "sacrifice" and point especially toward the need for greater male sacrificial investment. As it stands, it is not quite clear how her current emphasis is related to her earlier work with Browning. From Browning's perspective, her earlier work in *From Culture Wars to Common Ground* answers the very questions she raises in *The Equal-Regard Family and Its Friendly Critics*. From Miller-McClemore's perspective, it does not. This is an interesting discussion that involves the full parameters of the American family debate, an issue that goes beyond the scope of this study. Browning's involvement with family issues merits a separate book unto itself. And as I have previously mentioned, this is precisely what the energetic family and legal studies scholar John Witte, along with his colleagues Green and Wheeler, have provided.[34]

Contrasting Erikson and Kohut

Self-fragmentation is central to both Erikson's identify confusion and Kohut's injured self. Erikson's primary focus on identity crisis

---

[32] Ibid.

[33] Browning et al., *From Culture Wars to Common Ground*, 286.

[34] Witte, Green, and Wheeler, eds., *The Equal-Regard Family and Its Friendly Critics*.

revolves around the struggles of adolescence. While this incorporates some earlier, pre-Oedipal concerns, identity confusion clearly goes beyond this early experience. For instance, in the stage of trust and mistrust, Erikson highlights the significance of early experience for later identity. But these pre-Oedipal issues do not tell the whole story. Social and historical factors also play a key role. As Browning writes, "Social factors such as rapid social change, the dislocation and confusion inflicted on families living in a highly differentiated and mobile society, and the pressures on adolescents and young adults for complex syntheses of sexual, vocational, political, and ideological commitments all work with, intensify, and even freshly aggravate old serious and not so serious preoedipal deficits."[35] In other words, addressing pre-Oedipal issues alone is not good enough. One needs a multidimensional approach that also takes into consideration later issues and developments. As important as pre-Oedipal issues are, one needs to also understand the significance of later developments.

Browning argues that Kohut is more restrictive in his view of the essential problems of the self and its treatment: "Kohut keeps his eyes directly on the therapeutic interview and what it reveals about both the deficits in the early formation of the client's self and the deficits in the selves of surrounding parental figures."[36] There is little emphasis on sociological and cultural factors. In fact, Kohut sees this as a distraction from the central focus—an empathic immersion in the client's experience. *Narcissistic injury, for Kohut, is deeper and more pervasive than identity confusion in Erikson.* Perhaps the issue could be put this way: For Erikson, stresses in later life can greatly add to identity confusion; for Kohut, stresses in later life resurrect narcissistic injuries of the pre-Oedipal period. Thus, Kohut constantly goes back to pre-Oedipal experience as the determining factor in self-cohesion. Browning offers a challenge to this exclusive pre-Oedipal emphasis: "One also suspects that Kohut would look for preoedipal

---

[35] Don S. Browning and Terry D. Cooper, *Religious Thought and the Modern Psychologies*, 2nd ed. (Minneapolis: Fortress Press, 2004) 185–86.

[36] Ibid., 186.

deficits and imagine that he found them when in reality the stresses were later, more situational, and more relative to the incomprehensively complex, pressured, and unsupported tasks of coping and synthesizing that we place on people in modern societies throughout the life cycle, but especially on adolescents and young adults."[37]

For those who work primarily in psychotherapy, Kohut may be much more helpful than Erikson, yet for those interested in the broader issues of psychology and social change, Erikson may be more appealing. Again, Erikson's use of multiple observational standpoints makes him more amenable to psychology departments. While he favors the standpoint of free association, introspection, and empathy, Erikson also believes psychoanalysis should be more broadly connected with the social sciences. As Browning puts it, "Hence, in addition to the insights gained directly from the analytic interview, Erikson makes more objective observations of children playing, borrows concepts from biology (epigenetic principle), and does participant-observation anthropological studies. And he sees all this as resources for the enrichment of psychoanalytic theory."[38]

For Kohut, however, there is only one adequate epistemological starting point—introspection and empathy. Psychoanalytic epistemology moves from external words, symbols, and acts to an introspection of the therapist's own experience, then empathically back to the patient's experience. This movement always checks its accuracy with the patient's experience. Browning insightfully describes Kohut's rejection of social scientific epistemologies for understanding psychoanalysis.

> Psychological knowledge within the context of analysis is built on the careful development, testing, and revision of introspectively derived and empathically amplified knowledge of the other person. At the same time, Kohut rejects the use of all other disciplines external to the introspective and empathic situation provided by the psychoanalytic interview—for instance, biology, anthropology, sociology—

---

[37] Ibid.
[38] Ibid., 187.

unless they can somehow be used as guides to the understanding of introspectively denied materials.[39]

For Browning, Kohut's emphasis on the exclusive epistemological foundation of analytic empathy is unnecessarily narrow. He believes that this methodology can be supported by additional perspectives without being diluted. For him, Erikson's concept of identity can contain Kohut's findings:

> It is my opinion, however, that Erikson's concept is large enough to encompass both the self in its archaic formations and the self in its sociological definitions, and therein rests its power. Furthermore, the two perspectives are not really separate fields; the parental figures that help form the nuclear self and the self of the child being formed both stand in these sociocultural fields. These fields influence from the very beginning both the parental shapers and the infantile self being shaped. One would want to break up the fields only if one had made a prior decision to erect a science of the human totally from the perspective of the preferred interventional strategy of psychoanalysis (that is, individual treatment built around free association and transference), a decision that the Kohutian school has clearly made. For then the truth is what one can see from the perspective of what one does within a particular specialized mode of treatment. But from the perspective of other disciplines that must necessarily preside over multiple forms of intervention—social work, the ministry, government—it is precisely such bridging concepts as those found in Erikson that are so valuable.[40]

While Kohut seemed to insist that all data for psychoanalytic self-psychology had to come from clinical experience, he did not, in fact, completely stick with that assumption. He seemed to have a growing appreciation for infant studies. And certainly the work of contemporary Kohutians has embraced such significant developmentalists as Bowlby and Stern. Some traditional adult

---

[39] Ibid.
[40] Ibid., 187–88.

psychoanalysts at first had difficulty fully accepting the early developmental studies of "baby watchers," as they were sometimes called. Following Freud's lead, they chose to analytically reach back into childhood from comments and experiences reported by adults. Gradually, however, the important observational work of children's development has been included in nearly all psychoanalytic institute training programs. The old tension between adult psychoanalysis and child development studies seems to have waned.

While observational data is important, for Kohut, it does not constitute psychoanalytic data. Extrospective data collection observes, measures, and documents external behavior. It understands human beings as objects that can be studied, a process that is similar to other natural sciences. The emphasis is upon controlled, repeatable, objective observations. In order for psychology to match the epistemology of the harder sciences, it must strictly apply this observational perspective. Academic psychology, therefore, often turns into a scientific study of human behavior and leaves altogether untouched the inner world of personal experience and meaning. But this approach will never provide psychoanalytic data—the data of subjective experience. Knowledge of someone's personal history, observations of their external behavior, and even observations of their verbal behavior will not provide psychological data about their inner world of experience. The data may be very useful, but it is the wrong method to understand the individual's private experience. Access to inner experience is available only through introspection and the empathic journey into someone else's experience. Empathy, then, is vicarious introspection. It is careful, focused listening and thinking one's way into another's world. This is an act of imagination that must be carefully matched with another's own experience. Ernest Wolf expresses Kohut's strong conviction about empathy: "Indeed, Kohut's statement that the very idea of human mental life is 'unthinkable' without the ability to know by means of empathy… becomes the cornerstone for the possibility of constituting the field of psychoanalysis. The empathic vantage point becomes the organizer for all observations made."[41] Thus, psychology, for Kohut, is primarily the study of complex emotional states; empathy is the appropriate data-gathering tool for these emotional states.

As Kohut intensely developed his creative ideas on the self, he seemed indebted only to Freud, even as he was departing from the master. Charles Strozier, in his outstanding biography of Kohut, makes the following point:

> Certainly the articulation of how his notions of the self departed from Freud's drive-based system became the obsession of his life. At least with Freud, Kohut acknowledged his debt. But with other thinkers he often talked and wrote as though there was no one ever who had written anything that remotely fitted into the tapestry of ideas he was weaving. All ego psychologists become epigones of Freud's flawed system. Erikson, whom he had never liked, was dismissed now with a wave of his hand…. Kohut's need to distance himself from all other thinkers was the only way he could protect his creativity.[42]

Kohut moved from a specific focus on the problem of narcissistic personality disorders to a more general conviction that the struggle with self-injury and narcissism is a universal concern. Thus, disorders of the self become the underlying current of various psychological problems. Stated another way, psychological disorders can be largely understood as a lack of self-cohesion or self-fragmentation. This regression to a less coherent self involves a feeling that one is "falling apart" or "coming undone." Self-fragmentation occurs on a continuum. It involves a loss of self-esteem, a feeling of emptiness accompanied by depression and anxiety. In its extreme forms, of course, it involves a decomposing psychosis in which one feels completely incoherent and fragmented. As Wolf puts it, "Fragmentation means regression of the self toward lessened

---

[41] Ernest S. Wolf, *Treating the Self: Elements of Clinical Self Psychology* (New York: Guilford Press, 1988) 20.

[42] Charles B. Strozier, *Heinz Kohut: The Making of a Psychoanalyst* (New York: Other Press, 2001) 244.

cohesion, more permeable boundaries, diminished energy and vitality, and disturbed and disharmonious balance…. The experience of a crumbling self is so unpleasant that people will do almost anything to escape the perceptions brought about by fragmentation"[43] Again, psychological problems stem from a sense of self-injury. This self-injury may camouflage itself by becoming quite exhibitionistic and seemingly arrogant. Kohut scholar Ernest Wolf describes the inner tension of self-fragmentation:

> The subjective experience of a regressing, fragmenting self is so painful in loss of self-esteem and anxiety that emergency measures are instituted to reverse the process. Attempts to boost one's self-esteem often take the form of some sort of self-stimulation, or one provokes or manipulates the environment to supply the needed selfobject experience in order to maintain some structural cohesion to one's self. The resulting behavior often has great social impact and may lead to antagonistic or otherwise counterproductive reverberations. It is annoying for most people to have to listen to a lot of bragging or to witness someone's arrogant attitude, even when one recognizes that such behavior clearly means that someone is suffering and trying to prevent a worse calamity. Much of the irritation of people with each other, the quarrels that tear up marriages, and the misunderstandings that lead to loss of spouse, friend, or job can be traced back to the ups and downs of self-esteem when individuals with fragile *selfs* try to use others to make themselves feel stronger and more whole.[44]

When one experiences a threat to the self, there is always a temptation to "act out." The attempt to find a "coherence fix" is ever present. In the face of fragmentation or the subjective feeling of "coming undone," one may grasp at anything that helps provide a temporary sense of unity. Wolf describes the relationship between "acting out" and threats to the self.

> "Acting out" is a variety of symptomatic behavior. The experience of loss of self that is associated with deep regressions and

---

[43] Wolf, *Treating the Self*, 39.
[44] Ibid., 42.

fragmentations is so painful that individuals will do almost anything to avoid it. From this arises the imperative urge for acting out as a way to ameliorate the fragmented self-experience. Frantic lifestyles, drug abuse, perversions, and delinquency all serve as desperate measures to hold on to some self-organization and avoid sliding into a fragmented state.[45]

Kohut gradually came to believe that the best way to deal with narcissistically injured individuals, even when they display extreme forms of exhibitionistic pride, is to offer empathic mirroring. This empathic process seeks to get beneath the grandiose pole of the self's posturing and acknowledge the deep injury propelling the inflated image. While Freud had argued that narcissists were nearly impossible to treat because they were stuck in self-love, Kohut did not believe that narcissism is about self-love at all. It may be about self-obsession, but this obsession is frequently a painful one that craves acceptance. The point is to transform the original, narcissistic grandiosity of the child into ambitions and achievements worthy of adult investment. Early narcissistic injury blocks this transformation of grandiosity into worthwhile goals. This occurs when one is not adequately mirrored, prized, and given a robust sense of attention. Thus, in the earliest period of life, a deprivation of attention leads to the nagging self-doubts that promote adult narcissism. Again, it is appropriate for the child to be grandiose and attention-seeking. When this need is met, the child's grandiosity typically moves toward realistic goals and ambitions. However, when this need for attention is not met, a child can stay stuck in a craving for attention, a craving that can surely burden adult relationships. And the sad reality for adults with severe narcissistic injury is that the very thing they continue to crave (affirmation and attention) is rendered unlikely by their overly zealous attempts to capture it. Put simply, they drive others away with an incessant need for attention and affirmation. Other adults grow weary of being an adoring audience as the narcissistically injured talk on and on about themselves. Kohut

---

[45] Ibid., 43.

strongly believes that narcissistic disturbance emerges from earlier deprivation of attention.

> When we analyze adults who suffer from narcissistic disturbances—individuals who make incessant demands for gratification, we may get the impression that they were spoiled as children. We reason: there was continuous drive-satisfaction, so those people became fixated on their drives and that is why they became sick. But that's not so. They didn't become fixated on the drive because they were spoiled, because of drive-satisfaction. They became fixated on drives because their budding selves were overlooked, were not responded to. They turned to drive-gratification (and later remained fixed on it) because they tried to relieve their depression— they tried to escape the horrible feeling that nobody was responding to them. Such people may have had mothers who satisfied their drives continuously, yet failed to respond with pride and pleasure to the child's independent self.[46]

Kohut gradually let his theoretical cat out of the bag: The drives are not primary, but instead, secondary, disintegration by-products of self-injury. In making this proclamation, he denied what had been absolutely central in traditional psychoanalysis—the key role of the Oedipus complex. Rather than being the "complex" that works out the innate drives of sex and aggression, the Oedipus period (not complex) only becomes problematic when self-injury has already taken place in the pre-Oedipal period. As Kohut scholar Marcia Dobson reminds us, Oedipus lived comfortably in Corinth until he received an insult from a drunken man at a dinner party: "You're a bastard!"[47] After these wounding words, he visits a Delphic oracle and asks the interesting question, "Who am I?" The oracle tells Oedipus that he will kill his father and marry his mother. Oedipus

[46] Heinz Kohut, *The Chicago Institute Lectures*, ed. Paul Tolpin and Marian Tolpin (Hillsdale NJ: Analytic Press, 1966) 199–201.
[47] Marcia Dobson, "Freud, Kohut, Sophocles: Did Oedipus Do Wrong?" Paper presented at the 29th Annual International Conference on the Psychology of the Self, Chicago IL, 26–29 October 2006.

then heads toward Thebes in an attempt to escape this fate. Oedipus is nearly run off the road by an older man, and retaliates by killing the intruder (who turns out to be his father). Oedipus enters Thebes and guesses the riddle of the Sphinx, thereby becoming the King of Thebes. He marries the queen, who turns out to be his mother. Oedipus realizes that he has unwittingly fulfilled the fate pronounced by the oracle.

For Freudian psychology, this story is the centerpiece for understanding the human condition. It reveals both the sexual and aggressive drives, and expresses the psyche's fundamental conflict. A sexual attraction to one's mother is met with fear of retaliation by one's father. The Oedipus story thus reveals an unconscious wish and conflict. A Kohutian interpretation, however, would insist that Oedipus's first struggle was with a feeling of insignificance and self-injury. He was insulted and spiraled into shame and self-doubt. The insult was deep enough, Dobson reminds us, to take a long journey to visit a Delphic oracle.[48] This comment, though delivered by a drunk man, must have triggered his own self-doubt. Oedipus could have simply attacked the intoxicated man and been done with it. However, this comment sent him on a deep pursuit of his true identity. Put in psychoanalytic terminology, Oedipus was motivated more by disintegrating anxiety than by castration anxiety.[49] A sense of self-rejection and self-fragmentation was deeper and preceded his so-called sexual and aggressive drives toward his parents.

Kohut's conviction that *pre*-Oedipal issues are deeper and more pervasive than the Oedipus complex, as much as anything else, set him at odds with the psychoanalytic community. It challenged the very fabric of drive theory, a theory the ego psychologists had tried to maintain even as they included the importance of environmental factors. Erikson, as we have seen, never went as far as Kohut in denouncing the basic drives. For him, the human condition revolved around coordinating the instinctual tendencies with the surrounding

---

[48] Ibid.
[49] Ibid.

social world. Erikson would have never used the language of "by-product" to describe a drive. Kohut distanced himself so far from Freud's biological model that he began to look more and more like a humanistic psychologist, at least to traditional psychoanalysts.

This leads us, then, to an important question: What *is* the difference between Kohut and a humanistic psychologist such as Carl Rogers? Both emphasized the radical role of empathy in understanding another person; both insisted that the self is primary in understanding the human condition; both recognized that early experiences of rejection or inattention propel one into profound self-doubts that create problems throughout life; and both argued that psychotherapy must promote an atmosphere in which one feels deeply valued and understood. Yet unlike Rogers, Kohut would never agree that empathy itself is enough to produce therapeutic efficacy. Rogers's approach proclaimed that the therapist simply creates the therapeutic conditions for which the client can reconnect with the actualizing tendency and move toward growth. These therapeutic conditions became foundational for counselor education programs throughout North America. They included empathy, unconditional positive regard, and congruence or genuineness. For Kohut, this approach lacked the psychoanalytic foundation for offering interpretation. Rogers saw no need for interpretation because the client will come to his or her own self-discoveries when provided with an empathic atmosphere. For Kohut, while the interpretations need to be *empathic ones*, they nevertheless involve helping the person see the underlying psychodynamic processes in his or her life. For Kohut, Rogers's approach, however valuable, ultimately ends up leaving the patient empty-handed. Rogers's highly democratic approach to therapy downplayed the therapist's expertise as inter-preter; Kohut understood the therapist as an expert in intrapsychic dynamics, a guide and interpreter for the patient. Detached clinical aloofness without empathy is worth little; but empathy void of any interpretation is also very limited. In fact, interpretation is an advanced form of empathy.

In many respects, it is not just psychoanalytic self-psychology that began to look like humanistic psychology; the object-relations perspectives of Fairbairne, Guntrip, and Winnicott preceded and looked similar to the human potential movement. Ronald Fairbairne, from Scotland, regularly argued that the drive toward objects is more significant than the drive toward pleasure or gratification. Rather than seeking energy discharge, the deeper concern is human connection. And Winnicott, especially, revealed the impact of Romanticism on his own theory when he talked about a "true" and "false" self. Philip Cushman describes the significance of the true and false self for Winnicott:

> He thought the determination about which self would be predominant in the overall shape of the child's individual way of being in the world was the most fundamental issue in the life of the individual. It is fragile, this true self, quite vulnerable to danger, and indispensable to the life of the individual. It is imperative that the true self be allowed to unfold without external restriction or impingement; the fear of exploitation of the true self is the child's greatest terror. The true self develops in the child who is the product of the proper holding environment. In the safety and reliability of the mother's attention and concern, and in the "potential space" of play, the infant experiences the freedom to be spontaneous, expressive, and creative. The core essence of this little being, whatever it is, is allowed to come out and be expressed and presented to the world, to grow naturally, according to its own timetable and with its own very personal qualities. The true self flows, naturally flows, intuitively toward the light.[50]

The "good enough" mother will provide the "holding environment" in which the young child can move toward the authentic self. An inauthentic or false self will emerge when a child is not given an adequate environment. This may occur from too much or too little stimulation, from abandonment or engulfment.

---

[50] Philip Cushman, *Constructing the Self, Constructing America: A Cultural History of Psychotherapy* (Cambridge MA: Perseus Publishing, 1995) 257–58.

Trauma and Narcissistic Disruption

As Allen Siegal reminds us, for Kohut, the question is not "Who is narcissistic?" Instead, the question is "Whose narcissistic development has been disrupted by trauma?"[51] In other words, the developmental defect in narcissism is the key factor, and *not* the narcissism itself. The simple reason for this is that everyone moves along a narcissistic line of development. Mature, undisrupted narcissism moves from grandiose fantasy to more realistic ambitions. The gradual shift to a more reality-based cluster of goals is based upon the empathic, optimal frustrations provided by the caretakers. Make no mistake: Kohut places enormous weight on the significance of these primary caretakers. As Kohut and Seitz put it:

> The most important source of a well functioning psychological structure, however, is the personality of the parents, specifically their ability to respond to the child's drive demands with non-hostile firmness and non-seductive affection.... If a child is exposed chronically to immature, hostile, or seductive parental reactions toward his demands, then the resulting intense anxiety or over-stimulation leads to an impoverishment of the growing psyche, since too much of his drive equipment is repressed and thus cannot participate in psychic development.[52]

The goal is to gradually experience optimal frustration *without* experiencing self-injury and its accompanying sense of fragmentation. In short, the aim is to avoid trauma. Trauma disrupts the natural transformation of early grandiosity into healthy ambition. The grandiosity goes underground, remains archaic, and makes unrealistic demands for constant admiration.

---

[51] Allen M. Siegel, "Basic Course: Heinz Kohut," Paper presented at the 29th Annual International Conference on the Psychology of the Self, Chicago IL, 26–29 October 2006.

[52] Heinz Kohut and Philip F. D. Seitz, "Concepts and Theories of Psychoanalysis," in Paul Ornstein, ed., *The Search for the Self*, vol. 1 (New York: International Universities Press, 1978) 370–71.

Trauma is a very significant word for the Kohutian vocabulary. It refers to the impact and intensity of an experience rather than to the content of the experience. In other words, there is no way to "objectively" measure trauma. The very idea is ludicrous because of the vast differences in individuals' subjective experience. The cohesiveness and solidarity of the self are the most important factors in facing trauma. A cohesive self is better able to manage affect and regulate tension. Allen Siegel states this point well:

> Trauma, a concept central to the psychoeconomic perspective, occurs when an affect overwhelms the mind's capacity to maintain its balance. Kohut teaches that trauma refers to the intensity of the affects surrounding an event rather than to the content of the event itself. Trauma is relative to the nature and maturity of the psyche. Timing is crucial, since the intensity of a trauma depends upon the vulnerability of new structures at the time of the traumatic event, both in childhood and in the course of an analysis.[53]

The simple rule of thumb is this: *A vulnerable, fragile, and less cohesive sense of self will be easily overstimulated and traumatized.* And a second rule is this: If we want to learn about trauma, we need to talk with someone who has been traumatized. Empathy, and not detached observation, will tell us about trauma and its effects.

Once again, for Kohut, empathy is essential because even the most difficult narcissistic patient has been mirror-deprived. David Augsburger insightfully states this point:

> …narcissism—the self over-concerned with itself—is the self's attempt to substitute self-indulgent self-care for the appropriate care by a significant other which is absent or woefully inadequate. The self-centered behavior of the narcissist arises from too little self-esteem and self-valuation, not from too much. It is the impoverished self that

---

[53] Allen M. Siegel, *Heinz Kohut and the Psychology of the Self* (London: Routledge, 1996) 29.

hungrily grasps for attention and affirmation (no matter how smoothly presented or artfully expressed).[54]

As we have seen, Kohut believes that excessive attention and flattery is demanded later in life precisely because it was not offered earlier. Adult relationships become a search for mirrors. Without any ability to assure oneself or self-soothe, the adult narcissist is dependent on others to provide narcissistic supplies. While even healthy individuals need ongoing support and affirmation from others, they have also learned to affirm and validate themselves. The injured narcissist, on the other hand, *desperately* needs others so much that they become instruments of self-gratification and not persons with whom they can interact.

Kohut's emphasis on the unempathic and injurious source of narcissism differs dramatically from the more drive-oriented approach of Otto Kernberg.[55] Instead of offering an empathic response, Kernberg thinks that analysts need to confront and challenge the grandiosity of the adult narcissist. Kernberg does not believe that narcissism is a fixation at an earlier state of development. Instead, narcissism is linked to unconscious rage that narcissists hold against those who abandoned or humiliated them as children. There is a close relationship between narcissism and resentment or even revenge. The narcissist has enormous rage. And further, adult narcissism, for Kernberg, is fundamentally different than childhood narcissism. Adult narcissists are deeply envious and may attempt to destroy anyone who surpasses them. Childhood narcissism involves "showing off" for someone the child loves. It can be satisfied. The attention is enjoyed. There is a nonaggressive, even humorous, quality to it. Children can be both narcissistic and love their parents. But for Kernberg, none of these things are true of adult narcissism. It is fundamentally different and therefore not a "fixation" or "arrest"

---

[54] David Augsburger, *Helping People Forgive* (Louisville KY: Westminster-John Knox Press, 1996) 76.

[55] Otto Kernberg, *Borderline Conditions and Pathological Narcissism* (New York: Jason Aaronson, 1975) 270–342.

of narcissistic development. For Kernberg, Kohut's theory does not adequately incorporate issues of destructive rage, envy, and resentment. The difference between Kernberg and Kohut surely revolves around the issue of drives. For Kernberg, we have built-in, destructive tendencies that often attempt to devalue another. We want to eliminate the very person who seems to cause our envy. The inclination to devalue others, then, emerges from an excessively aggressive drive with which we must come to grips.

Kohut, however, believes that we devalue others only because of an injured self. We have been devalued, so we devalue others. The primary reality, though, is injury and not destructive aggression. Abandonment, loneliness, and self-loathing are the deeper issues beneath our negative attitudes toward others. Narcissistic rage is very real, but as we have seen, Kohut believes it always emerges from deprivation. It is not a natural outgrowth of our biological tendencies. It is a disintegrative by-product. As Kohut states it, "The baby cries, and the baby cries angrily when whatever needs to be done is not done immediately. But there is no original need to destroy; the original need is to establish equilibrium."[56] While healthy aggression is part of our innate potential, destructive aggression does not arise naturally as other bodily needs arise. Instead, destructive aggression always arises from frustration. Kohut finds the notion of inherent violent drives to be both inaccurate and brutal. Individuals become fixated on drive gratification because of a lack of emotional response, not because of a biological inclination. As Volney Gay describes, "From a moralistic point of view, the patient's rage is wrong and unjustified. From an empathic, analytic point of view these rageful responses, like fragmentation experiences, must be understood as signs of the patient's profound narcissistic suffering."[57]

Kohut, Selfish Consumerism, and Generativity

---

[56] Kohut, *The Chicago Institute Lectures*, 199.

[57] Volney P. Gay, *Understanding the Occult: Fragmentation and Repair of the Self* (Minneapolis: Fortress Press, 1989) 41.

Philip Cushman argues that we must approach self psychology as we approach all psychology: Place it within its historical context and not reify it as if it is a timeless truth about the human condition. More specifically, Cushman argues that self psychology is an outgrowth of Western consumerism. In fact, Cushman fears that the exhibitionism and grandiosity encouraged by Kohut in childhood do not so easily fade away. They do not, argues Cushman, "transfer" into worthwhile goals. Instead, this grandiosity continues as an ongoing hunger. In short, it pushes a feeling of entitlement in which the adult, hungry self relentlessly searches for narcissistic supplies. As Cushman writes,

> Kohut is often praised for his creative ideas regarding the importance of grandiosity and omnipotence in infant development. He regarded them as universal but temporary phases in the natural unfolding of the self. But how temporary are they? Are they temporary stages in the life of the infant, or are they learned ways of being, long-term patterns of adjustment that are indispensable to our consumer society? Where would our economy be today if Americans did not consider themselves entitled to every consumer item they can purchase or find credit for? Where would the celebrity, culinary, exercise, diet, and cosmetics industries be today if adults did not feel driven to be unique, to stand out from the crowd, to comply with the fashion industry's standard of beauty, to be noticed and powerful and famous. In other words, where would these industries be if adults were not exhibitionistic and grandiose, hungry for mirroring and merging with celebrities or politicians? Is it just a coincidence that the very qualities that Kohut described (and thus implicitly prescribed) as indispensable to healthy infant development do not appear to recede but instead become major motivators in the consumer activities of adults?[58]

Cushman believes that Kohut leaves us with a view of the self as a consummate consumer—digesting its selfobjects, incorporating

---

[58] Cushman, *Constructing the Self*, 273.

them, and then leaving them behind. Genuine relating to others is secondary to *using them* for selfobject purposes. In other words, relationships become a matter of what others can do for the self. How can others enhance one's own experience? How can others advance one's own cause? Cushman believes that Kohut's theory reduces other people to "commodities" to be used by the self for its own purposes. The good qualities of others are "metabolized" for the purposes of building a more solid self-structure. At the end of the day, relationships are mere "food" for the primary goal—the emergence of a robust and vital sense of self. For Cushman, Kohut did not historically contextualize the empty self he saw in treatment. Instead, he treated this empty self as the timeless problem of the human condition. He argued that this emptiness is an essential part of human being, an inevitable aspect of normal development. He universalized this condition and failed to grasp the social and political factors that gave rise to this "psychological" problem. By focusing on the intrapsychic dynamics of the empty self, Kohut reinforced the political status quo, unwittingly aided a consumerist culture, and moved attention away from the social dimensions of our lives. For Cushman, Kohut was too apolitical, too ahistorical, and too self-absorbed. He ended up perpetuating the very narcissism he sought to heal. Thus, Cushman stands in a tradition of social thinkers who accuse much of American psychology with creating a preoccupation with the self at the expense of moving toward where real change is needed—the social and political sphere.[59] Kohut's view of the self, for Cushman, is much too romantic:

---

[59] See, for instance, Edwin Schur, *The Awareness Trap: Self-Absorption Instead of Social Change* (New York: McGraw-Hill, 1976); Martin Gross, *The Psychological Society* (New York: Simon and Schuster, 1978); Wendy Kaminer, *I'm Dysfunctional, You're Dysfunctional: The Recovery Movement and Other Self-Help Fashions* (New York: Vintage, 1993); Charles Sykes, *A Nation of Victims: The Decline of American Culture* (New York: St. Martin's Press, 1992).

Kohut, so much under the influence of romantic thought, wrote as though the self is concrete, real, and immensely salient; it is alive, growing, expressive, willful; it is the center of one's initiative, the embodiment of one's self-conscious subjectivity, the container of one's genetic blueprint, the core of one's being. The self is properly built in a specific manner, and if that process isn't followed, if the self is deprived of certain types of "provisions," the self will suffer in various characteristic ways that will lead to the absence, fragmentation, or rigidity of certain psychic "structures" that Kohut thought are indispensable to the mature shape of the self.[60]

Cushman's complaint is that by turning the self into a "thing," Kohut made it a commodity like any other commodity.

It is ironic that a person who worked so hard to create an experience-near, empathic understanding of the nature of self-injury should be accused of turning the self into a "thing." Judith Guss-Teicholz's excellent work, *Kohut, Loewald, and the Postmoderns: A Comparative Study of Self and Relationship*, is helpful here:

Since Kohut consistently avoided attributing a "thingness" or a "location" to the self, and since he consistently spoke of the *sense* of coherence and continuity rather than of coherence and continuity per se, I think it might be accurate to say that coherence and continuity were for him primarily experiential phenomena, regularly associated with psychic health; therefore he set up both as developmental achievements and treatment goals.... Kohut's self was, above all, an experiential self, and his notion of self structure was always directly linked to its experiential base and experiential consequences.[61]

Teicholz goes on to ask whether it is even ontologically possible to "go about the business of living without a subjective sense of cohesion."[62] One does not have to view the self as a "thing" in order to appreciate the inner experience of continuity, cohesion, ambitions,

---

[60] Cushman, *Constructing the Self*, 275.

[61] Judith Guss Teicholz, *Kohut, Loewald and the Postmoderns: A Comparative Study of Self and Relationship* (Hillsdale NJ: Analytic Press, 1999) 58.

[62] Ibid., 55.

goals, and values. Teicholz argues that Kohut saw the importance of the self's continuity and sense of cohesion precisely because of what many postmoderns proclaim—we are surrounded by the dangers of self-fragmentation and the push toward inward multiplicity. But it is wrong to assert that Kohut reified the self into a fixed, rigid, and coherent "thing." "To say that we need a *sense* of coherence and continuity denies neither the experience of multiplicity, the human potentiality for fragmentation and discontinuity."[63]

Cushman is not content to critique self psychology as the only carrier of an excessive focus on self. None of the other therapies fare very well either:

> If anything, more popularized theories such as addiction theory, twelve-step self-help groups, and the pop psychology embrace of trauma theory as the sole cause of adult psychopathology are even more consumer-oriented than past psychoanalytic theories. For instance, addiction theories characteristically argue that the individual has been transformed into an "addict" through the continual ingestion of a drug, the bad commodity. Addicts are then thought to be powerless in the face of the commodity and in order to regain control over their lives their only hope is to abstain from consuming it. But they cannot achieve abstinence solely by their own efforts; they cannot withstand the siren call of the bad commodity until they appeal and in fact *surrender* to a "higher power." Only in this way, it is argued, will consumers regain control over their lives, because once the commodity is consumed it overpowers the consumer. In this view, the commodity is all-powerful.[64]

Thus, with a broad wave of the hand, Cushman seems to dismiss much of contemporary psychotherapy as well as the experience of millions of people in twelve-step groups, people who have regularly reported a lack of control once they ingest a mood-altering substance. Are these people simply the creation of a consumerist culture? Pushed aside altogether is the possibility that some individuals may

---

[63] Ibid., 53.
[64] Cushman, *Constructing the Self*, 276.

159

have genuine biochemical predispositions to be addicted to chemicals.

Critiques of psychotherapy as promoters of narcissism—as ways of turning us away from the *real* problems in the social and political sphere—need to be critiqued. Cushman's work, while helpful and insightful, misses in Kohut an underlying care for future generations, a genuine concern for the nurturing of younger minds. Browning picks up this theme in Kohut and argues that while it is not as explicit as it is in Erikson, it is nevertheless present in Kohut as well.

Thus, while Cushman accuses Kohutian theory of using others for the primary purposes of one's own self-development, Browning disagrees. He argues, rather convincingly, that Kohut develops a sense of mutuality that is close to that of Erikson. While neither Kohut nor Erikson announce that they are moving from a description of what is healthy to a principle of moral obligation, the underlying ethic is present. We *ought* to care for future generations. Kohut puts it this way: "Optimal parents—again I should rather say: optimally failing parents—are people who, despite their stimulation by and competition with the rising generation, are also sufficiently in touch with the pulse of life, accept themselves as transient participants in the ongoing stream of life, to be able to experience the growth of the next generation with unforced and nondefensive joy."[65] Kohut also talks about being "warmly committed to the next generation, to the son in whose unfolding and growth he fully participates—thus experiencing man's deepest and most central joy, that of seeing a link in the chain of generations."[66] How does one square these convictions with Cushman's thesis that Kohut uses others for the purpose of advancing a narcissistic agenda?

In good hermeneutical fashion, however, Browning reminds his readers that neither Erikson nor Kohut would have "come upon" the

---

[65] Heinz Kohut, *The Restoration of the Self* (New York: International Universities Press, 1977) 237.

[66] Heinz Kohut, "Introspection, Empathy, and the Semi-circle of Mental Health," *International Journal of Psychoanalysis* 63 (1982): 403.

notion of generativity without an effective history that nudged this conviction. For both of them, it seems as if generativity is a moral good that happens to match a natural human impulse. Yet for Browning, nature alone is not enough to guarantee the care of future generations. While Browning appreciates the biological push toward generativity (noted by both Erikson and evolutionary psychology), this natural inclination needs the added support of symbols and a community of discourse. But Erikson is not wrong in arguing that *generativity has instinctual foundations*. It is simply that Erikson sometimes conflates the language of instinct with the language of ethics. Browning quotes Erikson to make this point: "Generativity, as the instinctual power behind various forms of selfless 'caring,' potentially extends to whatever man generates and leaves behind, creates and produces (or helps to produce)."[67] Also, Browning reminds us, Erikson, like William James, is an instinctual pluralist. Erikson sees a patterned sequence of instinctual tendencies throughout development. There is no single over-arching instinct or master motive.

Erikson, Kohut, and Anxiety

While Kohut and Erikson understand the pervasiveness of anxiety in ways the humanistic psychologists do not, Browning argues that Kohut still puts an unnecessary strain upon himself by tracing all adult anxiety back to its pre-Oedipal roots. As we have seen, adult problems are problematic because they resurrect pre-Oedipal anxieties related to self-fragmentation. Kohut's emphasis on these earliest experiences comes dangerously close to minimizing later developmental problems with anxiety and insecurity. Later issues seem merely to push the earlier, pre-Oedipal issues to re-emerge. Browning does not think Kohut adequately grasps the newer forms of anxiety that emerge during the life-cycle. Instead, everything is related back to pre-Oedipal fragmentation.

---

[67] Erik H. Erikson, *Insight and Responsibility* (New York: W. W. Norton, 1972) 131.

In a previous publication, *Reinhold Niebuhr and Psychology*, I contrasted Niebuhr and Kohut on the self and its anxieties.[68] While I had grown appreciative of Niebuhr's theological anthropology for understanding psychotherapy, Browning's work greatly enhanced this view. When examining Kohut's view of anxiety, Browning once again employs the Kierkegaard/Niebuhr emphasis on our ontological insecurity. This anxiety exists for the postanalyzed as well as the pre-analyzed. Niebuhr argues strongly that this anxiety is not reducible to a specific psychological source such as unempathic parents. To repeat, Niebuhr never condemns self-regard, but he believes that anxiety inevitably, but not necessarily, provokes *excessive* self-regard. Analysis, even Kohutian analysis, will not get rid of this temptation. The reason is that this undue focus does not result from a psychopathology we can cure. Even if the pre-Oedipal issues of our lives are largely healed, we will encounter new levels of anxiety throughout our lives. The newer anxieties do not represent a mere return to the pre-Oedipal issues; even a highly cohesive self will struggle with anxiety and be tempted to treat the other as a means toward greater security. To eliminate this form of anxiety is to eliminate life itself. We're stuck with it. This excessive self-regard cannot always be tracked back to a specific preOedipal injury. Niebuhr is most direct on this point: "It also tempts psychiatry to reduce all forms of egotism to vestiges of childhood egocentricity, which greater experience will correct. Thus an approach to the self that is therapeutically adequate for pathological aberrations of selfhood is incapable of comprehending the real problems of the self on either the practical or the religious level."[69] Excessive self-regard is not reducible to failures in our interpersonal relationships. Those failures may surely exacerbate this undue self-focus, but for Niebuhr, they do not cause it. Niebuhr is forever warning about the dangers of

---

[68] Terry D. Cooper, *Reinhold Niebuhr and Psychology: The Ambiguities of the Self* (Macon GA: Mercer University Press, 2009) ch. 4.

[69] Reinhold Niebuhr, *The Self and the Dramas of History* (New York: Charles Scribner's, 1955) 11.

turning a theological problem into a psychological one. Even if psychologically healthy, we will still be tempted by the anxiety of finitude. But Kohut does not spend much time dealing with this form of anxiety. Browning states this issue with both clarity and accuracy: "Kohut is not very interested in the problem of the relatively healthy adult self. He is not interested in the problem left over after a generally high degree of self-cohesion has been accomplished. Kohut loses interest at precisely the place where Niebuhr begins. Because Kohut's interest is in early development, the emphasis upon self-transcendence, although present, is small."[70] Again, Kohut is concerned with what makes the self incohesive, a process he believes points to very early experience. Later fragmentations point toward earlier developmental deficiencies. Browning argues that theologians can be faulted for not grasping the developmental nature of the self and presenting the human condition as if we've always been adults. Yet if this is one danger for theology, so too, psychologists can leave us with the idea that if we have a smooth developmental process with caring parents, there will be no problems whatsoever with anxiety tempting us to act in excessively self-interested ways. To state it once again: Both Niebuhr and Browning balk, and balk loudly, at the idea that human sin is reducible to pre-Oedipal issues. Instead, we must also consider the "left over" problems, the postanalyzed, and "post-cohesive self" dilemmas of life. Kohut's study of anxiety is perhaps overly focused on the nonempathic failures of parents.

Browning believes that Erikson more effectively deals with the lifelong anxieties associated with transitional moments of our lives, including our adult lives. Put directly, adulthood has its own form of anxiety-producing concerns. It does not simply trigger older, pre-Oedipal issues. Each stage of life pushes us with its own particular crises. Browning describes Erikson's grasp of a lifelong anxiety which transcends early childhood struggles.

---

[70] Browning and Cooper, *Religious Thought and the Modern Psychologies*, 193.

Whether it is the transition from trust versus mistrust to autonomy versus shame and doubt or the later adult transitions from generativity versus stagnation to integrity versus despair, the anxieties accompanying the subtle decisions to cope with the new circumstances of life are increasingly evident throughout the life cycle due to the pangs of freedom. Erikson could write passionately and sensitively about existential anxiety, metaphysical anxiety, and "ego chill" as he did in *Young Man Luther* (1958). He knew he was describing something that was both continuous with but certainly not exhausted by a child's fear of losing a parent or the experience of fragmentation to the self due to a parent's unempathic responses.[71]

Our anxiety, then, results from what *might* happen as much as what *did* happen. Excessive self-focus can emerge from anticipatory anxiety as well as previous self-injury. Niebuhr, while challenging the prideful pretentions of excessive self-regard, knew quite well that it masks a deep and pervasive anxiety. Distrust is always the flip side of inordinate self-focus. The ultimate "remedy" for this ontological anxiety is a trust in the Ground and Source of our lives. This trust will never eliminate the ambiguities of our condition. That is why it is called "trust" rather than "certainty." But it is finally a hope that all life, not just our own specific existence, has redeeming purpose.

[71] Ibid., 195.

4

Jung, Self-Realization, and Evil

"In the final analysis, we count for something only because
of the essential we embody, and if we do not embody that,
life is wasted."—Carl Jung

The great Swiss psychiatrist, Carl Jung, believed very strongly that
his life was guided by a transpersonal direction, a "calling" he was
"obligated" to follow. While he was not controlled by this inner voice,
he recognized that his life would be utterly miserable if he did not
follow this inner purpose. This sense of direction is transpersonal
because it moves beyond the influence of parental instruction, early
life experience, or even later cultural pressure. It is a kind of
"blueprint," an innate set of potentials that beckon us to fulfill. For
Jung, each person is "whole" from the very beginning. The task of life
is to allow this wholeness to express itself. This process of self-
realization is very similar to the process of self-actualization we
examined in chapter 2. It seeks expression, wants to be fulfilled, and
often demands our attention. It is inherently within us as an oak tree
is in an acorn. In fact, Jung finds Plato's notion of the *daimon* a most
convincing mythical expression of our destiny. The inner voice of the
daimon, once again, must not be confused with the voice of
conscience instilled by parents and culture. It is an internal authority,
a pattern unique to each of us. The idea that we are ethically
obligated to follow this inner blueprint is called *eudaimonism*. This is a
deep form of self-loyalty, a commitment to fulfill a transcendental
purpose for our lives. This is clearly what Jung had in mind when he
frequently talked about living our own myth. David Norton, who has

strongly influenced Browning with his book *Personal Destinies*, puts this issue well: "When an individual allows himself to be deflected from his own true course, he fails in that first responsibility from which all other genuine responsibilities follow, and whose fulfillment is the precondition of the least fulfillment of other responsibilities."[1] Norton doesn't like the term "self-realization" because he believes the term "realization" suggests that the self's potential did not exist prior to our creative acts. This would make Jung's position closer to Sartre, who believed we create ourselves in each new moment, since we have no "essence." For Jung, we each come into this world to fulfill a basic destiny, a purpose that transcends the particularities of our individual biography, but that clearly includes those particularities. The point here is significant: We are first and foremost obligated to fulfill this mission, purpose, and direction in our lives. This form of self-loyalty or integrity precedes any other ethical acts. Thus, we are exhorted to "become who we really are." But again, this call from the Self, for Jung, moves beyond the narrow confines of the ego. As Jungian analyst James Hollis states, the Self is "Carl Jung's metaphor for that inherent, unique, knowing, directive, intelligence that lies so wholly beyond our ordinary ego consciousness. The metaphor of the Self arises from our intuitive knowledge that something within each of us not only monitors our organic biochemical processes, develops us from less complex to more complex creatures, but, much more, seeks that state of being that is the apparent purpose of our incarnation in the first place."[2] This command also recognizes the possibility of being disloyal to our *daimon*, ignoring its voice, and moving against the direction it wants to unfold. Integrity, or following this internal sense of transpersonal direction, is more than psychological wisdom; it is an ethical imperative. As Norton writes, "According to self-actualization ethics it is every person's primary

---

[1] David L. Norton, *Personal Destinies: A Philosophy of Ethical Individualism* (Princeton: Princeton University Press, 1976) 9.

[2] James Hollis, *Finding Meaning in the Second Half of Life* (New York: Gotham Books, 2005) 4–5.

responsibility first to discover the *daimon* within him and thereafter live in accordance with it."[3]

Thus, Jung saw his life work as helping individuals recover their lost wholeness. We do not "accumulate" our personality part by part or build it from scratch; we already possess it and simply need to express it. As Calvin Hall and Vernon Nordby explain, "What he must do throughout his life span, Jung says, is to develop this inherent wholeness to the greatest differentiation, coherence, and harmony possible, and to guard against it breaking into separate, autonomous, and conflicting systems."[4] So Jung, like Heinz Kohut, is interested in strengthening the psyche to keep it from fragmenting. Psychosynthesis is the ultimate goal of analysis. Individuation, much like self-actualization, is the process by which our consciousness becomes individualized and distinct. The goal of individuation is greater consciousness. The *daimon* is the inner guide toward this greater awareness.

Norton, however, writing in the mid-1970s, suggests that it is precisely this Jungian notion of an inner voice that largely has been lost to most contemporary persons:

> Strangest to our ears is Jung's very conviction of the presence of the inner voice itself, for most of us today have no sense of an oracle within. Indeed, I offer it as our ranking malaise that that about which we instinctively believe we can be most certain—ourselves—is in fact our sorest bewilderment. We are apprehensive that an ear turned to our inwardness will detect at most only meaningless murmurings, that a resort to the inner self will be a dizzying tumble into a bottomless pit. Fearing this, we anchor ourselves upon external things, we cast our lot with the fortunes of objects and events that appear to be untainted by the disease of selfhood—if necessary, cleansing them of fingerprints, depersonalizing them in order to that they may better bear our weight. Turning our backs to the void, we become infinitely distractible by outward things, prizing those that

[3] Norton, *Personal Destinies*, 16.
[4] Calvin Hall and Vernon J. Nordby, *A Primer of Jungian Psychology* (New York: New American Library, 1973) 33.

"demand" our attention. We secretly treasure the atmosphere of world crises, for the mental ambulance-chasing it allows.[5]

In spite of this malaise, however, Jungian analyst and scholar James Hillman is able to write, twenty years after Norton's comments, a best-selling book on the *daimon*.[6] I suggest that this book, as well as Jung's thought in general, is attractive to many people precisely because they are not willing to "give up on" a sense of transcendental purpose in their lives. Hillman's book is a clear invitation to pay attention to our own sense of "calling." We are each "answerable" to an innate image, an inherent direction, a fundamental purpose in our lives—this is Hillman's central message. This internal image is a key factor in our development. Hillman believes that psychology has ignored this sense of blueprint because it has exaggerated the so-called deterministic nature of our early emotional environments. As he puts it, "Our lives may be determined less by our childhoods than by the way we have learned to imagine our childhoods."[7] Or a bit later in his book he states, "For we are less the victims of parenting than of the ideology of parenting; less the victims of mother's fateful power than of the theory that gives her that fateful power."[8] Hillman urges us to follow the direction of many ancients, especially Plato and Plotinus, who believed that our souls have a companion, a built-in direction for our lives. The myth that that our soul elected our particular parents, time of birth, and so on, tells a psychological truth many have experienced as they reflect on their lives. "You are born with a character; it is given; a gift, as the old stories say, from the guardians of your birth."[9] A literalistic mindset has caused us to devalue the significance of myth. But myth, for Jung and Hillman, has a redemptive psychological function. We must pay

---

[5] Norton, *Personal Destinies*, 4.

[6] James Hillman, *The Soul's Code: In Search of Character and Calling* (New York: Random House, 1996).

[7] Ibid., 4.

[8] Ibid., 77.

[9] Ibid., 7.

very careful attention to this internal voice and watch for its manifestations. If we neglect it, it will not leave. Hillman writes, "A calling may be postponed, avoided, intermittently missed. It may also possess you completely. Whatever; eventually it will win out. It makes its claim. The *daimon* does not go away."[10] This inner guide has also been called our "genius" by the Romans. Western religious people have understood it as the will of God for one's life. In all these emphases there is a unified emphasis on finding an "appointed" path to one's life. Hillman reflects on the loss of uniqueness and individual purpose in contemporary psychology.

> ...psychology does admit that we each have our own makeup, that each of us is definitely, even defiantly, a unique individual. But when it comes to accounting for the spark of uniqueness and the call that keeps us to it, psychology too is stumped. Its analytical methods break down the puzzle of the individual into factors and traits of personality, into types, complexes, and temperaments, attempting to track the secret of individuality to substrata of brain matter and selfish genes. More strict schools of psychology kick the question right out of the lab, packing it off to parapsychology for the study of paranormal "callings," or to research stations in the distant colonies of magic, religion, and madness. At its most bold, and most barren, psychology accounts for the uniqueness of each by a hypothesis of random statistical chance.[11]

Hillman even goes on to say, "Why not keep within psychology proper what once was called providence—being invisibly watched and watched over?"[12]

If Jung wants to speak metaphysically, he needs to say so. In other words, he can't make metaphysical claims and then turn around and say that he is only talking about psychological experience. Put directly, if we are "called," then who or what is doing the "calling"? Like Jung, Hillman takes us right to the edge of

---

[10] Ibid., 8.
[11] Ibid., 11.
[12] Ibid., 13.

theology but then retreats back into the world of "psychological experience." Nevertheless, Hillman *does* offer an important point: Even though he does not want to have a direct ontological discussion about God, he points out that a number of people have had a deep and abiding sense that their lives are guided by a transpersonal power.

Browning argues that Jung, too, while understanding himself primarily as a phenomenologist of religion, lapsed into ethical and religious thinking. Jung, perhaps as much as any other twentieth-century psychologist, appreciated metaphorical language. In fact, his work applauds myth for telling a story about the human condition that descriptive, empirical investigations cannot access. Jung's comment is a bold one: "Thus, it is that I have now undertaken, in my eighty-third year, to tell my personal myth. I can only make direct statements, only 'tell stories.' Whether or not these stories are 'true' is not the problem. The only question is whether what I tell is *my* fable, *my* truth."[13] Escaping myth and metaphor is impossible and undesirable.

Browning believes that Jung is similar to, but more complex than, Maslow, Rogers, and other self-actualization theorists. Clearly, Jung argues for an "inner telos" or purpose of the human organism, a process that moves toward balance and wholeness. Yet, as Browning suggests, this personal growth toward our innate potential is not quite as "natural" or "organic" as Rogers and Maslow portray it. As we saw in chapter 2, Rogers argues for a singularly directed, biologically based motivational tendency that has no competitors, as long as an empathic environment is provided. For Jung, however, one often pays a heavy price for following this innate pattern. The path has its share of conflict, ambiguity, and ambivalence. It does not biologically "unfold" in a joyful, easy manner. Nevertheless, as we have seen, there is a strong push in the direction of self-realization. The *daimon* within will not be easily dismissed. It wants to express its inherent purpose.

---

[13] Carl Jung, *Memories, Dreams, Reflections* (New York: Vintage Books, 1989/1961) 3.

Browning believes that Jung is sometimes inconsistent about this process of individuation. At times, argues Browning, he speaks as if individuation is a simple process of the unconscious archetypes (the inherited forms or patterns of which the mind organizes experience) following their natural direction toward wholeness. When Jung emphasizes this dimension of self-realization, he seems to insinuate an almost self-regulating function to this process. It is our destiny. At other times, however, Jung seems to describe self-realization as a rigorous, ethical process in which we must select aspects of the archetypal unfolding. In other words, it's not a simple automatic unfolding. We have to make tough choices. So Browning asks on what basis Jung makes these choices. He answers that Jung makes these difficult decisions on the basis of a nonhedonistic ethical egoism. This essentially means that while pleasure is not the highest aim, our own sense of self-fulfillment *is*. Thus, Jung is clearly within the eudemonistic group. We have a personal responsibility to realize our own potential.

Archetypes and Cognitive Science

While the archetypes are universal, we each have a unique combination of them. Individuation involves the actualization of our unique cluster of archetypes. As Jung writes, "The meaning and purpose of this process is the realization, in all aspects, of the personality originally hidden away in the embryonic germ-plasm; the production and unfolding of the original potential wholeness."[14]

Jung rather famously put the idea of a collective unconscious on the intellectual map. It immediately distinguishes Jung from other psychologists. For Jung, evolution provides the blueprint for the psyche just as it provides the blueprint for the body. The mind has been pre-structured by evolution. We are not simply tied to our individual past; instead, we are also tied to the collective past of our entire species. Jung, because of his emphasis on locating the mind

---

[14] Carl Jung, *Collected Works*, 21 vols. (Princeton: Princeton University Press, 1983) 7:108.

within the longer evolutionary process of humankind, is somewhat similar to the evolutionary psychology position we examined in chapter 2. As such, he will not be warmly embraced by avid social constructionists. While the personal unconscious consists of the particular, individually repressed or rejected aspects of one's personality, the collective unconscious is akin to a large pool of primordial images and symbols, many of which have been culturally repressed. These images go all the way back to humanity's beginnings. They reappear in dreams, artistic images, religious symbols, and other imaginative thought. We are each the beneficiaries of this ancestral past. These images are not particular memories that spring to mind from the distant past. One doesn't suddenly panic because he or she "remembers" an ancestor being chased by a lion. These symbols and images are more like a grid or structure by which we interpret our experience.

Even though these inherited images of the collective unconscious are in the background, they are dependent upon the particular experience of each person to pull them forward. The images need our experience in order to reveal themselves. This is why, for Jung, we need a rich variety of experiences if these images are to speak to us. The contents of the collective unconscious, then, are activated by human experience. These contents are called "archetypes." It is important to understand that archetypes are images of the mind, but they are not fully developed pictures. They are not that ambiguous and clear. Everyone draws upon the same pool of archetypal images because these images are universal. However, the particular manner in which the archetypes cluster together are unique to each person. It is this archetypal expression that both *wants* to come forth and *should* come forth. Hence, its discovery and expression is not simply an interesting finding; it is an obligation, even an ethical duty that requires the ego's cooperation.

Browning is less interested in the work of Hillman and others who "mystify" and "spiritualize" Jung and primarily interested in how the academy looks upon Jung.[15] For Browning, this matters more than the activities and claims of various psychotherapeutic healers. How does Jung's notion of archetypes and the collective unconscious square with what biologists, neuroscientists, and ethologists are discovering? Browning writes, "Jung is emerging from several decades of being viewed as a befuddled genius who spent his life rummaging through ancient mythology and his own dreams in an effort to reconstruct an alternative to the Christianity that he saw collapsing all around him."[16] It is worth noting here that Browning's apologetic mode, as opposed to a purely confessional mode, can be seen in his approach to Jung as well as to Christianity. He seeks points of contact between Jung's therapeutic ideas and academic psychology, with its related disciplines. Browning is not content with confessional statements about Jung's healing or Jung's impact on a greater sense of purpose in one's life. Instead, he wants to engage the apologetic task of bringing Jung into a public discussion with critical reason. That is, while Browning takes seriously the claims of Jungians who say that one can only understand Jungian insights from within the Jungian narrative, Browning wants to move toward a more public and distanciated position as he brings Jungian thought to the tables of other disciplines. Stated differently still, it is not enough to be a Jungian "true believer." While Jungian thought, like every other perspective, begins in faith, it needs to take the additional step of public conversation and risk a public analysis. I make this point with complete earnestness because a number of Jungian groups see themselves as quasi-churches or perhaps an alternative to traditional religious communities. Jung's metaphysical system, more readily than other psychological perspectives, lends itself to a community of faith. Whereas other psychologies, as we have seen, contain hidden assumptions about the ultimate context of our lives, Jung is much more transparent about his religious interests. More and more, within

---

[15] Don S. Browning and Terry D. Cooper, *Religious Thought and the Modern Psychologies*, 2nd ed. (Minneapolis: Fortress Press, 2004) 146–48.

[16] Ibid., 146.

Jungian circles, he is flatly called a "theologian." Nevertheless, some Jungians have tried to hold to the idea that Jung was only describing religious experience and not really saying anything about ontology. As we shall see, it is clear that Jung frequently moved from psychological experience to statements about the totality of existence. Philip Rieff states this issue as follows:

> Accepting as the leading premise of his psychology the failure of established religions in the West, Jung looked back on his entire life as the fortunate unfolding of a counter-myth, one that saved him from the fate of his father. In his development, from the dreams and visions of childhood on to the hypotheses of old age, Jung traced the convergence of divinely inspired messages and scientific intellection into a religious psychology—that form of faith he considered best adapted for use in the twentieth century.[17]

As many have realized, myth gains a new respectability in Jungian thought. Myth is the source of much wisdom, a wisdom lost to the demythologizing tendencies of Western positivistic science. As Browning explains, "In spite of his own self-understanding as a scientist taking a purely phenomenological approach to the study of psychology, Jung lapsed into both religious and ethical judgments at every turn."[18]

Browning is interested in connecting Jungian theory with the work of social anthropologist Victor Turner and psychiatrist Anthony Stevens.[19] These two thinkers, in particular, suggest ways in which Jungian archetypes are being reconsidered in light of evidence from the harder sciences. Stevens, for instance, believes that advances in neurobiology and ethology suggest that something akin to the Jungian archetypes may indeed be very real. In other words, there are probably universal structures of consciousness that orient and

---

[17] Philip Rieff, *The Triumph of the Therapeutic* (New York: Harper and Row, 1966) 109.

[18] Browning and Cooper, *Religious Thought and the Modern Psychologies*, 146–47.

[19] Victor Turner, "Body, Brain, and Culture," *Zygon* 18/3 (18 September 1983); Anthony Stevens, *Archetypes: A Natural History of the Self* (New York: Morrow, 1982).

predispose individuals toward certain images and symbols. Stated differently, evidence points toward universal, biological structures of the mind that have evolved through natural selection. As Browning points out, these universal structures have also been described by Plato, Kant, and Kepler, but they are now enjoying a firmer biological foundation. Noam Chomsky in linguistics, Konrad Lorenz and Kiko Tinbergen in ethology, and Robin Fox in anthropology—these are some of the people Browning mentions.[20]

One of the reasons Browning is enthusiastic about Stevens's work is that it offers biological support for the Jungian archetypes *without reducing the Jungian vision to strictly biological and deterministic processes.* In other words, Stevens's biological emphasis is not at the expense of self-reflection and human freedom. In spite of this affirmation, however, Browning believes that neither Stevens nor Jung fully understands the role of ethics in his perspective. When it comes to this issue of one's theory of obligation and means of ethical decision-making, Browning relentlessly pushes a human vision until it reveals its underlying assumptions about human fulfillment and how it plans to get there.

Stevens also uses the work of John Bowlby to help make his case. Bowlby rather famously highlighted the notion that all infants have an inherited need to attach to primary caretakers. Fortunately, the primary caretaker (usually the mother) has a similar need. This enduring emotional bond is to a specific person, and discomfort occurs when this caretaker is not available. When attachment is successful, it offers a secure base from which the child can then adventure. Rather than creating a situation of ongoing dependency on the caretaker, secure attachment provides a child with the security to explore, take risks, and become more independent. Dependence, at least in its unhealthy form, results from insecure attachment and *not* from "too much" attachment. The reciprocal attachment between the parent and child greatly aids the child's survival.

---

[20] Browning and Cooper, *Religious Thought and the Modern Psychologies*, 147.

Rather than finding all his answers in psychoanalysis, Bowlby turned to ethology, the study of how animals adapt and secure their lives, to understand species survival. Konrad Lorenz, Karl von Frish, and Nikko Tinbergen developed ethology in the mid-twentieth century. They were especially concerned with "imprinting," which refers to how a newborn animal responds to the movements of another animal in close proximity to it when it is born. The newborn connects with, follows, and imitates a moving object. For instance, when a duck hatches, it immediately connects and bonds with the first moving object it encounters. This is usually its mother. Imprinting is thought to occur in any species in which the need for parenting is great. Lizards, for instance, don't need imprinting because they are born rather self-sufficient.

Human infants are able to elicit from their primary caretakers a desire to care for them. Gestures and "cute" features have a way of hooking caretakers into wanting to nurture the infant. These "hooking" features are called innate releasing mechanisms. This is nature's way of ensuring that the species survives. Even stiff and detached adults can be reduced to putty in the hands of some babies. We *need* to take care of them nearly as much as they need our care. This reciprocity is biologically rooted. Babies respond to the soft, warm feeling of skin and cloth. They respond to eyes and like looking at them. Especially after about eight weeks, babies like to make eye contact. Babies respond to smiling and their smiles almost always elicit a smile from an adult. Babies also like the sound of soft voices. In turn, adults respond to the soft feel of babies. Most adults like to have babies grasp them. Adults especially find watching a baby laugh to be quite pleasurable. And cries universally make adults want to pick up the baby and comfort him or her. Lorenz frequently described the characteristic of "babyishness" as eliciting adult nurturing behavior. This characteristic of "babyishness" usually involves an extra large head, extra large eyes, big forehead, fatty and rounded features, puffy cheeks, no visible cheek bones, and soft and dimpled hands and fingers. Many studies have indicated that even when adults have "babyish" features, we may feel a greater urge to view them as innocent and care for them.

Stevens points out the similarities between Bowlby's understanding of attachment and Jung's perspective on the archetypes:

> Once one conceives of these archetypes as the neuro-psychic centers responsible for coordinating the behavioral and psychic repertoire of our species in response to whatever environmental circumstances we may encounter, they become directly comparable to the innate releasing mechanisms responsible for Lorenz' "species-specific patterns of behavior" and Bowlby's goal-corrected behavioral systems.[21]

This new possibility of a more scientific grounding for a Jungian theory of archetypes, says Browning, is exciting to some Jungian theorists and perhaps threatening to others. But it does offer the possibility of outside collaboration for the Jungian perspective. Just as some *kerygmatic* theologians are suspicious of bringing in outside material to "legitimate" or "demonstrate" the Christian message, so some Jungian "confessional" therapists may be suspicious of going outside the Jungian worldview to secure Jung's thought. Stated differently, for some Jungian "true believers," like Barthian "true believers," the message is self-authenticating and does not need outside reinforcement from another worldview. For the academic community, rather than simply the therapeutic community, this cross-over is quite fascinating. We must remember that Browning is usually speaking with an academic, public audience in mind.

Browning also points out that Jung may offer a bridge between the more biologically oriented ego psychologists and the more relationally oriented object relations theorists. Jung's theory of "the complex," in particular, may help us understand how our specific relationships help us actualize archetypal images of connection. It grounds the object-relational approach in biological inclinations and

---

[21] Stevens, *Archetypes*, 17.

helps provide our relational needs with a biological source—the archetypal structures in our minds.

In spite of some scientists' new interest in Jung, his popularity remains strongest among those individuals who see themselves on a spiritual journey toward wholeness. The popularity of Bill Moyers's interview with Joseph Campbell on mythology, Jung's influence on twelve-step spirituality, the connection between Jung and the mytho-poetic dimension of the men's movement, and the multitude of people who find in Jung a helpful guide in recovering from some of the abuses of institutional religion—all these persons find a source of inspiration in Jung. The Jung Society in my hometown (St. Louis) has more than tripled within the past year. As many liberal Protestant churches have combined a concern for spirituality with social ethics, some have turned to Jung as a guide for intrapsychic guidance and healing. Few programs in spiritual direction can avoid dealing with Jung. Jung particularly comes alive for people in the second half of life. Many best-selling "personal growth" authors have directly or indirectly based their work on Jung. References to Jung have flooded books on spirituality. Thomas Moore, Robert Bly, Joseph Campbell, and Sam Keen are but a few of the thinkers who have drawn deeply from Jung.

Browning points out that both myth and his own experience are key factors in the development of Jung's psychology. The task of greater self-awareness or fuller consciousness employs our practical intelligence. As Browning points out, "Sacrificing one's ego (and the superficial twentieth-century rationality to which it is beholden) so that the deeper rationality of one's unconscious archetypes can speak forth is, to Jung, a simple matter of practical moral intelligence. It just makes good practical moral sense. Here psychology as science and the processes of life converge for the purposes of practical moral living.[22] It does not take Browning very long to ask which type of ethical vision Jung supports; his perennial concern with ethics trumps his interest in Jung's voice on the spiritual journey.

---

[22] Browning and Cooper, *Religious Thought and the Modern Psychologies*, 149.

Destiny and Personal Choice

In contrasting Jung with the humanistic psychologies of Rogers and Maslow, Browning believes that the Swiss psychiatrist has a more complex model of individuation and growth. It is less automatic—a little less "natural"—and seems to require a tad more of James's "strenuous life." There is more conflict, internal polarity, and ambivalence than Rogers and Maslow admit. Nevertheless, Jung's view involves a very powerful force pushing the human organism toward wholeness and fulfillment. This force is trustworthy; in fact, Jung's trust in this innate growth potential is almost as strong as Rogers's deep belief in self-actualization. Stevens, also, boldly states that "individuation is an expression of that biological process— simple or complicated as the case may be—by which every living thing becomes what it was destined to become from the beginning."[23] Stevens goes on to suggest that the ego can never fully incorporate the wholeness of the Self. Some distortion and fragmentation is inevitable. Archetypal intent is never perfectly embodied.

Browning highlights one of Stevens's most significant passages:

> Here lies the essence of the critical distinction which must be made between *individuation* and the biological unfolding of the *life-cycle*. The two processes are, of course, interdependent in the sense that one cannot possibly occur without the other, yet they are fundamentally different. The life-cycle is the indispensable *condition* of individuation; but individuation is not blindly living out the life-cycle: it is living it consciously and responsibly, and is ultimately a matter of ethics. Individuation is a conscious attempt to bring the universal programme of human existence to its fullest possible expression in the life of the individual.[24]

Note that for Rogers and Maslow, we *naturally* act as we *should* act. If the right emotional conditions are present, self-actualization is as natural as breathing.

---

[23] Stevens, *Archetypes*, 64.
[24] Ibid., 141–42.

Perhaps we should ask a question that some humanistic psychologists might well ask of Browning: Does he exaggerate the extent Rogers understands the self-actualizing process as an automatic, biologically determined tendency? Rogers fought determinism all his life. Does Rogers really believe that with the right therapeutic conditions in place, there is no internal resistance to growth? Browning would no doubt respond that while Rogers recognizes the existence of some degree of anxiety and fear within the person, this is an "outside-in" problem. In other words, our anxiety and resistance to growth is always rooted in the emotional environment. Rogers does *not* recognize the deeper Kierkegaardian and Niebuhrian anxiety, which results from simply existing as a self-conscious, finite creature. While Rogers at times seems influenced by Kierkegaard, Browning would argue that Rogers did not read Kierkegaard deeply enough. There is no place for ontological anxiety in Rogers's thought. As we saw in chapter 2, the singularly directed actualizing tendency has no internal competition. Rogers does not speak of an *essential* anxiety; instead, anxiety results from distorted relationships. Thus, there is not an intrapsychic resistance to growth and development, a resistance that longs to secure itself in a very insecure world. The implication in Rogers's thinking is that if we could but clear up the conditions of worth, we could raise completely self-actualizing children—children who are not tempted by any internal anxiety to act in unhealthy ways toward their neighbors. To say it differently, Browning disagrees with Rogers's basic assumption that our natural, essential, or "original" condition is one in which anxiety never poses a problem. Following Niebuhr, Browning believes that anxiety is part of our essential condition, an inevitable part of being self-reflective, limited creatures.

Browning pinpoints the basic ambiguity in both Stevens and Jung: On the one hand, they use "destiny talk" to describe the process of "becoming who we are." Again, this seems to be an inevitable unfolding, a biologically rooted tendency not unlike the organic image of the humanistic psychologists. On the other hand, the task of individuation is presented as an ethical one—definite struggle that involves selecting which archetypal patterns should be actualized. Browning asks a straightforward question: "Does Jung also see the individuation process as distinguishable from the simple biological unfolding of the life cycle? Is the natural unfolding of the life cycle in the life process for Jung the 'condition' as Stevens would say, of the more focused and necessarily ethical process of individuation (hermeneutical philosophy would call it an ethical-interpretive process)?"[25]

Browning turns to Jung's *Two Essays on Analytical Psychology* to search for an answer to this ethical ambiguity. While Jung seems to swerve back and forth between the view that individuation is a naturally unfolding process and the view that individuation involves ethical deliberation, Browning is convinced that Jung finally makes self-fulfillment the final ethical factor in his moral reasoning. Self-fulfillment is what we are called to embody and obligated to achieve. While there *is* a danger of consciousness over identifying with an archetype and becoming "possessed" by it, Jung ends up trusting the natural direction of the human organism toward greater wholeness. There is an internal, trustworthy direction and purpose that culminates in self-expression. Will we perfectly embody fulfillment? No. But the direction can be trusted. This process may involve sacrifice, particularly as we follow the Self beyond the particular concerns of the ego. As Browning says, "Consciousness is necessary not to order or form the archetypes in ways they would not naturally go; consciousness and its functions of reflection, choice, and sacrifice are necessary to remove the obstacles and avoid the pitfalls that might block or divert the natural inclinations of the archetypes to express their uniqueness."[26]

Browning wants to know how this inclination toward self-fulfillment is coordinated with the self-fulfillment of others. In short, how does one care for others *while* one is individuating? Jung's major

---

[25] Browning and Cooper, *Religious Thought and the Modern Psychologies*, 159.
[26] Ibid., 163.

concern in caring for others returns to intrapsychic work—namely, the limiting of our own projections onto others. Rather than providing an interpersonal strategy for increasing our care for another, Jung turns our attention toward the unaccepted and alienated parts of our own psyche, our own shadows. It is the unaccepted and disowned aspects of ourselves that we project onto others, thus making the task of caring for them very difficult. In other words, Jung is more concerned with the "enemy within" than with an outside enemy. In fact, he tends to reduce all hatred to a projected form of self-hatred. He implies that embracing the full range of who we are will eliminate shadow-projection and hence remove the obstacles to loving others. But this seems to reduce the process of interpersonal reconciliation to intrapsychic integration.

Further, when Jung discusses sacrifice, he refers primarily not to our sacrifice for another, but instead, the sacrifice of our own ego for the sake of the higher Self. In this process, we are to follow the example of Christ. But for Jung, we cannot depend on Christ's sacrifice for ourselves in any sort of redemptive way. Instead, we, like Christ, must make our own sacrifice by dying to the needs and demands of the ego and following the call of the Self. Hardship and ego surrender are part of this calling. But this sacrifice is not the difficult task of negotiating our own needs with those of others so much as moving beyond the securities of the ego in the name of a deeper calling. In this sense, the surface needs of the ego are the great tempter on the spiritual journey. The goal is a deep sense of joy and contentment and not a shallow sense of pleasure. As Jung said, "It is no easy matter to live a life that is modeled on Christ's, but it is unspeakably harder to live one's life as truly as Christ lived his."[27] Even though Jung advocates a loyalty to the deeper Self rather than to the superficial world of the ego, for Browning, this sacrifice to the higher self is technically still a form of ethical egoism. Describing Jung, Browning says that "using the rhetoric of sacrifice, the will of God, and sacrality, Jung dresses up in religious clothes a form of

---

[27] Carl Jung, *Collected Works*, 11:340.

ethical egoism."[28] This comment will no doubt infuriate some Jungians who see this higher call as a transcendent and ego-sacrificing journey, a spiritual movement that doesn't deserve to be placed within an ethical category highlighting the needs of the limited ego. For instance, Jungian analyst and scholar Mario Jacoby insists that it is wrong to argue that Jungian analysis promotes narcissism because narcissism always has to do with the specific needs—usually grandiose ones—of the ego:

> There is some question of whether psychotherapy and analysis, both of which aim at self-knowledge and the search for the self-may be regarded as indulgence in a kind of narcissistic wallowing—an accusation not infrequently heard. Cynics might say that, just as there are women and men who sell their services to satisfy the sexual needs of others, so there are analysts who play the part of good and sympathetic listeners to satisfy the narcissistic needs of others, and get paid very well indeed for doing so! A Jungian analyst, however, has no difficulty in countering the charge that analysis revolves around the insatiable ego. The obvious response is that an analysis revolves not around the ego but around the self, and thus is neither narcissistic in itself nor encouraging of narcissism. What Jung means by the self, of course, is the center of the personality, a person's inner core "with its individual and social destiny"—and concern with that fundamental core of being often seems to promote a relativization of ego demands.[29]

Jungian analyst James Hollis states this issue even more boldly:

> This work upon which you embark is far from an exercise in narcissism or self-indulgence. (And don't let anyone tell you it is!) The quality of our relationships, the quality of our parenting, the quality of our citizenship, and the quality of life's journey can never be higher than the level of personal development we have attained. What we bring to life's table will be a function of how much of our journey we

---

[28] Browning and Cooper, *Religious Thought and the Modern Psychologies*, 164.

[29] Mario Jacoby, *Individuation and Narcissism: The Psychology of Self in Jung and Kohut* (London: Routledge, 1991) 21.

have made conscious, and how much courage we were able to muster to live it in the real world that life has presented to us. This more conscious journey, which demands a life of spiritual and psychological integrity, is the only journey worth taking. After all, the diverting, addictive alternatives are all around us, and their sad evidence suggests that a more effective route must lie in the risk of looking within for a change.[30]

Browning, however, is not using the term "ethical egoism" in a manner that necessitates a narcissistic and ego-preoccupied perspective. Instead, he means an ethical stance that considers the fulfillment of the individual person the most important ethical criteria. He carefully distinguishes between hedonistic and non-hedonistic ethical egoism. In short, nonhedonistic ethical egoism moves beyond the comforts and pleasures of the ego, but nevertheless sees self-fulfillment as the ultimate goal of life, and hence, the most important ethical criteria. If we instead use the term "ethical Selfism" rather than "ethical egoism" to accommodate Jung's terminology, the point remains that individual fulfillment trumps other ethical consideration.

Some Jungians, no doubt, would still object. They would perhaps say that even in the ego-sacrifice of Jesus as he faced the cross, he was obeying the call of a higher self and not ethically negotiating the impact this call might have on his mother, his disciples, and others close to him. This call transcended even neighbor love and followed the dictates of integrity, wholeness, and the fulfillment of one's sense of purpose. As James Hollis puts it, "The directive, purposeful energies that govern our lives are themselves in service to meaning, though a transcendent meaning that often has little to do with our narrow frame of conscious understanding."[31] Jungians insist that this fulfillment of a transcendent purpose, this following of the deeper voice of the Self, simply cannot be identified as a form of ethical egoism. The ego hardly has the final word here.

---

[30] Hollis, *Finding Meaning in the Second Half of Life*, 34.
[31] Ibid., 5.

This call is an ultimate summons that may contradict the fulfillment of the ego. Jung's constant insistence that we must move beyond the realm of the ego, Jungians might argue, makes it problematic and confusing to call Jung an ethical egoist. "This is the essence of what Jung means by individuation. It is a service not to the ego, but to what wishes to live through us. While the ego may fear this overthrow, our greatest freedom is found, paradoxically, in surrender to that which seeks fuller expression through us. Enlarged being is what we are called to bring into this world, contribute to our society and our families, and share with others."[32]

Nevertheless, Browning brings his critique of nonhedonistic ethical egoism to Jung, the same critique he powerfully developed against the humanistic psychologies. The personal fulfillment of the individual is privileged over other considerations. For Browning, this is an ethic of personal fulfillment. Ego sacrifice in the name of serving the larger Self is not the same as sacrificing for others. Ethical egoism, whatever its form, always has the difficult task of telling us how we should handle situations in which our own personal fulfillment might interfere with another's. Thus, Browning asks, "Does he believe that he can meet the archetypal needs of others through actualizing his own because finally there is an ultimate hidden harmony of all archetypal possibilities? It is my belief that Jung does envision such a world, and he does so in spite of his apparently rebellious insistence that the shadow and the reality of evil must not only be integrated into the self but be acknowledged to exist in the godhead itself."[33] Browning's concern, again, is how we coordinate our own archetypal fulfillment with that of others. The concern with self-fulfillment certainly has its place. It is also very important as one develops greater self-awareness, but it is a transitional ethic in preparation for a larger ethical task of relating my own self-realization with that of others. Browning describes this transitional ethic as follows:

---

[32] Ibid., 12.

[33] Browning and Cooper, *Religious Thought and the Modern Psychologies*, 165.

Seen from this perspective, the ethical egoism of self-actualization and self-realization becomes a transitional ethic designed to heal and mobilize a fragmented and distorted self so that it will be free, more spontaneous, and have more ready access to its energies and potentialities for the task, finally, of serving a more worthy ethical goal. The goal of individuation can be placed within alternative moral theories and need not be put to the service only of a non-hedonistic ethical egoism of the kind Jung himself apparently thought was the necessary end of psychological growth.[34]

A greater sense of self-awareness, a more robust sense of self-potential, then, are important factors we must bring to ethical decision-making. Indeed, we may need to "bracket" other issues while solidifying and exploring a sense of self during the liminal phase of psychotherapy. This is a crucial and important transition; however, it is not the end of the road because this solidifying of the self will not guarantee ethical decisions. Again, "our need to actualize our archetypes into a balanced and integrated self does not itself dictate how this need could be morally organized with other needs that I may have or with similar needs for self-actualization that others may have. Such also is the case with our tendencies and needs to actualize our archetypal inheritance."[35] Thus, Browning wants to alter Jung's goal of self-realization to include a consideration of the needs of others. So, "The final goal of individuation would be to actualize into a consciously balanced self the uniqueness of our archetypal needs but to do so in such a way as justly and mutually to coordinate this actualizing with the archetypal needs of the neighbor."[36]

In this view, sacrifice would occur merely as the ego forfeited its immediate needs to the higher self; instead, even the higher self may be called to sacrifice some of its own fulfillment in the name of the fulfillment of another. This is a form of sacrifice Browning believes that Jung did not fully acknowledge.

---

[34] Ibid., 167.
[35] Ibid., 168.
[36] Ibid.

As I hope my comments about Browning and Jung reflect, this issue is far from over. Many Jungians do not like what they understand to be their painstaking journey of ego-sacrifice called "ethical *ego*-ism." Yet Browning would argue that even if we believe this ego-transcending call is the will of God, we still must coordinate it with the needs and fulfillment of others. It does not automatically solve our ethical dilemmas. Further, even what we call our "call to a Higher Self" can also be infiltrated and tempted by ontological anxiety. Jungians would, of course, agree that we are always tempted to regress to the ambitions and controls of the ego. We do not make a once-and-for-all commitment to the Self and thereby permanently dismiss the clamoring of the ego.

Wholeness and Evil: A Problem in Jung

Browning believes that Jung's understanding of human fulfillment is based on a faulty view of human wholeness. This view of wholeness tries to incorporate evil in a way that is ultimately confused. Browning believes Jung developed a sophisticated version of ethical ego *while holding an ambiguous view of evil as sometimes ontological and sometimes not*:

> In order to facilitate self-acceptance in both himself and his patients, Jung tried to incorporate evil into his understanding of both human wholeness and divine perfection. In doing this, he often lapsed into a kind of double-talk that revealed he was not so much making a serious point as he was tweaking the nose of an overly rationalistic and moralistic culture. Insofar as he was playing the role of cultural trickster, we can forgive him his inconsistencies. But to the degree he presented his view on wholeness, both human and divine, with the seriousness of a scientific writer, we have no alternative but to tweak his nose in return as well as the noses of all his followers who take his vision of life so seriously.[37]

For Browning, Jung goes back and forth between seeing evil as an ontological structure in the heart of reality (even contained in the

---

[37] Ibid., 151.

Divine) and on the other hand seeing evil as the individually and culturally despised dark side or "shadow." When Jung speaks about evil as an ontological reality, he moves even beyond Freud's and the Manichaens by placing good and evil at the center of the Divine essence, as well as the human self. In such a view, both God and creation are not good but *both* good and evil. Browning does not believe this view of evil is Jung's final perspective (nor do I) even though Jung sometimes sounds this way. Instead, he believes that Jung's thought reinforces the goodness of creation and human aspirations, and therefore sees evil as more related to a distorted will—a position not dissimilar from the general inclination of the Jewish and Christian tradition.

Browning gets right to the heart of what he considers a contradiction in Jung's view of evil, at least on the surface. On the one hand, Jung pushes for the actualization of all archetypal potentialities. On the other hand, he seems to divide reality both psychologically and ontologically into a dualistic perspective of good and evil. This seems to reach not only the very essence of humanity, but it also describes the Divine essence. Browning remembers that the humanistic psychologists were free to encourage the actualization of all potential because that potential is fundamentally *good*. But what happens when that potential is *both* good and evil? Is Jung encouraging the realization of "evil" potential as well as good potential? Won't this be destructive to ourselves and others?

Perhaps Jung should not be taken literally when he uses this "good" and "evil" language. Browning writes, "It is difficult to tell, however, whether Jung is speaking here about evil and good in an absolute or relative sense."[38] Browning wants to know whether or not Jung's dualism is ultimately complementary: "Are the two sides mutually reinforcing, balancing, and corrective to one another? Or are they in genuine opposition to each other as are Freud's *eros* and *thanatos*?"[39]

---

[38] Ibid., 170.
[39] Ibid., 172.

Browning finds much in Jung's vast writings to suggest that he is using evil in a more relative manner. He quotes Jung in an important passage about the shadow:

> If the repressed tendencies, the shadow as I call them, were obviously evil, there would be no problem whatever. But the shadow is merely somewhat inferior, primitive, unadapted, and awkward; not wholly bad. It even contains childish or primitive qualities which would in a way vitalize our existence, but—convention forbids! The educated public, flower of our present civilization, has detached itself from its roots, and is about to lose its connection with the earth as well.[40]

Here Jung suggests that both the personal and the collective shadow are not *in themselves* evil, but *appear* evil because they are cut off from everyday consciousness. The shadow may be primitive and inferior, but it is not purely evil. This means that evil is not ontologically "bad" in a moral sense. Instead, it is a rejected dimension of consciousness that does not meet the personal and cultural standards of decency. Because it has been cut off, it appears worse than it really is. Mr. Hyde is not inherently evil; he is evil only from the vantage point of Dr. Jekyll's daylight consciousness. Once integrated into Jekyll's daytime reality, Hyde's nocturnal activities can be used constructively. If this is Jung's final position, Browning is right that "much of Jung's rhetoric about evil seems excessive."[41] Especially in *Memories, Dreams, and Reflections*, Jung seems to hold a far less dualistic and more compatible view of good and evil. We are told not to think in terms of absolute good and evil. Browning identifies a key Jungian comment: "A sheer will for destruction is not to be expected…. In all my experience I have never observed anything like it, except in cases of severe psychoses and criminal insanity."[42] Thus, it is not our natural inclination to act destructively. Destructive behavior results instead from distortion.

---

[40] Jung, *Collected Works*, 11:78.

[41] Browning and Cooper, *Religious Thought and the Modern Psychologies*, 173.

[42] Jung, *Collected Works*, 11:457.

Browning therefore believes that Jung's final position on human distortion and alienation is much closer to Christianity than one might at first realize. There is no *essential* or *necessary* evil in the human condition; destructiveness results from a violation of our this basic nature, a distortion of our created being, an estrangement from our original possibilities. Unlike Freud, Jung did not seem to believe we have ontological tendencies toward evil. But as we have seen, his language is notoriously ambiguous in getting to this point. Put in theological terms, Jung does not think evil is a part of creation but is instead a distortion of that creation. Browning describes the usefulness of Jung's concept of the shadow when we do not assume that evil is innate within the human condition.

> This point—that unless people are aware of their shadow they will project the evil they fear in themselves to events in the social world beyond—is an important truth to acknowledge. And there is little doubt that this is the central contribution Jung is trying to make to the reduction of strife in human affairs. Jung is trying to get us to look inward, become introspective, and acknowledge that genuine evil lurks within. The use of introspection to discern one's own evil—a central part of the Christian and Jewish concern with confession (in ways that Jung sometimes seems to forget), is absolutely central and one of the great themes in psychoanalysis and analytic psychology. But we can argue that humans have a capacity for genuine evil and that this capacity, often buried in our shadow, needs to be confronted and acknowledged without, at the same time, going so far, as Jung sometimes did, as to make evil in humans an absolute, substantial, and autonomous reality. We can present good arguments to support the contention that humans have the capacity for genuine evil without becoming excessive and saying that they are psychologically and ontologically within the grips of a moral dualism of a substantive and even ontological kind.[43]

While this evil is not ontologically given, it *is* a distortion for which we are each responsible. In other words, we cannot blame our

---

[43] Browning and Cooper, *Religious Thought and the Modern Psychologies*, 174.

destructive inclinations on a force completely outside of ourselves. Jungian analyst John Sanford writes, "Modern man prefers to believe that the evils of our time somehow do not exist in the human soul or spiritual sphere, but have political or economic causes, and could be eliminated by a different political system, or education, the correct psychological conditioning or one more war to wipe out the enemy, for he does not want to see that the enemy is to be found in the devils and demons in himself."[44] Ultimately, then, we can blame neither our biology nor our society for all of our destructiveness.

Brief Summary of Browning on Jung

To summarize, Browning believes that the brilliance of Jung, and especially his view of archetypes, is enjoying a serious reconsideration in neuroscience. More scientists are taking seriously the idea of archetypal patterns within the evolving brain. Browning believes that Jung's ethical stance, after careful analysis, still ends up being a form of nonhedonistic ethical egoism because it privileges individual fulfillment over the needs of others. Also, while Jung is quite ambivalent in his discussion of evil, Browning believes that Jung does not actually ontologize evil and, instead, ends up with a view of evil as human distortion, a view compatible with a Judeo-Christian perspective.

---

[44] John Sanford, *Evil: The Shadow Side of Reality* (New York: Crossroad, 1981; 2nd ed., 1989) 15; For an analysis of Sanford's contribution to the issue of evil, see Terry D. Cooper, *Dimensions of Evil: Contemporary Perspectives* (Minneapolis: Fortress Press, 2007) 149–58.

5

Browning's Contributions:
Interview and Concluding Statement

In this final chapter, I will (a) present Browning's direct responses to several questions I posed for him, and (b) conclude with a summary of the many contributions he has made to the dialogue in psychology and religion.

An Interview with Don Browning

By nearly anyone's standards, you have been a pivotal figure in psychology's dialogue with theology in the second half of the twentieth century, and on into this century. What have been some of the most significant shifts in the field you have seen since your student days studying with Seward Hiltner at Chicago?

There are, of course, many shifts. I cannot cover them all. I will focus on one aspect of the theoretical conversation about how to relate theology and psychology. Seward Hiltner, who started the program at Chicago, was a proponent of what he called the "perspectival method" for relating psychology and theology. In this model, psychology and theology were two different frameworks for the interpretation of the same data—human experience or, as Anton Boisen said, the living "human document." It was the data—this human document—that provided the integration of two disciplines. Hiltner wanted to make certain that theology did not dominate psychology and that psychology did not dominate theology. Both had a place in interpreting human behavior. He was especially interested in finding a seat at the table for the minister and chaplain in the interdisciplinary team of the modern general hospital and the then-prevalent psychiatric asylum. The perspectival model was as much a diplomatic maneuver as it was an epistemological framework. It made doctors comfortable to think that ministers and theologians would not try to dominate case conferences. And it made ministers and chaplains comfortable to think—or at least hope—that doctors and psychiatrists would listen to, and perhaps find value in, their insights into the case being discussed.

The major shift has been from a perspectival to a hermeneutic perspective. A hermeneutic view gives more attention to interpreting the human document in light of the classic monuments of a religiocultural tradition, first the tradition of the client and then also that of the professional, be it minister, doctor, or psychologist. This gives more first-order interpretive status, not just to Christianity, but to the collage of Jewish, Christian, and Greek ideas that were synthesized in various ways in early Christianity and somewhat differently in the Church Fathers, the Roman Catholic medieval theologians, and even in the Protestant Reformation. Most modern psychological systems in the West today reflect some variation on this religiocultural conglomerate. Rather than relying on Hiltner's perspectival view, which assumes two rather autonomous disciplines mutually interpreting the same data, today's dialogue is more likely to see modern psychology as a distanciated (in contrast to "objective") framework that still needs locating within a larger religiocultural interpretive perspective over which Western theology and philosophy chiefly reign. Hence, the various psychologies become different forms of that distanciated submoment of explanation that still require more encompassing worldviews, narratives, and ethics—the stuff of theology.

A consistent theme throughout your career has been looking for the hidden assumptions and "horizons" in various psychological theories. Why do you think this is so important?

Very early in my teaching and research at the University of Chicago, I concluded that the modern psychologies were not as neutral and value-free as they pretended. We knew that the various schools did not always agree on the meaning of health, brokenness, hope, and cure, but the problem seemed to me to go beyond simple differences of scientific opinion. Very different worldviews and systems of ethics could be discerned in these psychologies if one brought a theological-ethical mode of analysis to them. I began reading the metaphor theory of George Lakoff, Mark Johnson, Sallie McFague, Ian Barbour, and Paul Ricoeur. I became fascinated by the ways deep metaphors of harmony, life against death, control, design, and care ran through the various major clinical psychologies such as humanistic psychology, Freud, Jung, Skinner, Kohut, and Erikson. Not only did they suggest worldviews and quasi-religions that invited faith, they often implied an ethic.

Views of health in these psychologies were seldom value-free but merged into normative views of the good life. Many of the modern psychologies had built on, yet distorted, aspects of the Judeo-Christian tradition. That did not mean that they were wrong, but these differences did invite, I argued, a theological, ethical, and philosophical analysis and critique. And I pursued this critique, especially in *Religious Thought and the Modern Psychologies* (1987, 2004) and much later in *Christian Ethics and the Moral Psychologies* (2006). Even my work in *A Fundamental Practical Theology* (1991) and the Religion, Culture, and Family Project assumed and relied on this early interest in examining the value orientations of the social and psychological disciplines.

You have often suggested that modern psychologies have more than an underlying philosophy in their theories; instead, they also frequently have a quasi-theology. What do you mean by that?

I touched on this in my answer above. It would be wrong to say that these psychologies are full religions. A religion not only requires a worldview and a sense of the sacred, but it also must exhibit some institutional patterns, rituals, systems of socialization, and methods for developing leaders. The psychologies are not religions in this full sense. But they have many of the elements of religion, hence the justification for calling them quasi-religions. I mentioned above some of the deep metaphors that run through the various dominant psychologies—metaphors of an underlying harmony in life found in the humanistic psychologies, the balance of opposites and harmony in Jung, life against death in Freud, teleological design metaphors in the later Kohut, and care and generativity metaphors in Erikson. Paul Watson, Stanton Jones, and you, Terry, as well as a few other scholars have found additional metaphorical dimensions in the modern psychologies. Sometimes these metaphors get elaborated into larger narratives about the beginning, middle, and end of life, or about life's origins, fall, and restoration. When this happens, these psychologies induce a kind of faith and trust, from both consumer and therapist, about the meaning of life—a faith that is analogous to what we call religious faith. A therapeutic relation is not just a relation of client to therapist. It is a developing faith on the part of the client in the view of life opened up by the therapist.

In the early and mid-1970s, you became concerned about the underlying ethical models in various forms of psychotherapy. You particularly focused on how ethical egoism shaped the direction of highly individualized therapies. As a result, your book The Moral Context of Pastoral Care *(1976) was a pioneering critique of what several later social theorists would also say. How do you see this "turn to ethics" as a crucial part of your work?*

I hope that you are right that other theorists have joined in this ethical analysis of the psychotherapies. There indeed have been other scholars working on this, but on the practicing ground of psychotherapy and pastoral counseling, I am less sure that progress has been made. The problem centers on the ambiguous way the word "health" is used in the modern psychologies and psychotherapies. Health is a valid concept for the psychologies, and psychotherapy should help enhance psychological health. But there is a lack of clarity about the borderline between health and ethics. On the whole, psychological health refers to a relatively conflict-free sphere of human agency. Many people requiring counseling are in conflict, and therapy should help them reduce conflict so that they can make decisions more freely and act more positively. This often entails restoring certain degrees of self-confidence and self-regard. This is good, and all helpful therapy must do this to some extent.

But this modicum of freedom, agency, confidence, and self-affirmation can easily be converted to an overemphasis on self-regard and a de-emphasis on other-regard. Both within psychotherapy and pastoral counseling the legitimate therapeutic interests in appropriate self-regard (what Reinhold Niebuhr called "ordinate" in contrast to "inordinate" self-regard) can get frozen into a more generalized attitude toward life that elevates self-regard above all else. This is when various forms of ethical egoism (hedonic or nonhedonic) become the cultural deposit of the therapies. I have followed and extended analyses by Philip Rieff that have shown how this implicit moral stance has often spilled over the boundaries of the fifty-minute therapeutic hour and, in the literature of the psychotherapies and the ethos that surrounds them, an ethical-egoist view of moral obligation has emerged as a more generalized cultural ethic.

Since I believe that ordinate self-regard is important even for healthy other-regard, I have promoted a love ethic of equal regard in which both other and self should be treated as ends—as children of God—and never as means alone. This, I contend, is the meaning of

Christian neighbor love. This is not a simple ethic of reciprocity in which my acts on behalf of the other are conditioned on the other doing good to me. It is an ethic of mutuality in which both other and self are expected to treat each other as ends and to actualize the good for one another. Self-sacrifice—in situations of conflict, finitude, and sin—has a role in this ethic of equal regard, but not so much as the goals of genuine love but as a mobilizing and transitional ethic designed to restore once again mutuality and equal regard. Obviously, the contemporary psychologies and psychotherapies have much to contribute in restoring the agency and self-regard needed for adequate acts of love as equal regard. But they also need to understand that the greater goal of healthy self-regard is a genuine love ethic of equal regard. Healthy self-regard alone does not automatically lead to equal regard and the transitional capacity for self-sacrifice. An ethic of equal regard requires the religiocultural belief that the other is valued as an end in himself and made in the image of God.

You often distinguish your method of "critical hermeneutics" from a more general hermeneutical approach. Paul Ricoeur seems to be pivotal for your own framework. How have you put together Gadamer's hermeneutical approach with the addition of Ricoeur's understanding of "distanciation"?

Ricoeur is significantly influenced by Gadamer. He takes over Gadamer's view of human understanding as basically a matter of practical dialogue between question and answer—between the problematics of our contemporary situations and our effort to find orientation and answers from the inherited wisdom of the past. The wisdom of the past is where we must begin; this is all that we have, even if it must be critiqued and refined and reshaped for a more adequate approach to the future. Understanding the wisdom of the past is interpreting a past that already has shaped us. The past is not dead; it is in us as part of what Gadamer called our "effective history." Understanding this storehouse of wisdom is like a practical moral dialogue between the questions of the present and the answers that have been delivered to us by our effective history. All of this comes from Gadamer, and Ricoeur buys almost all of it. In so doing, he joins Gadamer in relativizing the aspirations for complete objectivity found in the modern sciences, what Gadamer calls "method" in the title of his great book *Truth and Method.* Gadamer makes the stunning point that the beginning points of inherited wisdom—what he sometimes calls "pre-understandings" or "prejudices"—are essential for understanding. We understand something in relation to these "pre-understandings" even if we later refine or alter them in light of new experience and evolving situations. This is why these pre-understandings should be permitted into the task of arriving at genuine human understanding. The quest for pure objectivity found in the modern social sciences abandons or disregards the importance of these pre-understandings.

But Ricoeur makes an important modification to Gadamer. He introduces the concept of "distanciation" as a way of restoring some of the features of objectivity. According to Ricoeur, we never achieve pure objectivity in the human sciences, and if we did we would lose understanding since it requires the horizons of our pre-understandings. But we can achieve relative degrees of "distance." This can often help us clarify assumptions and knowledge about the more naturalistic dimensions of human experience—our desires, needs, and bodily capacities and limits. This is important because even the wisdom of the past—even our religious wisdom—often assumes knowledge of the rhythms of nature that modern science can clarify even more. But these clarifications only have their full meaning when placed within the larger frameworks of understanding arrived at through practical dialogue with the effective history and pre-understandings of an inherited tradition.

This relativized appreciation for the distanciating functions of science is what Ricoeur contributes to Gadamer. There is a turn to hermeneutics in various expressions of psychology today, but it should not forget the contributions of distanciated scientific investigation as a subordinate dimension of human understanding.

Your approach to doing practical theology emphasizes both the idea that all thought begins in faith, along with the idea that we should make public arguments for those convictions. This seems to combine elements of two conflicting perspectives, postliberalism and a revisionist approach. Can you elaborate some on this?

Yes, you are right. As I acknowledged above, I agree with thinkers such as Gadamer and Ricoeur and other nonfoundationalists such as Richard Bernstein and Robert Bellah that all genuine human understanding begins with the formations of the past—the traditions that have shaped us. I guess this makes me something of a postliberal. But I do not stop here; there are revisionist, or what David Tracy called "critical correlational," components in me as well. We grow up being shaped by those inherited traditions even before we acquire our more mature capacities for critical reflection. Even then, we can critique only that which has been previously given to us. We cannot empty ourselves completely of the past and then do critique; we then have nothing to analyze, nothing to criticize, and nothing to fault or correct. So, yes, as do most modern theologians as well, I agree with the proposition that faith precedes knowledge. In this, I am a nonfoundationalist in contrast to an Enlightenment foundationalist who might think we gain reliable knowledge only by first emptying ourselves of the prejudices of the past.

The pre-understandings of the past are not blind. They contain genuine moral, metaphysical, and scientific insights into thick and multidimensional chains of thought embedded in a tradition. This is true even of what is conveyed by our religious traditions. Understanding what has shaped us means unearthing the tradition-embedded rationalities of the past, analyzing them, critiquing them in light of the more abiding and tested themes within a tradition, and articulating them in more systematic ways in contemporary situations of public discourse. In my decade-long research on the family in western theology and culture, I began to grasp the complicated and multidimensional perspectives on marriage, kinship, and childhood found in the Christian tradition—perspectives that combined naturalistic description, principles of moral obligation, and narrative frameworks around the doctrines of creation, covenant, and eschatological fulfillment. I became struck by how contemporary social-scientific study of family was blind to the richness and embedded rationality of this tradition. I also became convinced that Christian family theory could be reintroduced to contemporary discourse about the future of marriage, family, and children in modern societies. Christian theology can and should present plausible reasons—not foundationally scientific reasons—that engage contemporary debates over the family.

You have clearly affirmed some of the foundational work that evangelicals are doing in relating psychology to religion. How do you see this work as more instructional, at least in some ways, than what is happening in mainline groups?

Although the dialogue between psychology and theology began, for the most part, in mainline theological centers, it has in many ways broadened, if not basically moved, to more Protestant evangelical centers and scholars. I do not want to overstate this transition, but I think this is to some extent true.

Why has this happened and is it good? It has happened for several reasons. Mainline discussions became more and more captured and confined to the immediate requirements of pastoral care and counseling. With only a few exceptions, more theoretical investigations subsided. Furthermore, evangelical scholars have always had a higher regard for the empirical, partially due to their deep concern for the "factuality" of the Christian faith. This led them to take empirical scientific psychology more seriously then many mainline scholars. But soon, the strain and sometimes sharp tensions between simplistic empiricism and many evangelicals' strong Christian beliefs came into overt conflict. Hence, in recent years in the work of Stanton Jones, Stephen Evans, David Meyers, Robert Roberts, Steven Sandage, and several others, a new and robust theoretical discussion has emerged in explicitly evangelical circles. Although I consider myself part of the mainline Protestant tradition and something of a theological liberal, I respect this new evangelical conversation, have contributed to its symposia, and learned much from its new theoretical probes.

I like to think that the critical hermeneutic model that you and I developed in the second edition of *Religious Thought and the Modern Psychologies* (2004) has contributed to this evangelical conversation. My only criticism of this new trend in evangelical circles is that it often is content to end with securing the use of modern psychology in evangelical communities without compromising the faith. In some cases, as in the work of Stanton Jones and Ray Anderson, it goes beyond this more defensive goal and attempts to influence secular psychology. And this is good. But the evangelical conversation often fails to develop a sufficiently differentiated language that not only includes confessional avowal but also phenomenological description and empirical modeling and testing. Critical hermeneutic phenomenology might help evangelical theorists bridge that gap between confession and scientific modeling and research. Most secular psychologists still hear evangelical researchers as mainly apologetic "true believers" who want to bring psychology back under the tent of a flat-footed Christian domination. This skepticism is a shortcoming of the secular psychologists, but it also means that the new evangelical contributions to the theology-psychology dialogue need more differentiated languages in order to communicate their insights. They must go beyond the message that psychology needs God, which often seems to tone-deaf secular psychologists as the essence of what evangelicals have to say in the dialogue between theology and psychology.

For many years now, you have directed the University of Chicago's Religion, Culture, and Family Project. This work has led you toward a very energetic, interdisciplinary connection with Emory School of Law and other institutions as you have explored issues surrounding the family. What prompted this enormous investment of your time and energy, and why do you feel it is so important?

In the late 1980s, I sensed that there was an emerging culture war over the family that the churches were ill-equipped to address. I convinced the Division of Religion of the Lilly Endowment Inc. to give me a multiyear grant to develop an interdisciplinary practical-theological research project on the situation of families and religion in present-day U.S. society. I have described how that endeavor was both a practical theological project and a research project at one and the same time in the second chapter of *Equality and the Family: A Fundamental Practical Theology of Children, Mothers, and Fathers in Modern Societies* (2007). We commissioned monographs and symposia on biblical, historical, economic, feminist, legal, and ecclesial perspectives on families. I coauthored with Bonnie Miller-McLemore, Pam Couture, Bernie Lyon, and Robert Franklin a summary book called *From Culture Wars to Common Ground: Religion and the American Family Debate* (1997, 2000). One of the most important books in our series was on the interaction between Christianity and law in shaping the direction of family and marriage in Western societies. It was written by Emory University legal historian John Witte and called *From Sacrament to Contract: Marriage, Religion, and Law in the Western Tradition* (1997). Later John Witte invited me to lead an Emory University faculty seminar on Sex, Marriage, and Family in the Religions of the Book as part of a larger research project funded by the Pew Charitable Trust. I did this in 2001–2002 in the School of Law of Emory University, and since then I have been related to that and other programs located there.

In fact, much of my writing in recent years has dealt with both American and international law on family issues. But I still keep an eye on theology, psychology, and the social sciences when I do this research. I often analyze legal theory of family much like I did the modern psychologies in *Religious Thought and the Modern Psychologies* and other works. I review how secular law regards the Christian tradition, how a legal theory uses the social sciences, and what kinds of psychological and naturalistic assumptions it makes about men and women, husbands and wives, and parents and children. What I do with the law today seems very similar to what I have done, and still do, with the modern psychologies. I also find a kind of drift toward the therapeutic in the law. Sometimes this has beneficial consequences, but often it undermines the very thing that law must understand and protect, i.e., the role of institutions in modern life even with regard to families.

You also may have in mind my involvement with the American Assembly, a think-tank located at Columbia University founded over fifty years ago by Dwight Eisenhower while he was president of that institution. The American Assembly has developed a sophisticated methodology for bringing diverse Americans together to form consensus statements on complex issues facing American life. In 1999, shortly after the conclusion of the first phases of the Religion, Culture, and Family project, the Assembly asked me to join with Gloria Rodriguez, a leader in social service work to Hispanics, to write the background book for the 2000 Assembly on issues facing the American family. We did this in a book eventually published as *Reweaving the Social Tapestry: Toward a Public Philosophy and Policy for Families* (2002). This brought the Religion, Culture, and Family project directly into the forefront of public policy debates on the family since this book and the consensus statement attached to it were widely distributed to members of the U.S. Congress, governors, and mayors throughout the nation. I like to think this book demonstrates how a practical theological research project can turn into a form of public theology influencing both public policy and law. Even this book and report implicitly exhibit some of the features of a critical hermeneutical approach to practical theology and social commentary.

Where do you see the theology and psychology dialogue headed as you think about the future?

The theology-psychology dialogue will continue to make issues pertaining to therapeutic intervention central to its concern. But it will expand. New advances in evolutionary psychology, cognitive science, and neuroscience have implications for psychology in general, theories of the self, the psychology of religion, and even psychotherapy. Already the philosophical debate about the implications of these new disciplines for personhood is raging in many quarters. Theology is in the discussion, but mainly in circles once interested in the theology-science discussion that formerly centered mainly on the sciences of physics and biology. Now scholars working on the wider relation of theology and science are attending more and more to psychology in the form of neuroscience and evolutionary psychology. I predict that scholars working on the relation of theology to psychology with mainly therapeutic interests will now begin to merge with this wider science-theology debate. This will make the science-theology debate more practical and the theology-psychology discussion even more theoretical. I hope that a decent balance between the theoretical and practical can be maintained as this new configuration begins to take place. And I hope that the practical life of the church and culture are not ignored in the process. Working on these issues from the perspective of family needs, family formation, and interventions in families has helped me, I like to think, keep this balance. History will determine whether this is true.

Some postliberals would no doubt argue that even though you distinguish the notion of "distanciation" from "objectivity," you nevertheless appeal to a somewhat "neutral" bar of reason to resolve conflicting interpretations. They would see this move as impossible because there really are no standards of rationality that are not tradition-saturated.

How might you respond to your postliberal friends who question your apologetic?

I agree that there are no standards of rationality that are not influenced by tradition. But I think that the phrase "tradition-saturated" is a bit too strong a statement. The closer a tradition gets to saying something about nature, or the rhythms of nature, in its interpretations and statements, the more it must confront the clarification of what they say by the distanciating epistemological accomplishments of science, including the psychological sciences. Of course, the sciences only earn a gradual and partial distanciated space; they are in the beginning of their work on any topic influenced by our various inherited traditions of interpretation. But science's various efforts do accomplish some distance from these tradition-embedded interpretations. Hence, they put pressure on a tradition's assumptions about nature and on various additional meanings within a tradition that are dependent in part on these views of nature, its directions, constraints, and patterns.

Hence postliberals go too far in their disconnection from science. They are not foundationalists; neither am I. They are nonfoundationalists, as I am as well. But I do believe that the distanciated moments of science can help resist the total relativity of postliberalism and nonfoundationalism and can also help make refinements to the different points of view within a tradition, demonstrating that some strands of a tradition have more rationality than others. In several recent writings on the conflict between strong *agape*, *caritas*, and *eros* views of Christian love, I have shown how insights from Erikson's theory of generativity, the concept of kin altruism from evolutionary psychology, and the origins of empathy from social neuroscience suggest why the *caritas* view of Christian love is the strongest. It shows how the love of others—even sacrificial love—builds on very early natural empathy we have to the pain of others, the natural affections of kin altruism, and then extends these natural tendencies into adult generativity. God's grace builds on and helps extend some of our natural inclinations to the love of others, even nonkin, the neighbor, the stranger, and even the enemy.

How might you respond to any liberation and feminist pastoral theologians who perhaps see your work as too abstract, too disconnected from the concrete perspectives of suffering people?

It is true that my later work beginning with *Religious Thought and the Modern Psychologies* (1987, 2004), *A Fundamental Practical Theology* (1991), *From Culture Wars to Common Ground* (1997, 2000) has been primarily about the theoretical framework of the dialogue between theology and psychology and method in practical theology. It has been about establishing those subjects as systematic disciplines that are simultaneously theoretically sound, culturally relevant, and practical. My earlier work in *Atonement and Psychotherapy* (1966), *The Moral Context of Pastoral Care* (1976), and *Religious Ethics and Pastoral Care* (1983) was much more directly practical. Even then, since these books challenged pastoral counselors to be much more aware of the moral and cultural dimensions of their work, many pastoral counselors, accustomed to the uncritical absorption of the implicit ethical egoisms of the various modern psychotherapies, may have found this work jarring, abstract, and not very useful. In fact, even in these books, I was simply trying to change the angle of vision of pastoral counseling and psychotherapy rather than coming up with totally new clinically articulate tools.

Throughout my career, I have been primarily working on the theoretical and practical frameworks for pastoral care, pastoral psychotherapy, practical theology, and the dialogue between theology and the social sciences to answer the criticisms of the classic theological disciplines that the pastoral disciplines were weak—in fact, nondisciplines—that hardly deserved to be represented in seminaries, let alone university divinity schools or departments of religion. What I write may not seem relevant to the beginning ministry student about to face his or her first pastoral counseling encounter. But for the overall health and direction of these disciplines, and for the young minister's basic sense of direction in using the social sciences in ministry, I hope and believe that my efforts have and will prove useful.

In some ways, your work has been a call to Protestants to take more seriously the Catholic understanding of nature's relationship to grace. You speak frequently about how grace builds upon, and fulfills, some natural inclinations. To state it in another way, I see your work, from Atonement and Psychotherapy *onward, as a rigorous challenge to the Barthian radical disconnection between grace and nature. Do you think this is accurate?*

I do think this is mostly accurate. That does not mean that I do not also value aspects of Barth's thought. There are analogies between Barth's emphasis on the priority of revelation over reason and nature and Gadamer's and Ricoeur's strong emphasis on tradition. In both points of view, we are seen to be shaped significantly from the outside, be it by revelation or tradition or revelation mediated by tradition. But my position claims that our natural inclinations shape us as well. We are shaped both from the inside outward and from the outside inward. On the inside, we bring to experience many positive natural inclinations—natural empathic responses, inclinations toward kin altruism, a natural sense of trust and hope—all of which can contribute in the right environment to the development of mature generativity, equal regard, and even the self-sacrificial love required to restore equal regard when sin and finitude undermine it. Of course, we possess as well selfish, hostile, and ambiguous tendencies toward in-group fidelities. Although even these impulses can be adaptive goods, but when exaggerated by ontological anxiety (as both Niebuhr and Tillich have pointed out) they can sow the seeds of sin and destruction.

General or common grace—the grace that comes through God's revelation in creation—is indeed the source of all of these inclinations, but God's grace in the revelation of Jesus Christ builds on, draws out, and empowers our more positive moral inclinations. This dialectic between revelation and nature seems to be missed by Barth. It was more accurately grasped in the natural-law theory of his contemporary Emil Brunner. And, before that, it was possibly best stated in Thomas Aquinas. One way to conceive of the goal of the contemporary dialogue between psychology and theology is to update Aquinas's use of the psychobiology of Aristotle with fresh insights from aspects of psychoanalysis, object relations theory, social neuroscience, evolutionary psychology and other tested social-science perspectives. I can say this as a liberal Protestant because I also would bring a Protestant sense of critique to my use of Roman Catholic theology. In the end, I will remain a Protestant.

Concluding Statement:
A Summary of Browning's Major Contributions

By anyone's standard, Don Browning has been an enormously eclectic and interdisciplinary thinker. His began his career in religion and psychological studies, a position from which he and Peter Homans probably staffed most of the psychology and religion Ph.D. programs in the United States. He gradually came to see the significance of ethics and became an important ethicist, particularly in connection to the social sciences. As far back as 1976, he alerted psychotherapists to the often neglected role of ethics in their work. He steadily maintained an interest in the science and religion discussion, an interest that eventually led to his invitation to give the John Templeton lectures on Science and Religion at Boston University in fall 2008. In his own methodological work, he became a solid scholar in the Continental philosophical traditions of phenomenology and hermeneutics. He brought a philosophical sophistication to pastoral theology and practical theology not shared by many. He began a huge project at that University of Chicago dealing with the family, culture, and religion, a project that brought him into contact with a wide variety of social scientists and ethicists around the world.

This involvement in culture and family studies helped generate a deep interest in law and religion, an interest shared by his legal colleague and friend from Emory University, John Witte. As I indicated before, when I worked with Browning on my 2002 sabbatical, he had an appointment in Emory's law school. His interdisciplinary accomplishments are astonishing.

I have referred throughout this book to Browning as a horizon analyst because I believe that this is what he does best. This is the abiding theme that runs from *Atonement and Psychotherapy* in 1966 to his newest publication of the Templeton Lectures. But I would like to suggest some particular themes that I think represent some of the best fruit of his labors. There are many, many other things I could mention, but these stand out to me as central contributions.

First, Browning navigates well between scientific foundationalism and radical relativism. In other words, in his critical hermeneutical methodology, he is able to appreciate the significance of empirical evidence without falling prey to an Enlightenment view of "objective" reason. He respects science but not scientism. We can never empty ourselves of our orienting assumptions and the effective histories we have inherited. In fact, such a self-emptying process would render understanding impossible. We are firmly embedded in a tradition of interpretation. Our thinking process is never completely "pure" in an unmediated fashion. Experience is not that "raw." Instead, it is culturally influenced, which means that it is shaped by language and social matrix. To rid ourselves of this context is to rid ourselves of our humanity. Reason never stands so autonomously from culture that it bears no marks of its historical location, so the idea of an abstract, asocial, and apolitical rationality is not realistic.

If a return to an Enlightenment view of pure reason is one danger, radical relativism is certainly the other. While total objectivity is not possible, Ricoeur's notion of distanciation is not only possible, but very necessary. As we have seen, this is Browning's place for self-critique and the corrective influence of science. Without this submoment of distanciation, interpretation collapses into relativism.

Put another way, Browning believes the incommensurability argument has been exaggerated. This is a view that insists our epistemological starting points and interpretations are so different that there is little hope of any sort of public discussion. We are simply arguing "past" each other. While Browning acknowledges that we will never find a completely neutral bar of reason uninfluenced by cultural factors, it is quite unnecessary to therefore retire from any possibility of public discussion. This is where he is at odds with his postliberal friends, many of whom believe such a public discussion is impossible. Again, while he appreciates the postliberal emphasis on all perspectives beginning in "faith" assumptions, Browning does not believe that they have to simply remain there. There is a place for self-critique and appeal to a general, shared understanding. Browning accepts this apologetic task and believes that any perspective will quickly become sectarian without it. Our epistemologies are not so vastly different that we cannot reason together. If our perspectives truly were that incommensurate, then the entire point of a university would be lost. Surely an ongoing ideal of the university is the bringing together of multiple angles for a shared public discussion. This may *at times* seem futile because of very different starting assumptions. Nevertheless, it is important to maintain if one is seeking a greater understanding. Without this public discussion, there is no hope of intellectual bridge-building. Lest we fall prey to sectarianism, fideism, and obscurity, we must risk the idea of public dialogue.

Browning's use of science, then, is a submoment within a larger interpretation of the human condition. Science does not have a monopoly on all insights into the human condition, nor is it the final, all-consuming last word on life. But it offers an important critique of various aspects of our interpretive framework. The answer is not a return to Enlightenment scientism, a perspective that uncritically accepts science as the only angle of vision. This fails to see that science, too, is always embedded in a community of metaphors, assumptions, and selective attention. Science must be respected as an important part of a perspective's self-critique. This way, science can deeply aid the larger hermeneutic process. As we have seen, this is why Browning's position, like that of Ricoeur's, needs to be labeled a *critical* hermeneutical position, rather than simply a hermeneutical one. We eliminate the submoment of distanciation at our own peril. A "pure" phenomenology seeks to understand the uninfluenced ego of Descartes and Husserl. Again, it is a form of positivism that wants to make the untainted ego the foundation of all thought. For Browning, the ego is embedded in language, tradition, and symbols. We cannot start from scratch with a disembodied consciousness. Even before we begin this phenomenological description we have already been influenced by the narratives surrounding us. Also, *our practical interests* will enter into this understanding from the very beginning. We move from practice to theory and then back to practice. This critical moment of reflection allows science to play its key role in our understanding. Our epistemology can grant priority to understanding rather than to explanation and *still have a self-critical moment in the larger process of interpretation*. We do not have to choose between an uncritical embeddedness in tradition and the pretensions of foundationalist science.

As I have indicated, unlike Karl Barth, Browning believes that humanity possesses a readiness to hear the revelatory significance of the classics in our religious and cultural histories. These classics are both personal and public. Religious classics are also cultural classics. Following Tracy, Browning believes that the significance of the classics are potentially available to all people searching for meaning and truth. Here Browning's Protestant liberalism emerges in contrast to Barthian neo-orthodoxy: Reason is not so distorted or "fallen" that it is completely unable to recognize something of revelatory significance. These religious classics invite us into a dialogue. In fact, they command our attention. They insist on being heard. Yet these classics never simply overwhelm us with a prepackaged interpretation that eliminates the experience we bring to them. Neither science nor Scripture write, on a "blank slate." This is not the way understanding happens, and religious understanding is no exception. Browning disagrees with Barth's view that God's revelation comes with its own epistemological verification, and therefore needs no further public discussion. For Barth, any notion that God's revelation, the highest court of appeal, would need to be brought before the standards of human rationality is a very wrong methodological turn. In fact, for Barth, if we don't assume the inherent validity of God's revelatory word, we will spend our lives pointlessly wrestling with methodological concerns and never get to actual theology. Apologetic theology places entirely too much significance in human rationality. Browning, as well as the school he represented for half a decade (the University of Chicago), tends to balk at any notion that revelation is so self-authenticating that it does not need additional public discussion.

Browning's critical hermeneutical perspective walks a fine line between kerygmatic and apologetic theology. He clearly accepts that all perspectives begin in faith. He is not trying to do a constructive theology from the ground up as if we begin with empty heads and no assumptions. He also believes there is an important place for evidence, and particularly scientific evidence, within the larger interpretive process. Scientism denies its need for faith assumptions; fideism denies the need for scientific evidence, and Browning is in the middle between these two extremes. We must look backward (toward our orienting assumptions of tradition) before we can look forward. We need to move forward, and in the process, allow science to help correct and guide us with its empirical findings. We must critique science when its pretensions suggest that it is all we need, yet we must also *allow ourselves to be critiqued* by science, particularly when it brings data to help refine our understanding of the human condition. Does science offer us total objectivity? No. But does it allow an important step of self-critique and distanciation? Yes. While our reason is never a disembodied rationality that bears no marks of self-interest, it can nevertheless be employed to help us evaluate validity claims. Put directly: *There can be a modernist submoment even within a postmodern interpretation.* Distanciation is not inherently alienating as some postliberals claim.

Thus, psychology can be broadened into an interpretive discipline while at the same time having critical components of scientific scrutiny. Further, these critical investigations can help revise our interpretive assumptions. Our understanding of the concrete process of psychotherapeutic empathy, for instance, can aid in our understanding of Divine empathy. This argument in favor of a parallel between Divine and human empathy, which Browning first made in 1966, can now also include the findings of social neuroscience, attachment theory, and the clinical work of Heinz Kohut, among others. In other words, theology can learn from the concrete contributions of the human sciences. There are some continuities between human experience and the experience of the Divine. Grace can therefore be seen as a process that fulfills and completes nature rather than utterly contradicting it. While our natural inclinations are not sufficient, they can be built upon and completed. This is why Browning is comfortable with a religious humanism that does not recognize a radical split between Divine and human ways of being.

Second, in my estimation, Browning also navigates well between a biological and social emphasis, or the old conflict between nature and nurture. In other words, he brings our instinctuality and culture into a fruitful discussion. He is seduced *neither* by a radical social constructionism that practically eliminates biology *nor* by a biological orientation that leaves little room for culture's influence. While he refuses to embrace a biological or social determinism, Browning's perspective carefully weaves together the strong influences of both biology and culture in his estimation of the human condition.

As we have seen, Browning persuasively points out how Freud lifted his two-instinct theory (*eros* and *thanatos*) into a metaphysical realm by assuming that *all* life can be placed into these competing camps. Freud's final position, which is not far from Zoroastrianism, pointed beyond the meager realm of the human psyche and described a cosmic dualism. While Freud would be the first to insist that his was not a religious or even quasi-religious perspective, he nevertheless embraced a naturalistic ontology that moved beyond psychology into an all-inclusive framework. For Freud, this conflict exists as long as life itself goes on.

Rogers, Maslow, and humanistic psychology eliminate the double-instinct theory and collapse all life into a master move—the actualizing tendency. In their worldview, only one instinct is prominent—the natural urge toward growth and fulfillment. Yet Browning makes two philosophical insights into the humanistic psychologies that simply cannot be ignored. First, in order for humanistic psychology to be accurate, there must be a pre-established harmony that allows all people to self-actualize simultaneously. In other words, the humanistic psychologists do not address the issue of how one person's self-actualization might interfere with another's. What happens when an individual's self-fulfillment collides with his or her partner's? With the children's? With friends'? With the needs of the community? For Browning, the humanistic psychologies make ethical decision-making look a little too easy. In fact, they tend to dismiss the task of ethical decision-making as they assume that our drive toward growth comes ready-made with a biologically unfolding ethical guideline. *Perhaps no one has pointed out better than Browning that the humanistic psychologies are based on as much of an instinct model as Freud's theory.* Many do not associate the word "instinct" with the humanistic framework, but it is clearly there. It is a singularly directed, natural force toward growth and development, and this force for growth naturally tells us what we "should" do. Browning is critical of this mono-motivational approach for two reasons: (a) it doesn't take into consideration competing impulses that also coexist within each person, and (b) it does not offer any guidance for deciding what to do if one's own self-actualization conflicts with those of others.

Third, Browning borrows from the Kierkegaardian-Niebuhrian tradition to make another criticism of humanistic psychology that can also be applied to other perspectives. Browning argues that Rogers and his associates do not account for the problem of ontological anxiety, the anxiety that is not completely reducible to interpersonal factors. For Rogers, anxiety is a "fall out" of relational disturbance. In other words, anxiety is caused by the emergence of incongruence. Incongruence involves presenting a false self because we feel that being genuine would bring judgment and even alienation. Hence, we act in less-than-genuine ways and feel a discrepancy between our honest feelings and the "self" we present. This internal, dichotomous state leads us toward self-estrangement with its preoccupying anxiety. Our buried "genuine self" puts pressure on our false self-presentations as it threatens to come forth. Hence we feel anxious.

While Browning readily agrees that this is indeed a source of anxiety, he does not believe this portrait of anxiety tells the whole story. We also carry within us an ontological anxiety, a sense of insecurity that is simply part of our being. We are both biological creatures and self-transcending creatures. We can step outside ourselves and review our lives—our decisions, our vulnerabilities, and our ultimate death. This *condition itself* produces anxiety. This is not a condition that can be psychologically "fixed." As Niebuhr said so often, it does not have a specific psychological cause. Its source cannot be tracked down and eliminated. This is why psychotherapy cannot eliminate it. In fact, given the fact that ontological anxiety is the forerunner (not the cause) of excessive self-regard and preoccupation, one could say theologically that psychology cannot eliminate sin. The possibility of anxious, inordinate self-regard is built into the very conditions of human existence. Paradoxically, this excessive self-regard is not necessitated by our human condition. We are not biologically hard-wired to sin, but this is the direction in which the human condition inevitably moves. Out of our own anxiety, we reach out for forms of security that are not possible. Total security and finitude are incompatible, yet we nevertheless reach beyond the bounds of our finitude and try to establish a place of infinite safety. This is where sin happens. Thus, Browning would argue that while interpersonal anxiety can exacerbate and contribute to this more pervasive and inevitable anxiety, it does not *cause* it. Browning would further argue that while much of our anxiety can be quieted through the process of psychotherapy, there is always going to be an ever-present possibility of the postanalyzed or "therapized" self to engage in anxiously excessive self-regard. We never get "beyond" this possibility. It stays with us even if we have received the very best fruits of psychotherapeutic healing. As long as we are breathing, we are tempted.[1]

Fourth, Browning is able to incorporate insights from perspectives as radically different as Skinnerian behaviorism and evolutionary psychology. While Browning would certainly *not* agree with radical behaviorism that we have no instincts, he would nevertheless suggest that we need to pay attention to the manner in which Skinner describes our environmental conditioning. While this conditioning hardly tells the whole story, it still sheds light on our story. Similarly, while Browning balks at any evolutionary psychology that advocates a biological determinism, he believes evolutionary psychologists regularly point out important empirical findings about the nature of our instinctual tendencies such as kin altruism and survival. Cultural symbols and institutions can build upon these natural inclinations. Browning, as we have seen, dug out "evolutionary psychology" tendencies in the thought of an unlikely candidate—Thomas Aquinas. These natural tendencies aren't enough in themselves. They need the added reinforcement of cultural support. But nature certainly makes its contribution to culture. *Culture can build upon, direct, and complete our instinctual tendencies.* Culture can take a natural instinct such as genetic kinship and add an expanded ethic to it. Again, culture need not contradict our instincts;

---

[1] It is here, once again, that I have learned much from Browning about the significance of Reinhold Niebuhr for psychology. Browning's regular reliance on Niebuhrian theological anthropology as a helpful critique of psychotherapy nudged me toward the writing of the second volume in this trilogy of theologians and psychotherapists with Mercer (*Reinhold Niebuhr and Psychology: The Ambiguities of the Self* [Macon GA: Mercer University Press, 2009]).

it simply needs to lead them. Reason is necessary to deliberate precisely because we have so many instincts. Blindly following these instincts (Rousseau) or trying to smash them (Hobbes) is not necessary. We are ambivalent and ambiguous carriers of a multitude of instinctual patterns. Browning is suspicious of any master motive that renders the remainder of our instincts quiet or nonexistent. We're stuck with a variety of tendencies, and ethical decision-making is precisely about coordinating them along with the needs of others.

Browning does not believe that evolutionary psychology is going to go away simply because it is sometimes attacked by certain forms of social constructionism. While I've committed myself throughout this book to staying out of the debate over gender and family issues, it would seem that Browning does not want to see the issue of female equality become excessively tied to an antibiological view of gender that sees everything about our lives as socially constructed. Among other things, this view, for Browning, would be too antiscientific. We need to hear and critique what evolutionary psychologists are telling us about genes and culture. This means restraining ourselves long enough to at least hear what they are saying about gender before we look critically at the political implications of their findings. This is a very difficult tightrope to walk. Evolutionary psychologists insist that social constructionists are clinging to an outdated, blank slate theory of humanity and blocking science.[2] Social constructionists, on the other hand, insist that evolutionary psychologists have a sexist political agenda they are pushing in the name of science. As we have seen, for Browning, both perspectives have a contribution to make, and both also need to be critiqued.

Browning, following both William James and Reinhold Niebuhr, consistently argues for a plurality of instincts within each of us. We are not simply divided between two instincts (Freud), nor are we singularly driven by a single instinct (Rogers and Maslow) that

---

[2] See especially, Steven Pinker, *The Blank Slate: The Modern Denial of Human Nature* (New York: Penguin, 2002).

comes equipped with our ethical directions. Instead a plurality of instincts bargains for our attention. Our reason is capable of awakening one instinct to modify another. It is not the job of reason to redeem our instincts, as Freud thought, and it is not the job of reason simply to follow our instinct, as Rogers believed. Instead, a variety of instinctual tendencies need to be considered. We will have the always challenging struggle to decide what is the ethical thing to do amidst competing instincts. Thus, we have to consider both the choir of tendencies within us as well as the tendencies and needs of those around us. This is a strenuous and difficult decision.

Fifth, there is a consistent *nonromantic element* in Browning's thought. All notions of a "blossoming" self, a "hidden" self, a "buried" self, or a naturally developing self are strongly critiqued. Browning is much more impressed with James's hard-won definition of self that comes primarily from ethical decision-making. One's sense of self is much more negotiated rather than "discovered." No form of biological unfolding, automatic self-creativity, or "given" self can take away the difficult task of ethical decisions. We don't simply discover our "true self" and then wait for this discovery to provide us with a secret form of wisdom.

Browning realizes that Jung does not make this striving toward our inner telos as easy as Rogers portrays. In fact, he believes, as we have seen, that Jung is somewhat confusing in his depiction of this process. At times, the self seems to unfold naturally; at other times, the growth journey seems far more riddled with struggle. I read Jung as conveying a near-constant struggle between the safety, security, and status of the ego and the call of the higher self. The "self" calls us to a more rigorous journey. This call may be at odds with the comforts and easy identity of this world. Browning understands that Jungian individuation is indeed more complex and nuanced than humanistic self-actualization, yet Browning asserts that Jung, too, holds out a deep trust in the organism's natural push toward growth.

I have sometimes wondered if Browning's nonromantic view might have been slightly different if he had spent more time doing clinical work. In other words, does a "faith" in the naturally evolving "discovered self" emerge more easily as one watches the process from the vantage point of a close and personal encounter in psychotherapy? Does clinical work itself provide an avenue for understanding and appreciating this deep inclination toward growth and health? Some clinicians claim an access to the inner world of their clients or patients that is not readily available to academics whose vantage point is less empathic and less subjective. As a religiously informed social scientist at the University of Chicago, a person whose career was tied up with critiques of various perspectives, Browning is hardly going to be one who becomes intoxicated with a new method of healing. He is far too sober for that. This is in no way indicates that Browning is not warm, personable, and very mentoring in his approach with people. But he is perennially interested in how other departments and academic voices around a university might evaluate what a psychotherapy or religious claim is asserting. How will this provocative and inviting theory look in the daylight of hard public scrutiny? That has been his concern. Clearly, this stance has kept Browning from "going off the deep end" with any new trend. And this has surely been one of his most valuable services to ministry. His critical thinking skills are sharp; his vision into the underworld of assumptions is highly developed; and his suspicions of only seeing one side of the picture push him toward balance. He is interdisciplinary, learns from everyone, and writes in a nuanced fashion. His multidisciplinary proclivities can sometimes make his writing complicated. It is full of the kind of qualifiers that attest to his attempt to be fair-minded and consider as many perspectives as he can. He does not, however, immerse himself in the subjectivity of patients in the way an empathically attuned psychotherapist does. Someone like Rogers or Kohut would insist that it is in the process of doing the deep work of empathic immersion into another's subjectivity that we discover an emerging healthy, direction-seeking fulfillment. While Browning is not dismissive of this inclination toward growth, he simply believes that we have other inclinations as well. Nothing is "automatic" about human development.

Sixth, it is important to recognize that Browning does not think psychotherapists should start thinking about ethics as an "add on" to what they are already doing. Instead, he believes they are *already operating* on the basis of implicit ethical principles buried in their visions of human flourishing. Browning places ethics right at the center of psychotherapeutic theory. We cannot work with people without an image of health and human flourishing, and that image always contains ethical principles of obligation. All psychotherapies have hidden beliefs about how we "ought" to live, what we "should" do with our lives, and how we relate to others. A huge mistake of some forms of psychotherapy, for Browning, is the assumption that if we can simply be in touch with an inner principle of growth, our ethics will come naturally. A psychotherapist might tell us that we need to get away from all "should" statements, but at least indirectly, this very statement involves a "should." While guilt-ridden, tyrannical consciences have created many problems for which psychotherapy can surely help, the answer is not to create an amoral atmosphere in which ethical issues are not considered. Further, such an amoral atmosphere is not even possible. There is always a cluster of value assumptions and tacit ethical notions floating in *any* therapist's office. It is impossible to function without some sort of guiding assumptions. Thus, claims to complete value neutrality are impossible. A huge value assumption about the importance of self-understanding is clearly being made in every therapeutic interaction.

There are premoral goods we each seek, such as health, comfort, and job fulfillment. But for Browning, it is important to stress that these are *premoral* rather than moral issues. The healthy, wealthy, or skillful person is not necessarily a *moral* person. Moral goods have the additional task of deliberating and reconciling these premoral goods *both within the person and between persons*. Moral thinking, then, involves both an internal process of choice and an interpersonal process of coordinating those choices with the needs of others. For

Browning, psychotherapy has all too frequently confused and conflated premoral goods with moral goods. In other words, therapists have moved too rapidly from the healthy person to the morally ideal person. This premature movement has been largely facilitated by the huge assumption that health automatically comes equipped with its own natural moral striving. But for Browning, a lack of internal conflict (which is characteristic of mental health) does not automatically guarantee moral choices. Psychological health is an important premoral good, but it does not eliminate the further task of ethical deliberation. Both physical and psychological health can contribute to the moral good, but they do not automatically bring it about. An absence of internal conflict does not necessarily provide us with ethical decisions. Moral thinking will build upon and attempt to fulfill and order our strivings for premoral goods. It will be a referee between competing goods, as well as help negotiate our own needs with those of others.

Perhaps I need to state Browning's attitude toward psycho-therapy even more boldly: Browning recognizes and affirms the significance and importance of psychotherapeutic healing. He even believes it can help us clarify and better grasp the process of Divine healing. He is pro-therapy, but he is critical of any form of therapy that neglects or ignores the further process of ethical deliberation. More importantly, he is critical of any method of psychotherapy that assumes that a healthy personality will automatically, naturally, and biologically choose the right course of action. We will always have the more difficult task of coordinating our needs with those of others. We will also have the task of choosing between premoral goods that may contradict each other. With both of these tasks, we need to recognize the significance of ethical decision-making. In Browning's career, *he didn't simply turn from psychology to ethics; instead, he realized that psychology was already making ethical assumptions that needed to be made explicit and invited into a more deliberate discussion.*

These then, from my perspective, are some of the most significant aspects of Browning's contribution to the religion and psychology discussion. Others could surely put forth many, many other valuable insights. And this is only one aspect of the work Browning has done across many discipline borders.

I have many times suggested throughout these pages that Browning's work is too broad in scope to be fully analyzed in one volume. I have reminded the reader that my primary purpose is to examine the significance of Browning's keen insights into the discipline of psychology. Yet this analysis inevitably moves into larger areas and concerns, such as cultural analysis, family studies, law, and the broad field of ethics, to name but a few. As I have become more acquainted with Browning as scholar and friend, the more I have been deeply impressed with the breadth of his background and ability to think from such a multidisciplinary vision. He is at once a very generous and a carefully critical thinker. And he is, as I have tried to portray throughout these pages, primarily an analyst of the horizons out of which we live our lives. If one is interested in the broad discussions of religion, the social sciences (especially psychology), ethics, and culture, the work of Don Browning, in my estimation, is essential.

Index

abuse, seeking out, 126–27
academic psychology, 144
acting out, related to threats to the self, 146–47
action; as discharge of energy, 123–24; healthy vs. moral, 47–48
actualizing tendency, 77–78, 111–15
agape; building upon natural instincts, 77; Niebuhr's emphasis on, 76
aggression; as a dominant instinct, 62; externalization of, 63
American Assembly, 203
Analogical Imagination, The (Tracy), 23
analysis, ultimate goal of, 167
Anderson, Ray, 201
anxiety, 90–91; caused by emergence incongruence, 215; generated, when defenses are pointed out, 122; masked by excessive self-regard, 164; new forms and sources of, 161, 162–63; ontological, 215; as part of humans' essential condition, 180; promoting excessive self-regard, 162–63; response to, 69–71; resulting from distorted relationships, 180; resulting from seeing world realistically, 69; therapy causing, 128
Aquinas, Thomas, 106–7, 208, 216
archetypes, 171, 172, 174–75, 177
Aristotle, 106
art, resulting from primitive energies of the id, 124
atheism, current books on, 11–12
Atonement and Psychotherapy (Browning), 7, 80–81, 206, 207

attachment, 177; as goal, 126–27; secure, 175
attention, deprivation of, leading to narcissism, 147–48
Augsburger, David, 153–54
authoritarian communities, 52–53
authoritative communities, 52–53

babyishness, 176–77
baby watching, 126, 144
Barash, David, 92–93
Barbour, Ian, 194
Barth, Karl, 17, 21–22, 53–54; Browning's disagreement with, about God's revelation, 212; missing dialectic between revelation and nature, 208
Beck, Aaron, 3
behaviorism, 83–85
Bellah, Robert, 199
Berger, Peter, 135–36
Bernstein, Richard, 8, 27, 199
Black, Margaret, 62, 120–21, 123, 124, 125, 129
Blank Slate, The: The Modern Denial of Human Nature (Pinker), 98
Blessed Rage for Order (Tracy), 19, 23
Bly, Robert, 178
Boisen, Anton, 192
Bowen, Murray, 3, 132
Bowlby, John, 143, 175–76
Bridges, William, 42
Browning, Carol, 3, 4
Browning, Christopher, 4
Browning, Don; addressing contradiction in Jung's view of evil, 188; acknowledging influence

of Gadamer and Ricoeur, 30–31; advocating critical hermeneutical approach, 4; analysis of Rogers, 80–82; on anxiety, 71; apologetic mode of, 173; as archaeologist of concepts, 6; arguing for a plurality of instincts, 217–18; attitude of, toward different methods of therapy, 221; aware of science turning into scientism, 108–9; believing the incommensurability argument has been exaggerated, 210; believing Jung has a faulty view of human wholeness, 187; believing Jung's position on human alienation is close to Christianity, 190; believing that humanity is ready to hear the classics' revelatory significance, 211–12; bringing Jungian thought to other disciplines, 173; cautious approach of, to Habermas, 26; concerned with relationship between instincts and culture, 60; connecting Jungian theory with Turner's and Stevens's work, 174–75; contrasting Jung with Rogers and Maslow, 179; critical hermeneutical perspective of, 212; critical of humanistic psychology, 44–45, 214–15; on dangers of creativity without generativity, 134–35; defining religion, 195; depending on Ricouer's notion of distanciation, 53–54; desiring to expand understanding of human experience, 36; developing skills of philosophical investigation, 7–8; disagreeing with Rogers on matter of anxiety, 180; discounting the notion that all sin results from pre-Oedipal issues, 163–64; distinguishing pastoral counseling from secular psychotherapy, 49–

51; on elements of religion, 34; emphasizing idea of equal-regard marriage, 109–10; endorsing Tracy's revised correlational approach, 17; Erikson as favorite psychologist of, 117; on Erikson's approach to generativity, 133–34; on Erikson's concept of identity, 143; on Erikson's development of generativity, 136–40; on Erikson's enrichment of psychoanalytic theory, 142; evaluating Freud via Niebuhr and Tillich, 66–73; evolutionary psychology and, 105–10; fascinated by deep metaphors, 194; fitting between modernity and postmodernity, 57; on five levels of practical thinking, 31–34; on Freud turning metaphysician, 63–64; on the future of the theology-psychology dialogue, 204; on generative people, 132; as horizon analyst, 1; on human understanding beginning with formations of the past, 199; on importance of science at moment of distanciation, 29; incorporating insights from a variety of perspectives, 216; influence of, 1; influence on, of University of Chicago, 4–5; influenced by Norton, 81; on influence of metaphors, 32; interdisciplinary nature of, 219; interested in how others view Jung, 172–73; on James's approach to instinct, 111; on James's significance in discussion of human instincts, 115–16; on Jung bridging gap between ego psychologist and object relations theorists, 177–78; on Jung and ethical egoism, 182–83; on Jung and other self-actualization theorists, 170–71; on Kohut developing a sense of mutuality, 160; on Kohut's approach to psychoanalysis, 141–43; on Kohut's view of anxiety, 161–62; linking psychology and ethics, 40–45; methodology of, 53–54; Miller-McLemore's criticism of, on generativity, 139; on the moral psychologies, 51–53; moving away from strict definitions of human experience, 55; on moving conceptual claims to the public realm, 25–26; on nature and spirit, 72–73; navigating between scientific foundationalism and radical relativism, 209; navigating well between biological and social emphasis, 213; on Niebuhr's view of reason, 56; nonromantic element in thought of, 218; Norton's influence on, 165–66; on original sin, 91; philosophical approach of, 6–7; pinpointing ambiguity in Stevens and Jung, 180–81; pioneering the reconnection of psychology to ethics, 32–33; placing, with Tillich and Niebuhr, 2–3; position of, labeled as a critical hermeneutical position, 211; presenting distance between Freud's and Niebuhr's ethical convictions, 76, 77; promoting a love ethic of equal regard, 196–97; on Protestant Christianity's distance from Jewish legal roots, 45–46; on psychology being steeped in images, 10–11; on psychology and metaphor, 35; on psychology moving into religion, 37–38; on psychotherapy confusing premoral and moral goods, 220–21; on psychotherapy and ethics,

220; pulling together Erikson's vision of humanity, 118; pushing discussion back to philosophical anthropology, 10–11; questioning Clinebell on specificity of ethical guidelines, 46–47; questioning empirical psychologists, 11; on reason and instinct, 110; rejecting objectivity, 8–9; representing apologetic side of theology, 20; on Rogers as theologian, 7; on sacrificing one's ego, 178; on shifts in psychology's dialogue with religion, 192–93; on Skinner and ethics, 87–91; suspicious of any master motive, 217; Tracy's influence on, 14–20, 24, 25; on two models of psychology, 39–40; using science with the context of the human condition, 210; wanting to include needs of others as part of self-realization, 186; welcoming scientific approaches to life, 13–14; widely versed in a variety of disciplines, 1–2
Browning, Elizabeth, 4
Brunner, Emil, 208
Buss, David, 97

calling, paying attention to, 168
Campbell, Joseph, 178
caretakers, primary, importance of, 152
caritas, 205
child development; effect on, of emotional deprivation, 124–26; fantasy objects' role in, 127; seeking relationships, 126–27
children; absorbing values from others, 79; as image of mental health, 78–79
Chomsky, Noam, 175
Christian Ethics and the Moral Psychologies (Browning), 51, 194

Christian family theory, 200
Christian theology, addressing wider
    audience, 22–23
church, task of, to create moral
    systems, 47–48
Civilization and Its Discontents (Freud),
    61
classics; affecting pretheoretical world
    of psychologists, 34–35; influence
    of, 14–16
classic texts, influence of, preceding
    interpretation of, 23
Clinebell, Howard, 46–47
cohesion, 158–59
collective unconscious, 171–72
complex, Jung's theory of, 177–78
concupiscence, 68
conditioning, 83
confessional approach, 25
confessional community, engaging the
    surrounding culture, 30
confessional theology, 20–25, 55
confessional therapists, 177
congruence, 80
consumerism, Western, self
    psychology as outgrowth of, 156–
    58
conversation, 24, 30
Cooper, Terry, 195
counselor education programs, 150
Couture, Pam, 202
creation, 56
creativity, dangers of, without
    generativity, 134–35
culture; guiding instinct, 110;
    influence of, on individuals, 129–
    30
Culture of Narcissism, The (Lasch), 53,
    132
Cushman, Philip, 45, 151, 156–60

daimon, 165–70
Darwinism, relating psychology to,
    89–90

Dawkins, Richard, 11–12
death instinct, 62–63
defenses; creating symptoms, 126; role
    of, in ego psychology, 122–23
dependence, 175
Descartes, 211
descriptive psychology, 39–40
destiny, following, 165–66
detachment, 74–75
devaluation of others, 155
distanciation, 3–4, 27, 132–33, 193,
    198–99, 209–10, 213; generativity
    and, 137–38; science's importance
    for, 29
distrust, 164
Dobson, Marcia, 148–49
double-instinct theory, eliminated, 214
drive theory, 62, 66, 122, 124–25, 149–
    50

effective history, 9, 30–31, 131, 197–98
ego; Freud's use of term, 120;
    grandiose needs of, linked with
    narcissism, 183–84; moving
    beyond the realm of, 185; primary
    task of, 120–21; relying on id for
    energy, 123–24; sacrifice of, in
    name of serving the larger Self,
    185; surface needs of, 182
Ego and the Id, The (S. Freud), 120
Ego and the Mechanisms of Defense, The
    (A. Freud), 122
ego psychology, emergence of, 120–28
Eisenhower, Dwight, 203
Eliade, Mircea, 38
Ellis, Albert, 3
emotional deprivation, 125–26
emotional environment, importance
    of, for ego development, 125–26
empathy, 142–43, 80; interpretation as
    advanced form of, 150;
    psychotherapeutic, 213; as
    response to narcissistic injury,
    147–48; teaching about trauma

Index

and its effects, 153; as vicarious introspection, 144–45
empirical, definition of, 55
empiricism, 14, 97
emptiness, as part of human development, 157
End of Faith, The (Harris), 11
energy, build-up and discharge of, 123–24
environment, as source of human behavior, 84–85, 87
environmental-social dimension of practical thinking, 34
epigenetic principle, 118–19
Equality and the Family (Browning), 202
Equal-Regard Family and Its Friendly Critics, The (Witte, Green, and Wheeler, eds.), 109–10, 140
equal-regard marriage, 109–10
equity feminism, 104–5, 109
Erikson, Erik; addressing issues of psychology and social change, 142; attracting attention outside the psychoanalytic community, 128–29, 130; Browning's favorite psychologist, 117; conflating language of instinct and ethics, 161; contrasted with Kohut, 140–43, 149–50; ethics of, 117–18; focus of, on contextualizing identity, 128; on generativity, 132–35; as instinctual pluralist, 161; on the lower in man, importance of, 119; metaphors in work of, 195; not always welcomed in psychoanalytic community, 129, 130; perspective of, on identity, 143; recognizing lifelong triggers for anxiety, 163; similarity of, to Niebuhr, 118; underlying criticism of Freudian psychology, 129–31; vision of humanity, Browning pulling together, 118
eros. See life instinct

essentialism, 94
ethical egoism, 171, 182–87, 196
ethical living, occurring naturally, 44
ethology, 176
eudaimonism, 165–66
evangelical centers, psychology-theology discussion moving to, 200–201
Evans, Stephen, 201
evidence, defining, 97–98
evil, Jung's ambiguous view of, 187–90
evolutionary development, ego adaptation and, 124
evolutionary psychology, 91–101, 172, 216–17; Browning and, 105–10; marriage and, 107–8; offering important data on the human condition, 105–6; reductionism in, 109
excessive self-regard, 113, 162–63, 164, 215
existentialism, 112
explanatory psychology, 39
extrospective data collection, 144

Fairbairne, Ronald, 126, 130, 151
faith, comparison of, 18–19
faith assumptions, importance of, 5
faith preceding knowledge, 199
fantasy objects, child's turn to, 127
Faris, Ellsworth, 93
feminist theory, Pinker and, 103–5
Finger, Thomas, 66, 74
forgiveness, linked with the moral life, 48
foundationalism, 8, 52
Fox, Robin, 175
fragmentation, 152
Franklin, Robert, 202
freedom; corruption of, 48–49; freeing of, 49
Frei, Hans, 20
Freud, Anna, 121–22

Freud, Sigmund, 112; arguing that
loving the neighbor as oneself is
unrealistic, 75; believing that two
instincts dominated life, 62–63;
context for his discoveries, 65;
defining instinct, 60; depicting the
human psyche, 65–67; developing
focus on aggression, 61–62;
disregarding nature, 90; drawing
on Darwin, 123; on ethical living,
44; final position of, 213–14;
human self created from struggle
with instincts, 73–74; increasing
pessimistic view of the human
condition, 62; Kohut's debt to, 145;
as master of suspicion, 65;
metaphors in work of, 195;
moving toward structural theory
of the mind, 120–21; Niebuhr's
outlook on, 68–73; not knowing
ultimate context of human
experience, 64; parallels of, with
Hobbes, 61; seeing detachment as
solution to instinctual situation,
74–75; Tillich's outlook on, 66–68;
turning metaphysician, 63–64
Frish, Karl von, 176
From Culture Wars to Common Ground
(Browning, Miller-McLemore, et
al.), 139–40, 202, 206
From Sacrament to Contract (Witte), 202
fulfillment; ethic of, 185; human,
psychologists holding an image
of, 118
fundamentalism, mistakes of, in
reading sacred literature, 16
Fundamental Practical Theology, A
(Browning), 194
future generations, caring for, 160–61

Gadamer, Hans-Georg, 9, 14, 28, 131;
influence of, on Browning, 30–31;
influence of, on Ricoeur, 197–99
Gay, Volney, 155

gender feminism, 104–5, 109
Generative Man: Psychoanalytic
Perspectives (Browning), 117
generativity, 117–18; Erikson's
approach to, 132–35; gender
differences and, 138–39;
instinctual foundations of, 161;
relational, 138–39; religious
support for, 135–36
Gilkey, Langdon, 20, 48–49
God; distrust in, 70; involvement of,
with humanity, 140
God Delusion, The (Dawkins), 12
goods, competition for humans'
allegiance, 114, 115
Gould, Steven Jay, 96
grace, 46, 213; related to self-
acceptance, 80–81; relationship of,
with nature, 207
grandiosity, 152, 156
Green, M. Christian, 109, 140
Guntrip, Harry, 151
Guss-Teicholz, Judith, 158–59
Gustafson, James, 20

Habermas, Jürgen, 26–27, 28, 29, 31
Hall, Calvin, 167
Hardwired to Connect: The New
Scientific Case for Authoritative
Communities, 52
Harris, Sam, 11
Hartmann, Heinz, 123–26
Hauerwas, Stanley, 21
health, relation of, to ethics, 196
hedonistic ethical egoism, 184
hermeneutic perspective, 193
Hillman, James, 168–70
Hiltner, Seward, 192–93
history, personal, including
conceptual history, 9
Hitchens, Christopher, 11
Hobbes, Thomas, 61
Hoff-Summers, Christina, 103–4
holding environment, 127–28, 151

Index

Hollis, James, 166, 183–84
hooking, 176
horizon, 117–18
human behavior, study of, 9–10
human document, 192
humanistic psychology, 44–45, 214–15
human nature; created vs. distorted,
    68; debate over, 59–60; estranged
    vs. essential, 67
human potential movement, 151
humans; always interpreting, 8, 9–10;
    as blank slates, 16, 85, 90, 97; born
    into state of anxiety, 69; capacity
    of, for self-transcendence, 69; as
    children of tradition, 9; combining
    nature and spirit, 69–73;
    complexity of, 119;
    destructiveness of, 101; dispute
    regarding nature of, 94, 96–100;
    inherited nature of, 91–93; natural
    growth of, 78; no metanarrative to
    describe humanity of, 94–95;
    normative image of, 133;
    nurturing infants, 176–77;
    plasticity of, 101; returning to lost
    innocence, 66
husbandry, image of, as crucial for
    Skinner, 89–90
Husserl, Edmund, 28, 211

id, actions of, 120–21
identity; contextualizing, 128; cultural
    influence on, 129–30; struggle for,
    114–15
identity confusion, 140–41
id psychology, 122
imperfectability, fear of, 101
imprinting, 176
inclusive fitness, 106
incongruence, 215
individuation, 167, 179; as ethical task,
    181; final goal of, 186; Jung's
    inconsistency on, 171
inequality, fear of, 100

infant study, 126
injustice, eradication of, 44
innate releasing mechanisms, 176
inner guide, 168–69
inner voice, Jungian notion of, 167–68
innovations, dangers of, 132
instinct; associated with humanistic
    framework, 214; as cultural
    product, 93–94; Freud's definition
    of, 60; losing control, 90; lower life
    of, 134; mixed with consciousness
    and memory, 110; not the enemy
    of humans, 118–19; plurality of,
    107; reason and, 110–11
instinctual pluralism, 102–3, 110–16,
    161
integrity, 166
interpretation, involving dialogue
    between interpreter and text, 24
intertextuality, 25
intrapsychic work, 182
introspection, 142–43

Jacoby, Mario, 183
James, William, 36, 38, 55, 107, 161,
    217; disagreeing with Freud on
    instincts, 110–11; on finding the
    authentic self, 114–15; instinctual
    pluralism of, 110–16; seeing self as
    unified pluralism of potential
    selves, 113–14
Jesus, obeying the call of a higher self,
    184
Johnson, Mark, 31, 194
Jones, Stanton, 195, 201
Jung, Carl, 38, 111, 112; academy's
    view of, 173; ambiguity in work
    of, 180–81; applauding myth, 170;
    bridging gap between ego
    psychologist and object relations
    theorists, 177–78; contrasted with
    Rogers and Maslow, 179; dualism
    of, 188; feeling called, 165; holding
    compatible view of good and evil,

189; interested in strengthening
the psyche, 167; lapsing into
ethical and religious thinking, 170;
life work of, 167; metaphors in
work of, 195; placing good and
evil at center of the Divine
Essence, 188; popular among
people on spiritual journeys, 178;
popularizing the collective
unconscious concept, 171–72;
reducing hatred to projected self-
hatred, 182; on sacrifice, 182;
transparent about his religious
beliefs, 173–74; trusting in
human's innate growth potential,
179
Kant, Immanuel, 175
Keen, Sam, 178
Kepler, Johannes, 175
Kernberg, Otto, 154–55
Kerygma and Counseling (Oden), 81n34
Kierkegaard, Søren, 69, 180
kin altruism, 106–8
Kohut, Heinz, 118, 130, 131;
    contrasted with Erikson, 140–43,
    149–50; contrasted with Rogers,
    150; Cushman's impressions of,
    156–59; denying central role of the
    Oedipus complex, 148–49;
    discounting observational data as
    psychoanalytic data, 144–45;
    focused on pre-Oedipal issues,
    149–50; Guss-Teicholz's
    impressions of, 158–59; as
    humanistic psychologist, 150;
    importance to, of trauma, 152–53;
    indebted to Freud, 145; metaphors
    in work of, 195; offering
    phenomenology of selfhood, 128;
    placing great importance on
    primary caregivers, 152;
    psychoanalytical approach of, 128;
    on reasons for devaluing others,
    155; on self-fragmentation, 145–46;

using empathy to dealt with
    narcissistic injury, 147–48;
    viewing psychology as study of
    complex emotional states, 145
Kohut, Loewald and the Postmoderns
    (Guss-Teicholz), 158–59

Lakoff, George, 31, 194
language; different perspectives on,
    24; significance of, 23–24
Lasch, Christopher, 42–43, 53, 132
Lewontin, Richard, 96
liberation, 49; ideology of, 44; limits
    of, 45–48
liberation theology, 49, 101–2
life-cycle, biological unfolding of, 179
life instinct, 62–63
liminality, 41, 42
Lindbeck, George, 20
Locke, John, 97
Lonergan, Bernard, 19
Lorenz, Konrad, 175, 176
Lyon, Bernie, 202

marriage, 107–10
Maslow, Abraham, 78, 111, 214; Jung
    contrasted with, 179; portraying
    personal growth, 170
mass killings, source of, 100–101
McFague, Sallie, 194
McGrath, Alister, 12
McGrath, Joanna, 12
Memories, Dreams, and Reflections
    (Jung), 189
metaphors; deep, 194; essence and
    importance of, 31–32; religiously
    inspiring, 35
metaphor theory, 194
metaphysical assumptions, 31, 35
Meyers, David, 201
Miller-McLemore, Bonnie, 138–40, 202
Mitchell, Stephen, 62, 120–21, 123, 124,
    125

Index

modern man, nongenerative mentality of, 134–35
Montagu, Ashley, 93–94
Moore, Thomas, 178
Moral Context of Pastoral Care, The (Browning), 40–41, 195, 206
moral judgment, suspension of, 46
moral psychologies, helping moral philosophy and Christian ethics, 51
mother, primary task of, 127
Moyers, Bill, 178
mutuality, 134, 138–40; ethic of, 197; Kohut developing a sense of, 160
myth; gaining new respectability in Jungian thought, 174; redemptive psychological function of, 168–69

narcissism, 147–48; cause of, 153–54; childhood vs. adult, 154–55; confronting, 154–55; developmental defect in, 152; Kohut perpetuating, 157; linked to specific needs of the ego, 183–84; moving along a line, 152
narcissistic injury, 141–42
natural selection, as ultimate metaphor, 89
natural theology, 21
nature; lacking regulation, 90; relationship with grace, 207
Nature and Destiny of Man, The (Niebuhr), 68–69
negative reinforcement, 85–86
neurosis; cause of, in Freudian theory, 120–21; ego psychologists' view of, 126
New York Psychology Group, 2, 18
Niebuhr, Reinhold, 2, 6, 10, 36, 49, 55, 196, 217; on anxiety, sources of, 162–63; embracing emphasis on ontological anxiety, 113; emphasizing importance of self-sacrificial love, 76; Erikson's

similarity to, 118; on excessive self-regard, 70; on how the human condition can help people, 102; liberation theology and, 101–2; linking pride and mistrust, 70; on man's ideological taint, 13; outlook of, on Freud, 66–67, 68–73; seeing humans as combination of nature and spirit, 69–70, 73; supporting idea of instinctual pluralism, 110; theological anthropology of, 69; understanding human context and limitations, 89; view of reason, 56
nonhedonistic ethical egoism, 184
Nordby, Vernon, 167
Norton, David, 81, 165–68

objectivism, 8
objectivity, 8, 52
object-relations perspective, 151
object relations theory, 126–27
obligational level of thinking, 32–33
Oden, Thomas, 80–81, 113
Oedipus complex, 148–49
ontological anxiety, 215
ordinate self-regard, 196–97
original sin, 68, 91
other-regard, deemphasized, 196

parents, excessive focus on, as source of anxiety, 163
Parsons, Talcott, 42
pastoral care; antipsychological nature of, 43; bringing into realm of ethical discourse, 43–44; distinguished from secular psychotherapy, 49–51; including moral thinking and forgiveness, grace, and freedom from guilt, 45–46; practiced with little regard for socioeconomic problems, 42–43

231

Paul Tillich and Psychology (Browning), 2, 18
people, reduced to commodities, 157–58
Personal Destinies (Norton), 166
personality theory, taking into account biological tendencies, 92
personhood, reliant on relationship, 127
perspectival method, for relating psychology and theology, 192–93
philosophical anthropology, 10–11, 36
philosophical thought, emerging out of symbols, 10
philosophy, questions asked by, 17
Pinker, Steven, 90, 94, 98–101; arguing for instinctual pluralism, 102–3; feminist theory and, 103–5; implying that biologists are setting theological agendas, 108–9
Placher, William, 21
Plato, 165, 168, 175
Plotinus, 168
pluralism, 25
Pluralism and Personality (Browning), 81
Plurality and Ambiguity (Tracy), 19–20, 23
Pope, Stephen, 106, 107, 109
positive reinforcement, 85
positivism, 14, 24
postliberals, disconnected from science, 205
postliberal theology, 20
posttherapy life, 44
practical thinking, five levels of, 31–34
prejudices, 198
pre-Oedipal issues, 141–42
pre-understanding, 198, 199
pride, linked with mistrust, 70
primitive societies, therapeutic rituals of, 41
Protestant Christianity, similarity of, to psychotherapy, 32–33

psyche, strengthening of, 167
psychoanalysis, Hartmann's influence on, 123
psychological health, 221
psychology; broadened into an interpretive discipline, 213; falling into narcissistic mode, 53; falling prey to foundationalism, 38; fostering a religious outlook, 37–38; loss of uniqueness in, 169; as religion, 195; saturated in tradition, 10; steeped in images, 10–11; treating as science, 83–84; two models of, 39–40
Psychology as Religion: The Cult of Self-Worship (Vitz), 37
psychology-theology discussion, moving to evangelical centers, 200–201
psychosocial theory of human development, 129–30
psychosynthesis, 167
psychotherapy; culture of, critiqued, 42–43; ethical analysis of, 196; goal of, 80; secular, distinguished from pastoral care, 49–51; similarity of, to Protestant Christianity, 32–33
public theology, 19–20; vs. confessional theology, 20–25
punishment, 85–86

radical relativism, 209
reason, instinct and, 110–11
reductionism, 14, 109
reincorporation, 41
reinforcement, two types of, 85–86
Reinhold Niebuhr and Psychology (Cooper), 2, 162
relationship, as primary point of a drive, 126–27
religion; characteristics of, 195; elements of, 34; replacing, with science, 57; understanding of, necessary to cultural studies, 15

Index

Religion, Culture, and Family Project, 4, 194, 203
religion of the self, 37
religious classics, affecting the secular world, 15
Religious Ethics and Pastoral Care (Browning), 206
Religious Thought and the Modern Psychologies (Browning), 3, 81, 194, 201, 203, 206
repression, necessary for survival, 62
restraint, necessity of, 60–61
revised correlational approach, 17, 18, 29
Reweaving the Social Tapestry (Browning and Rodriguez), 203
Ricoeur, Paul, 1, 3, 194; on distancing ourselves from our assumptions, 29; distinguishing between objectivity and distanciation, 27–28; Gadamer's influence on, 197–99; influence of, on Browning, 30–31; relationship of, to Gadamer and Habermas, 28; on symbols giving rise to thought, 35
Rieff, Philip, 73–74, 174, 196
Roberts, Robert, 201
Rodriguez, Gloria, 203
Rogers, Carl, 7, 112, 214; believing in humans' actualizing tendency, 77–78; Browning's analysis of, 80–82; on childhood development, 79–80; contrasted with Kohut, 150; criticism of, 45; on ethical living, 44; on the important role of a therapist, 128; Jung contrasted with, 179; not accounting for ontological anxiety, 215; not recognizing deeper anxiety, 180; offering little place for tradition, 82; portraying personal growth, 170; refusing to acknowledge problem of ontological anxiety, 113; singular drive theory, 82

romanticism, 24
Rose, Steven, 96
rule-role level of practical thinking, 34

sacrifice, 138, 139–40, 182
Sandage, Steven, 201
Sanford, John, 191
Sartre, Jean-Paul, 94, 166
Schur, Edwin, 43
science; interpreting the world, 14; nonfoundationalist use of, 13–14; unable to lay down moral blueprints, 33
scientific foundationalism, 105, 209
scientific psychology, 39–40, 51–52
scientific thought, emerging out of symbols, 10
scientism, 11–12, 88, 108–9, 212
scientists, acting as philosophers, 13–14
secular individualism, 44
Seitz, Phillip, 152
self; choice of, 114–15; continuity of, 158–59; created from struggle with instincts, 73–74; emergence of, 218
Self, Jungian metaphor of, 166
self-actualization, 44–45, 77–82, 166–67, 179
self-discovery, 112
self-fragmentation, 140–41, 145–47
self-fulfillment, coordination with self-fulfillment of others, 181–82, 185, 187
self-hatred, 182
self-injury; avoiding, when experiencing frustration, 152; in the Oedipal period, 148–49
self-loyalty, 166
self-preoccupation, 70
self psychology, growing out of Western consumerism, 156–58
self-realization, Jung's portrayal of, 171

self-regard; excessive, 70, 113, 162–63,
    164, 196, 215
self-sacrifice, 138, 197
self-sacrificial love, 76
self-transcendence; biological
    inclinations as part of, 118–19;
    humans' capacity for, 69
separation, 41
sex, as a dominant instinct, 62
shadow, 189–90
Siegal, Allen, 152, 153
singular drive theory, 82
Skinner, B.F., 83–91, 94; bringing
    Darwinism to psychology, 89;
    desiring to predict and control
    human behavior, 87; disregarding
    nature, 90; on the environment is
    the source of human problems,
    84–85; as humanitarian, 86–87; on
    two types of reinforcement, 85–86;
    using image of husbandry, 89–90
Skinner box, 85
Smith, James K.A., 25–26
social change, 95–96; coexisting with
    science of human nature, 102–3
social conservatism, evolutionary
    psychology associated with, 98
social constructionism, 91, 93–98, 217
social Darwinism, 112
social sciences, quasi-religious
    dimension of, 34–36
sociobiology, controversy over, 98
Sociobiology Group Statement, 96
Spencer, Herbert, social Darwinism of,
    112
spiritual capacity, energy of, 72
Spitz, Rene, 125–26
Stern, Daniel N., 143
Stevens, Anthony, 174–75, 177, 179,
    180
stimulus-response theory, 83
Striver, Dan, 28
Strozier, Charles, 145
sublimation, 124

symbols, giving rise to thought, 35

tabula rasa, 97. See also humans, as
    blank slates
tendency-need level of thinking, 33–34
tension, reduction of, as major goal of
    life, 63
text, entering conversation with, 16–17
thanatos. See death instinct
theological anthropology, needing
    critical reflection, 29
theology; addressing questions of
    human existence, 17–18;
    correlational mode of, 17;
    engaging culture, 22; public vs.
    confessional approaches to, 20–25;
    task of, descriptive psychology
    compared to, 39–40
theology-psychology connection, 2–3
therapeutic relations, 195
therapy, undemanding nature of, 128.
    See also psychotherapy
Thiel, John, 21–22
thinking, saturated by language, 24–
    25
Thomas Aquinas. See Aquinas,
    Thomas
Tillich, Paul, 2, 6, 94; correlational
    method of doing theology, 17–18;
    outlook of, on Freud, 66–68;
    practicing revised correlational
    approach, 18
Tinbergen, Niko, 175, 176
Toulmin, Steven, 38
Tracy, David, 14, 199; on attempt at
    establish a universal theory, 25; on
    central task of contemporary
    Christian theology, 22–23;
    discussing the classics, 14–15;
    embracing hermeneutical
    approach, 19; hermeneutical turn
    in works of, 23; influence of, on
    Browning, 14–20, 24, 25; on
    interpreting experience through

language, 23–24; on public theology, 19–20; representing apologetic side of theology, 20; on Tillich's correlational approach, 17–18

transcendent purpose, fulfillment of, 184–85

transitional ethic, 185–86

Transitions (Bridges), 42

trauma, avoidance of, 152–53

trust, 164

Truth and Method (Gadamer), 198

Turner, Victor, 41, 174–75

twelve-step groups, 159–60

Two Essays on Analytical Psychology (Jung), 181

unconditional positive regard, 80

understanding, involving interpretation, 38–39

University of Chicago, 20; Divinity School at, 4–5; influence of, on Browning, 4–5

validity claims, 27, 29–30, 31

vitalism, 123

Vitz, Paul, 37

Wallwork, Ernest, 75, 77

Watson, J.B., 83–84

Wheeler, Amy, 109, 140

White, John, 5

wholeness; expression of, 165; Jung's faulty view of, 187

Who Stole Feminism? (Hoff-Summers), 103–4

Wilson, E. O., 99–100

Winnicott, Donald W., 29, 126, 127–28, 130, 151

Witte, John, Jr., 109, 140, 202

Wolf, Ernest, 144–47

Yale University, 20–21

Young Man Luther (Erikson), 164